Bloodstains

Canada's Multiple Murders

Diane Anderson

DETSELIG
ENTERPRISES LTD

Bloodstains: Canada's Multiple Murders

© 2006 Diane Anderson

Library and Archives Canada Cataloguing in Publication

Anderson, Diane
    Bloodstains : Canada's multiple murders / Diane Anderson.

Includes bibliographical references.
ISBN-13: 978-1-55059-322-8
ISBN-10: 1-55059-322-6

1. Serial murderers – Canada. I. Title.

HV6805.A53 2006   364.152'3092271   C2006-904756-1

Detselig Enterprises Ltd.   www.temerondetselig.com
210, 1220 Kensington Road NW   temeron@telusplanet.net
Calgary, Alberta   DETSELIG   Phone: (403) 283-0900
T2N 3P5   ENTERPRISES LTD   Fax: (403) 283-6947

We acknowledge the support of the Government of Canada through the Book Publishing Industry Development Program (BPIDP) for our publishing program.

We also acknowledge the support of the Alberta Foundation for the Arts for our publishing program.

SAN 113-0234
ISBN 1-55059-322-6   978-1-55059-322-8
Printed in Canada
                    Cover Design by Alvin Choong

Contents

"But I don't want to go among mad people," Alice remarked.

Alice in Wonderland

Introduction

Excluding gangsters, religious zealots, terrorists, despots, and hired assassins, there are three basic classifications of multiple murderers: serial killers, mass murderers, and spree murderers, though it has become increasingly common to clump together the latter two and call them rampage murderers.

Mass and spree murderers are described as human time bombs – individuals whose inner rage builds until they can no longer contain it and they erupt into a devastating blast of fury and violence. Short in duration, the eruption usually ends when the murderer takes his own life, termed murder-suicide, or when the murderer is killed by a police officer, otherwise known as suicide by cop. Mass and spree murderers differ only in terms of geography. Mass murderers kill as many people as they can at a single location while spree murderers move from site to site cutting down anyone unlucky enough to cross their paths. Harold Schechter describes the difference between the two by saying, "the spree killer is simply a mobile mass murderer."

Unlike rampage murderers, there is no universally accepted definition of a serial killer, although they are generally described as individuals who commit their crimes at more than one location, over an extended period of time, and who experience what is called a cooling off period, lasting anywhere from a few hours to several years, between homicides. Though the reverse doesn't hold true, if the cooling off period increasingly shrinks, a serial killer can escalate into a rampage killer.

Just as there is no universally accepted definition of a serial killer, there is no consensus on the minimum number of homicides a murderer needs to qualify as a serial killer. In the early 1990s, the FBI Crime Classification Manual settled for "three or more," the United States's National Institutes of Justice have chosen "two or more," and Canada's RCMP have decided on "more than one." Today there are those who would argue it takes only one murder for an individual to be considered a serial killer, provided it can be predicted that he, or less commonly she, would have killed again and again if not caught so precipitously.

In addition to being subdivided into serial, mass, and spree murderers, the law further divides multiple murderers into the psychotics and the psychopaths. According to the dictates of jurisprudence, psychotics are unable to differentiate between right and wrong, and, consequently, cannot be held accountable for their crimes. Exceedingly rare, psychotic killers are quickly apprehended because of their erratic behavior.

Psychopaths are a different breed altogether. Until apprehended and their masks of sanity lifted, psychopaths appear no different than the average person. Indeed, they are often perceived as charming (Clifford Olson), generous (Paul Bernardo), likable (Robert Cook), and gentle (Michael Vescio). Furthermore, unlike the psychotic, the psychopath is more than capable of differentiating between right and wrong. These type of murders, says Elliott Leyton, in his highly-acclaimed *Hunting Humans: The Rise of the Modern Multiple Murderer*, "know precisely what they are doing." Rather than being criminally insane, they are described as being morally stunted or morally insane. Stated another way, they are mentally sane and criminally responsible.

The one thing multiple murderers share is perverse motives. Unlike those motives plotted out in murder mystery and detective novels – passion, greed, revenge, love, and ambition – a multiple murderer's motive is less easy to understand. They may be motivated by hallucinations and/or delusions (the visionary), the pleasure of killing (the hedonist), the need to rid society of a specific type of person, e.g. prostitutes (the mission oriented), their need to exert power over their victims (it is called the power/control oriented), or by a need to avenge themselves against a society they believe has oppressed or victimized them.

Not surprisingly, Canada, like every other nation, has its share of multiple murderers; what is surprising is how many. While many of Canada's multiple murderers have become common household names – Clifford Olson, Paul Bernardo, Karla Homolka – there are dozens more who are almost unknown. Unless one lives or lived in the area where individuals such as David Shearing, Michael Vescio, and Dale Nelson committed their crimes, it is conceivable that the average Canadian has never heard of them.

Bloodstains: Canada's Multiple Murders discusses nine of Canada's most infamous multiple murderers, as well as one alleged multiple murderer who may very well prove to be Canada's worst.

One
Earle Leonard Nelson-Ferral

Earle Nelson Talks From Prison Death Cell

"And when did you reach Winnipeg?" the reporter asked.

"I never was here at all!" Nelson exclaimed. "I admit I am subject to spells of lunacy in which I function the same as in a dream and sometimes find myself in strange places. But I never hurt anyone in these spells. And I was certainly not even near Winnipeg before police brought me up here. That's all there is to that."

"But what about the witnesses?"

"Whenever I was called out for identification, they dressed me up in clothes similar to those found in the secondhand stores, like those that belonged to the man who was supposed to have done the crime. And they made me comb my hair back, even though I generally wear it parted. That blonde detective, Smith, was managing it."

Winnipeg Tribune
November 18, 1927

Wednesday, June 8, 1927, was an ideal day to be travelling; the temperature was neither hot nor cold, and the sky was sunny and clear. At 9:00 that morning, Mr. and Mrs. W. E. Chandler of Winnipeg, Manitoba, were motoring home from Detroit when they picked up a lone male hitch hiker and drove him as far as the outskirts of Emerson, Manitoba. From Emerson, the Chandlers were heading north while their passenger said he was heading south to Noyes, Minnesota, Emerson's sister town, five kilometres on the other side of the international boundary. After a pleasant trip, the Chandlers and their passenger made their farewells and parted company.

Whether he had lied or simply changed his mind, no sooner had the Chandlers driven away than their passenger began walking north. At 11:00 a.m., one kilometre out of Emerson, he hailed a ride from John and Harriet Hanna, who, like the Chandlers, were also bound for Winnipeg. Two hours later, John and Harriet dropped him at the junction of Pembina Highway and Corydon Avenue, in the heart of the city.

Though it had not seemed important at the time, both the Hannas and Chandlers would later recall that the pleasant, if reticent man with the perfect white teeth they had given a ride to that day wore a "jazzy," red-patterned sweater, a blue suit, a distinctive pair of tan sandals, and a light grey cap. They had no way of knowing that the clothes had previously belonged to Martin Sietsema, a Chicago businessman whose twenty-seven year old wife, Mary Cecilia, had been savagely raped and strangled by the cord of an electric appliance only five days earlier.

After bidding John and Harriet goodbye, the man in the jazzy red sweater sauntered down Osborne until it intersected with Broadway. Turning right, he followed Broadway to Main and turned right again. Strolling down Main, he peered curiously into the shop windows until he reached Jacob Garber's second-hand store. Attracted by Jacob's collection of second-hand clothing, he stopped and entered.

At the sound of the bell Jacob looked up over his glasses.

"Do you need any help?" he asked.

"These clothes I'm wearing are too fancy for the sort of work I'm looking for. Would you be willing to exchange them for a something else and a dollar in cash?"

Jacob ran his eyes over the gentleman's clothing and reluctantly nodded. He sifted through his racks and shelves, and picked out a shabby, blue herring-bone coat, a pair of dark cotton trousers, black shoes, and an old green cap. Taking a shiny silver dollar from the till he set it together with the clothes on the counter. His customer hurriedly changed into the clothes and pocketed the money.

Upon leaving the second-hand store, the man set out to find a place to spend the night, preferably a room in a boarding house, preferably run by an unsuspecting and defenseless landlady.

Between four and five that same afternoon, Mr. Woodcots – "a nice Christian man" with two rows of perfect white teeth that broadened into "a million dollar smile" – presented himself at Catherine Hill's Smith Street boarding house and asked for a room.

Catherine Hill, a grey-haired, rheumatic and heavy-set, nononsense woman of seventy-one years, eyed Mr. Woodcots's shabby, blue, herring-bone coat, his dark cotton trousers, dusty black shoes, and old green cap through the eyes of her devout Pentecostal faith, and she said, "Now mind. I don't allow my roomers to bring girls or liquor to their rooms."

"Oh, no!" cried Mr. Woodcots, offended by the suggestion of any impropriety. "I wouldn't think of anything like that. I am a religious man. I am a Roman Catholic."

Although Mr. Woodcots carried no luggage, could only pay one of the three dollars Catherine charged for her weekly rent, and was a confessed papist, his response so impressed the landlady she agreed to take him in. He could pay the balance due on his lodgings on Saturday.

Mr. Woodcots rose early the following morning. He made his bed "in a most particular manner" and departed. No one at the Hill boarding house saw him again until he poked his nose into Mrs. Hill's kitchen at 7:00 that evening. Taken aback to find Catherine's husband William seated with his wife at the table, Mr. Woodcots hastily apologized for not having the two dollars he owed and said he intended to go out and get it.

* * *

Over at nearby University Place, the Cowan family was going through a difficult patch. Mr. Cowan's lengthy recuperation from pneumonia had depleted the family's finances. In order to tide the family over until her husband was back on his feet, Mrs. Cowan had taken a cleaning job at the St. Regis Hotel. Anxious to contribute what they could to the family coffers, Margaret and Lola, two of the Cowan's four children still living at home, devised their own means of bringing in a little extra money; Margaret crafted artificial sweet peas from colored paper and Lola went out and sold them door-to-door.

After dinner on Thursday, June 9, only three days before her fourteenth birthday, "bobbed-haired, fair-headed," and "very pretty" Lola set out with a bundle of Margaret's flowers. She dropped into the St. Regis Hotel where she and her mother arranged to meet at the corner of Smith Street and Graham Avenue after Mrs. Cowan finished work. Until then, Lola would continue to peddle her flowers.

Somewhere on Smith Street Lola encountered Mr. Woodcots. He expressed an interest in Lola's flowers and told her, if she would like to accompany him back to his room where he kept his money, he would be happy to buy some. Eager to make a sale, Lola agreed. Together they climbed the stairs to Mr. Woodcots's second-floor room and Mr. Woodcots pulled the door tightly behind them.

Back on the corner of Graham and Smith, Lola's mother waited in vain.

* * *

The following day the temperature dipped to four degrees Celsius, unusually cool for Winnipeg during the second week of June. At her home on Riverton Avenue, dark-haired and slim, twenty-seven year old Emily Patterson, slipped a sweater over her housedress to ward off the early morning chill and began preparing breakfast for her husband William and their two sons, five year old Thomas and three year old James. When the family finished eating, William left for his job as a dispatch clerk with the T. Eaton Company, and Thomas and James went out to play in the backyard. With the house to herself, Emily cleared away the breakfast things and began her daily cleaning.

At 11:00 a.m., there was a knock at the door. Hoping it was someone come to inquire about the "Room For Rent" sign in the living-room window, Emily opened the door to a man in a shabby, blue herring-bone coat, dark cotton trousers, dusty black shoes, and battered green hat. As luck would have it, he *had* come to inquire about the room for rent.

Emily gladly invited him in.

When Emily Patterson's caller departed at half past noon, he no longer wore the clothes he had arrived in. He now wore William's brown whipcord suit, brown shoes, and grey felt hat. In the suit pockets he carried William's fountain pen and cigarette case, Emily's gold wedding band, and seven $10 bills. In his hands he carried a small yellow box.

Fifteen minutes later, a gentleman wearing a brown whipcord suit and grey felt hat entered Sam Waldman's second-hand clothing store on Main Street. He told Sam there was something wrong with his clothes; they did not seem to fit him right and he would like to purchase something more comfortable. Sam invited the man to browse around.

At 1:15, Sam's customer exited the make-shift change room at the rear of the store wearing a light grey overcoat, a grey suit, a blue shirt, a fawn-colored cardigan, a tie, a grey and white scarf, a beige cap, a leather belt, grey gloves, grayish-brown socks, and brown, bull-dog toed shoes. Beaming proudly at his splashy new image, he paid for the clothes with three, $10 bills and announced that what he now needed was a haircut and shave.

Happy to be of further assistance, Sam escorted his customer to the Central Barber Shop next door and introduced him to Nick Tabor, one of three barbers who worked in the shop. Nick told the man to take a seat, and for the next hour shaved the gentleman and cut his hair, taking care not to irritate what appeared to be a fresh cut on the top of his client's head.

Freshly shaved, shorn, and suited, Nick's customer needed but one last thing to complete his transformation. Pulling out a $10 bill, he settled his account with the Central Barber Shop and made straight for Chevrier's Clothing Store. There he paid Thomas Carton, the Chevrier's clerk, $4.50 for a champagne-colored fedora, "the snazziest he'd ever owned."

Looking every inch the well-bred gentleman, he rambled over to Portage Avenue and jumped on a streetcar bound for St. Charles, located immediately to the west of Winnipeg.

* * *

John Hofer and his wife were returning to their home at the Pigeon Lake Hutterite colony when a respectable looking gentleman slid into the streetcar seat beside them. Curious about the Hofers' attire, the gentleman introduced himself as Walter Woods and struck up a conversation, talking primarily of faith and religion. As the streetcar rumbled west, Mr. Hofer pointed to a package Mr. Woods was carrying.

"What's that?"

Walter smiled his million dollar smile and handed the package to Mrs. Hofer. "Look and see."

Mrs. Hofer carefully untied the brown wrapping paper and found a beige cap and a receipt from Waldman's Clothing Store.

Pleased to reward the Hofers for being as devoted a Christian as he was, Walter told the Hofers, "you can have it."

Surprised by Walter's unexpected offer, Mr. Hofer took the cap from his wife and turned it over.

"We have no use for it, but someone might like it. But why would you give it to me?"

Walter's answer was simple and brief. "I don't want it."

When the streetcar pulled into St. Charles station, the three companions got off to transfer to the Headingly streetcar. Upon discovering they had missed their connection, Walter told the Hofers not to worry, stuck out his thumb, and hailed a ride to Headingly for all three of them.

At 7:30 that evening, Hugh Eldon gave Walter Woods a lift from Headingly to Portage la Prairie. Though Hugh found nothing especially memorable about Walter's face, he did take note of his light grey overcoat, his grey suit, his brown bulldog-toed shoes, and his champagne-colored fedora.

* * *

An hour before Hugh Eldon picked up Walter Woods in Headingly, William Patterson returned home from work. He was surprised, but not alarmed, to find his house quiet and empty. Assuming his wife was away visiting friends and had taken Thomas and James with her, he made himself dinner. He was puzzled but as yet still not alarmed when Thomas and James came home alone from the neighbors a short while later. Not until after he cooked his sons dinner and put them to bed did he begin to grow uneasy.

William rang the police and asked if there had been any accidents involving a twenty-seven year old woman. Only half relieved by their assurances that there had not, he placed the receiver back in its cradle. Casting a glance into the dining room, he spotted his family's brown leather suitcase. Thinking it an odd place to find it, William crossed the room to examine it and discovered that someone had jimmied the lock and taken the seven, $10 bills he and Emily kept hidden inside. Verging on panic, William entered his sons' bedroom and knelt at the side of James's bed. Clasping his hands in prayer, he raised his eyes to the ceiling and asked God for strength, wisdom, and guidance.

God quickly responded. As William put out his hand to hoist himself to his feet, he "providentially" ruffled the bed skirt. Beneath the bed skirt he spotted a coat sleeve. Beneath the coat sleeve he found Emily.

The coroner's report noted that Emily Patterson's face was smeared with blood. A bruise to the top of her head had likely been caused by some sort of blunt instrument. Discoloration to her elbows, chest, and neck suggested that someone had pinned her down with his knees while he wrapped his hands around her throat and tightened them. A "gelatinous material" smeared across her right thigh suggested she had been "mistreated."

In brief, Emily Patterson had been strangled and raped.

A search of the house produced a number of significant finds. In addition to the $70, a small yellow box, Emily's gold wedding band, William's cigarette case, fountain pen, brown whipcord suit and grey felt hat were missing. Left in their place were a shabby, blue herringbone overcoat, a pair of dark cotton trousers, an old green hat, and a *Manitoba Tribune* "Room to Rent" clipping for 695 Langside Street.

Winnipeg police left no stone unturned in their quest for Emily Patterson's murderer. They searched all empty and abandoned buildings and asked railroad police to be on the lookout for strangers "beating" their way on the trains. They placed 695 Langside Street under twenty-four-hour surveillance and began a comprehensive, house-to-house canvass of all Winnipeg rooming and boarding houses. They reached Catherine Hill's Smith Street boarding house on Saturday afternoon.

"Have any of your lodgers left in recent days?' they asked Catherine.

Catherine shook her head. "No. No one but a young Highlander."

Elsewhere, news of Emily Patterson's murder was spreading faster than Red River flood waters. When it spilled into Main Street,

Sam Waldman recalled the grey felt hat, brown whipcord suit, and small yellow box a customer had left the previous day. He examined the contents of the box and discovered a bible, photographs, and several letters and cards addressed to Emily and William Patterson. Sam quickly rang the police and gave them a detailed description of the man who had left the items – a short dark man with brown hair, dark eyes, and a muscular build who was now dressed in a light grey overcoat, a grey suit, and a pair of brown bulldog-toed shoes.

Armed with Sam's description, on Sunday police re-canvassed all Winnipeg rooming and boarding houses. Their search brought them back to Catherine Hill's Smith Street boarding house where Catherine once again told them that none of her lodgers had recently left.

Not until after the police had departed did Catherine begin entertaining doubts. Why had Mr. Woodcots not used the clean towel she had set out for him on Friday, and why could no one at the boarding house recall seeing him since she herself had seen him at 7:00 on Thursday evening? Perplexed, Catherine trundled up the stairs to Mr. Woodcots's room and opened the door. Even a cursory glance told her the bed had not been slept in.

Two things about the discovery particularly alarmed Catherine. First, she had inadvertently lied to the police when she had told them that none of her lodgers had recently left. Second, Mr. Woodcots still owed her $2. Catherine pulled the blinds and opened the windows to clear the unpleasant smell from the room, and limped downstairs to share her concerns with her husband. After talking it over, Catherine and William agreed that William ought to stop in at the police station and report the incident on his way home from church later that evening.

Some time after William set out for church, Bernhard Mortenson, another of Catherine's lodgers, happened to pass beneath the second story stairwell of the boarding house. Glimpsing up through the banisters, he caught sight of what appeared to be an undressed mannequin under Mr. Woodcots's bed. Curious to know why Mr. Woodcots would have an undressed mannequin under his bed, Bernhard mounted the stairs to take a closer look. Suddenly he began shouting and waving his arms frantically.

"Mrs. Hill! Mrs. Hill! Front room! Upstairs!"

Best estimates placed Lola Cowan's death at three days earlier, probably sometime late Thursday afternoon or early Thursday evening. Like Emily Patterson, she bore the telltale signs of strangulation and rape. Her neck, elbows, and chest were bruised. Her body, which the papers were pleased to report was "remarkably well-developed for one so young," was nude, and blood smeared her inner thigh and buttocks. What no one could account for was evidence of Lola's fierce struggle with her assailant because on Thursday evening, neither Catherine, nor William, nor any of their boarders had heard a thing.

Suspecting a connection between Lola's murder and the murder of Emily Patterson, Chief of Detectives, George Smith, who had been heading the Patterson investigation, promptly dispatched the clothes left at the Patterson crime scene to the Smith Street boarding house. Catherine took one look at the sorry collection and positively identified them as the clothing worn by Mr. Woodcots.

As much as police may have wished to believe otherwise, Lola Cowan's murder, coupled with the murder of Emily Patterson, confirmed a suspicion they had been praying would turn out to be unfounded. Not only were they now convinced that the same man was responsible for both Winnipeg crimes, they were also convinced he was the same man police in a dozen American cities had been fruitlessly hunting for the past twenty-two months.

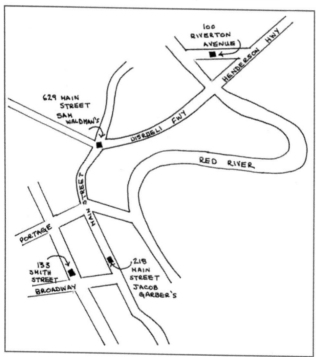

Map of Winnipeg streets where Lola Cowan and Emily Patterson were murdered.

Beginning with the August 23, 1925 murder and rape of sixty year old Elizabeth Jones in San Francisco, California, the man now thought to be terrorizing Winnipeg, and known to American police only as the "Gorilla" or "Dark Strangler," had left a trail of bodies over ten thousand kilometres, in twelve different cities, in nine different states. Unprecedented in magnitude, in only twenty-one months he had savagely murdered twenty-six (the precise number is unknown and there is no consensus on who his victims were) women and one infant boy; his victims ranged in age from seventy-six years to eight months.

On October 1, 1925, Elma Wells, age thirty-two, of San Francisco, was strangled then raped, and her naked corpse was crammed into a clothes closet. On October 18, 1925, Ollie McCoy of Philadelphia, the only black victim, was strangled in her living room and carried upstairs where she was raped. On November 7, 1925, May Murray of Philadelphia was strangled in her kitchen and carried to an upstairs bedroom where she was sexually assaulted. On November 11, 1925, Alena Weiner, age thirty-three, also of Philadelphia, became the third victim to be strangled downstairs, before being carried upstairs and raped post-mortem. Early in 1926, Lena Tidar, of Newark, was strangled with a man's necktie; on February 20, 1926, Clara Newman, age sixty, of San Francisco was strangled and raped. Less than two weeks later, on March 2, 1926, Laura Beal, age sixty-five, of San Jose was sexually assaulted after she had been strangled so violently by her dressing-gown cord the cord imbedded into her flesh.

Three months later, on June 10, 1926, Lillian St. Mary, age sixty-three, of San Francisco, was violated after she had been strangled with so much force nine of her ribs were broken. On June 24, 1926, Ollie Russell, age fifty-three, of Santa Barbara was raped after being strangled so savagely by a piece of cord the cord tore into her throat. On August 16, 1926, Mary Nisbet, age fifty-two, of Oakland was sexually assaulted after being murdered with such violence that her teeth were broken and the towel used to strangle her had puckered her neck. Three days later Isabel Gallegos, a seventy-six year old Stockton resident, was strangled by a pillow case but not raped. On October, 19, 1926, Beata Withers, age thirty-two, of Portland was raped after being strangled. Her body was crammed into a steamer trunk in an attic. Unfathomably, her death was thought to be a suicide. The next day Mabel Fluke, age thirty-seven, of Portland was strangled by a silk scarf that had been garrotted and knotted about her neck. She was found in her stench-filled attic three days later; like that of Beata Withers, Mabel's death was inexplicably considered a suicide. On October 21, 1926, fifty-nine year old Virginia Grant, the third Portland victim in as many days, was found hidden behind the furnace in her basement; her death was initially written off as the result of natural causes. On November 18, 1926, the day before her fifty-sixth birthday, Anna Edmonds of San Francisco was sexually assaulted after she was strangled. In Seattle on November 23, 1926, Florence Monks, age forty-eight, was choked to death but likely not raped; her body was found jammed behind her basement furnace. On

November 29, 1926, Blanche Meyers, age forty-eight, of Portland was strangled with the ties of her apron. Her corpse was sexually assaulted then shoved under a bed.

On Christmas Eve 1926, while her family made preparations for Christmas, Mrs. John Brerard, age forty-one, of Council Bluffs was strangled with a shirt hanging on her basement clothesline. Clumps of her hair were found stuck to the furnace, her body was crammed behind. On December 27, 1926, twenty-three year old Bonnie Pace, of Kansas City, was strangled and raped in an upstairs bedroom while her six year old invalid son lay helplessly on his bed in his bedroom below. The next day Germania Harpin, age twenty-eight, of Kansas City, was strangled and raped post-mortem; her eight month old son, Robert Harpin, was found dead in his crib. He too had been a victim of strangulation. On April 27, 1927, Mary McConnell, a fifty-three year old woman from Philadelphia, was found suffocated by a sock that had been forced into her mouth and strangled by a rag that had been twisted about her neck so tightly it had to be cut off. A month later, on May 30, 1927, Jennie Randolph, age fifty-three, of Buffalo was strangled with a kitchen towel. Her head had been pounded black and blue, and her corpse raped and shoved under a bed. On June 1, 1927, Fannie May, age fifty-three, of Detroit was garrotted by an electric cord and sexually assaulted after death. On the same day, in the same Detroit rooming house, Maureen Atorthy-Oswald, age thirty-nine, was strangled by a piece of ribbon, and on June 23, 1927, Mary Cecelia Sutsima was strangled and raped.

In all but two of his crimes, the Dark Strangler's *modus operandi* (MO) was roughly the same. He sought out a room for rent or a house for sale. On the pretext of renting or buying, he managed to get himself invited in. If he found the lady of the house alone, he strangled her and sexually assaulted her, usually post-mortem. After concealing the body, he helped himself to any cash, clothes, jewellery, or other items worth pawning, and vanished.

Though Lola Cowan's murder did not fit his usual pattern, police believed that because she had been strangled and raped after death, and because her body had been concealed beneath a bed, her death could be attributed to the Dark Strangler. Whoever he really was, he could now add another city, another province, another country, and another two names to his interminable list of victims.

Winnipeg police determined to stop him before he added more.

As heroic as their intentions were, the sober reality was that the Dark Strangler had been so successful at eluding police as he zigged and zagged his way across North American nobody even knew his name. "He is the fastest ghoul that ever wore shoe leather," said Chief Detective Smith.

Undaunted, police adopted the old adage "the best defense is a good offense." Using radio, posters, newspapers, telegrams, and any other tools at their disposal, they disseminated as much information to as many people as they possibly could. The same evening Lola Cowan's body was found, they interrupted a radio church service to make a special announcement warning people to be on the lookout for:

A man between twenty-six and thirty years of age, about five foot six or seven inches tall, and weighing about 150 pounds; large dark eyes, full face sallow complexion; clean shaven, dark brown hair and broad shouldered, evidently a transient of Jewish or Italian appearance, but might be any nationality. He was seen and identified wearing a light grey suit, neatly dressed . . . brown boots with bulldog toes.

They specifically cautioned women with houses for sale or rooms for rent against admitting any strangers.

On Saturday, June 11, at 3:00 in the afternoon, a man dressed in a light grey overcoat, a grey suit, a pair of brown shoes with bulldog toes, and a champagne-colored fedora, showed up at Mary Rowe's boarding house in Regina and rented a room under the name Harry Harcourts.

Harry remained at Mary's boarding house until 8:30 Monday morning, June 13, when he stepped out for breakfast at the New Wonder Café. Along the way he stopped to buy a copy of the *Regina Leader Post* and was dismayed to find an exhaustive description of the Dark Strangler plastered across the front page. Harry hurried back to Mary's and shed as many articles of clothing matching the description as he decently could. Leaving the boarding house, he hastened to a thrift shop where he exchanged his remaining clothes for a khaki shirt and a pair of blue bibbed overalls with white stitching. From the thrift shop he hurried to Barry Page's Royal Second Hand Store on Broad Street and traded his smart, champagne-colored fedora for a black cap and fifty cents. Still wearing the brown bulldog-toed shoes, he crossed to Fred England Jewellers and sold them a gold wedding band for $3.50.

At 10:00 a.m., a man wearing a pair of blue bibbed overalls with white stitching, a khaki shirt, brown bulldog-toed shoes, and a black cap, and going by the name of Virgil Wilson, showed up one and a half kilometres southeast of Regina. From there, Virgil hitched a ride to the town of Davin with Mr. W. E. Davidson, and then from Davin to Vibank with Lyle Wilcox. At noon, Isadore Silverman, a junk collector, picked Virgil up.

In exchange for food and lodgings, over the course of the next two days, Virgil helped Isadore salvage unwanted goods from district farmers. They spent Monday night in Arcola, Saskatchewan, and

Tuesday night in Deloraine, Manitoba. On Wednesday, June 15, the same day that both Emily Patterson and Lola Cowan were laid to rest at Winnipeg's Elmwood Cemetery, Isadore and Virgil drove to Boissevain, Manitoba where Virgil said goodbye to Isadore, telling him he planned to try and find work in the area. The moment Isadore sped away, Virgil sought out a general store, purchased a new straw hat, and made a bee line for North Dakota.

By the time Virgil Wilson was working his way to the border, Winnipeg police had managed to locate Hugh Eldon and John Hofer. From the information the two men provided, police suspected their fleet-footed quarry was bound for Regina and raised the alarm. Following Winnipeg's example, Regina police undertook a house-to-house visit of all rooming and boarding houses. On Tuesday, June 14, while Virgil Wilson and Isadore Silverman were scouting for junk on the farms between Deloraine and Boissevain, the police arrived at Mary Rowe's house. Yes, Mary told the police. She had had a short, dark-haired, sallow-skinned man stay with her over the weekend, but his name was neither Mr Woodcots nor Walter Woods, it was Harry Harcourt. Would they like to see his room anyway?

Amongst other things, police found in Harry Harcourt's room a light grey overcoat, a grey suit jacket, grey gloves, a grey and white scarf, and a copy of the *Regina Leader Post*, exposing its detailed description of the Dark Strangler.

* * *

Eight kilometres north of the North Dakota border, in the small community of Wakopa, Leslie Morgan was just getting ready to close his general store when a stranger in blue bibbed overalls with white stitching, a khaki shirt, brown boots with bulldog toes, and a straw hat entered. Having been inundated with news of the Dark Strangler, even though the stranger's clothing didn't match that of the broadcast description, Leslie grew suspicious of the stranger. Leslie sold the man two bottles of coke and a chunk of cheddar and patiently waited for him to vacate the store before ringing Constable Wilton Gray at the RCMP detachment in Killarney.

"I'm sure that the man wanted for them two brutal murders in Winnipeg just left my store," Leslie told Gray. "I'm sure he's headed for Bannerman."

Leslie rounded up a posse of Wakopa farmers and kept the suspect in sight while Constable Gray, accompanied by Constable Sewell, made for Bannerman at break neck speed. Five and a half kilometres north of the border, Constables Gray and Sewell caught up with the stranger. They took him back to Killarney where they relieved him of his socks, shoes, and belt, and locked him in a cell in the basement of the town hall.

Constable Gray was having difficulty associating the prisoner, the "easiest-going, simplest sort of chap you ever saw in your life," with the inhuman savage described by Winnipeg police. In addition to his gregarious and affable nature, the prisoner gave his name as Virgil Wilson and his clothing was wrong. Leaving Constable William Dunn in charge of their captive, Constables Gray and Sewell went to the telegraph office to request any updated information on the Dark Strangler, especially updated word on his clothing. In short order, their answer came back.

He is now dressed in a brand new pair of overalls stitched with white thread and with a bib, a khaki shirt, brown boots with bulldog toes, and an old black cap.

Surprised, exhilarated, and a tad self-satisfied to know they had Canada's most wanted fugitive in detention, Sewell and Gray returned to their detachment rooms. Minutes later, Constable Dunn burst through the door with the worst possible news. During Sewell and Gray's absence, Virgil Wilson had picked his lock and escaped!

The cry for help rang far and wide. Hundreds of police and civilian searchers flooded the countryside. Canadian and American border guards beefed up their patrols and a special train from Winnipeg, carrying bloodhounds and twenty trained officers, raced west. At daybreak, on the western edge of Killarney, a stranger in a pair of blue overalls with white stitching, a ratty green sweater, and a peculiar pair of shoes fashioned from hockey skates, approached Alfred Woods. Alfred asked the stranger if he was part of the search party.

"Sure am," said the stranger.

"Then you'll be pleased to know there's a special train with men and dogs headed this way."

In the distance, a train fast approaching blew its whistle and the stranger moved away. As he did, Alfred noticed the khaki shirt the man wore under his sweater. Realizing who the stranger actually was, Alfred made a dash for Doctor Beal's house across the road. Hearing his calls for help, Doctor Beal's sons ran forth to meet him.

Alfred pointed to the stranger and shouted, "It's the Strangler! I'll keep him in sight! You get the police!"

The Beal boys jumped in their car and sped towards Crystal City, eighty kilometres east, while Alfred took off in pursuit of the stranger. Soon Guy Ramsay, a second farmer joined him. Their quarry made for the railway tracks, but Alfred and Guy kept hard on his heels. After what seemed an eternity, the Beal boys and Constable William Renton pulled up. Alfred, Guy, and Renton made a run at the stranger, and the stranger hurled himself over a fence. Renton drew his revolver and followed suit. Realizing the odds were against him, the stranger surrendered. Renton hustled him into a patrol car as the special train from Winnipeg pulled into the station. At 7:00 in the morning of Friday, June, 17, Constable Renton delivered the Dark Strangler into the arms of the Winnipeg police.

When the special train puffed back into Winnipeg's Westside station ten hours later, four thousand people were on hand to cheer its arrival. "They were there," effused the *Free Press*, "to see a marauding jungle beast safely in the net; his claws trimmed and fangs pulled."

When the Dark Strangler was taken into custody, Canadians, mad to learn all they could about his background, were delighted when the news they received didn't disappoint. Virgil Wilson's real name was Earle Nelson, more accurately Earle Ferral. He had been born in San Francisco on May 12, 1897, to James and Francis Ferral. Before Earle was one, Frannie died of syphilis she had contracted from her husband; seven months later, Jimmy followed her to the grave.

After Frannie and Jimmy's deaths, Earle went to live with his maternal grandmother, Jennie Nelson, a widow with two children, Earle's Aunt Lillian and Uncle Willis. At the age of ten, when a bike he was riding was struck by a streetcar, Earle suffered a serious head injury and for almost a week wavered between life and death. His grandmother died the following year, after which Earle went to live with his Aunt Lillian and her husband Henry Fabian.

Earle's childhood oddities grew more pronounced as he matured into manhood and for all of his family's fire and brimstone preachings, he began to smoke, drink, brawl, whore, steal, and masturbate for hours on end. His criminal behavior eventually cost him two years, in San Quentin – 1915 to 1917 – for burglary.

Upon his release, Earle joined, and was discharged from, the military four times. Each of his attempts at trying to fit in with the rigorous demands of the navy failed miserably. Troubled by his incorrigible conduct and queer behavior, after Earle's fourth unsuccessful stint, the navy packed him off to Mare Island Naval Hospital which in turn packed him off to the Napa State Mental Hospital. From the time he arrived at Napa in May of 1918 until the time he was discharged in May of 1919, Earle escaped five times.

After his discharge, Earle's Aunt Lillian found him work as a janitor with St. Mary's Hospital. There, Earle met Mary Teresa Martin. Despite their thirty-six year age difference – she was fifty-eight and he was twenty-two – Mary and Earle, whom Mary knew as Evan Fuller, were married on August 5, 1919.

Not surprisingly, the marriage was a failure. In addition to their age disparity, Mary had difficulty coping with Earle's vulgar eating habits, his peculiar choice of clothes, his want of personal hygiene, his possessiveness and unwarranted jealousy, his unexplained absences, and his insatiable sexual demands. When she began to fear for her life, Mary left him.

Just as she was beginning to get her life back in order, police called Mary to inform her that on May 19, 1921, Earle had attempted to sexually assault a twelve year old girl named Mary Summers. In an attempt to prevent another prison term, Mary and Lillian instituted insanity proceedings against him. On June 16, Earle was sent back to the Napa State Mental Hospital. As he had done so many times during his previous institutionalization, on November 2, he escaped. On November 4, 1923, after a brief two day fling with freedom, he was recaptured and returned to Napa. On March 10, 1925, following sixteen disturbance-free months, he was officially released. Five and a half months later, Elizabeth Jones was murdered and raped in San Francisco.

When Earle Leonard Nelson – a.k.a. Earle Ferral, Virgil Wilson, Charles Harrison, Roger Wilson, Adrian Smith, Harry Harcourt, Mr. Woodcots, Evan Fuller, Mr. Williams, and other aliases – was apprehended at Killarney on June 17, 1927, he had murdered more people in a shorter time than any previous North American serial killer. Earle was thirty years old when he made his foray into Canada but he would not get any older.

On Tuesday, June 20, a coroner's jury indicted him for the murders of Lola Cowan and Emily Patterson. His trial for Emily's murder began November 1, 1927. Those Winnipegers who managed to jockey themselves into one of the prized seats in the filled-to-capacity courtroom, expecting Earle's trial to be sated with lurid tales of lust and wanton depravity, were sorely disappointed. By and large, it was as exciting as parliamentary debate.

The first day and a half were spent in jury selection. Jury selection was followed by a rehashing of details that spectators already knew by heart. Witnesses – the Chandlers, the Hannas, Jacob Garber, Sam Waldman, Isadore Silverman – were finally brought before the court to explain where they had picked up and dropped off the defendant and to identify clothing he had bought, stolen, and sold. For the umpteenth time, Catherine and William Hill retold their story of Mr. Woodcots's brief stay in their boarding house, and the discovery of Lola Cowan's body. An assortment of neighbors, doctors, photographers described finding, examining, and photographing Emily Patterson's body; law enforcement officials gave evidence concerning Earle's capture, escape, recapture, and identification, and witnesses were scrupulously and tiresomely cross-examined by Earle's defense lawyer, J. Stitt. The only real thrill came on Wednesday afternoon when William Patterson took the stand to recount the painful discovery of Emily's body.

Still, those in attendance *did* get a first-hand look at William Patterson's grief, and even though Nelson never took the stand, sitting for the most part bored and half asleep in the dock, the crowd did get a peek of the "marauding jungle beast." Unfortunately for those expecting some half-human creature, for his trial Nelson was dressed in a slate-grey suit, a polka-dotted tie, a cream shirt and a pair of highly polished black shoes, and he looked decidedly unbeastly. So unbeastly, in fact, his appearance inspired one female spectator to remark with undisguised astonishment: "Why, he's the best-looking man here!"

If, by Wednesday, the trial had proven to be less sensational than expected, Thursday's prospects looked better. That day court spectators would finally get a glimpse of Mary Fuller, Earle Nelson's wife, the she-devil who had eaten with, talked with, and fornicated with the devil incarnate.

Expecting perhaps a cigarette-smoking, gum-popping, bottled-blonde of loose morals and suspect reputation, wearing tall heels and short hems, what spectators got instead was a wizened old woman of sixty-six with white hair and thick-lensed spectacles, dressed in respectable shoes and a matronly black dress. While spectators craned and strained their necks to observe her more closely, for over an hour, Mary described her brief marriage to Earle, his shiftlessness and laziness, and his insane jealousy. Mary spoke of Earle's want of moral responsibility, his bizarre behavior, his eccentricities, his madness, and finally, her fear of him.

Despite compelling insanity arguments delivered by Earle's wife and Aunt, proof of his incarceration in insane asylums, and a particularly impassioned plea to the jurors by his defense attorney, beseeching them to show compassion and mercy for a man so obviously deranged, on Saturday, November 5, the jury choose to side with Crown Prosecutor Graham's assertion that "evidence of eccentricities and insane jealousy" is not proof of insanity and that showing mercy "is no part of a jury's deliberation," and found Earle Leonard Nelson-Ferral criminally sane and guilty of murder.

Earle Nelson went to the gallows professing his innocence on Friday, the thirteenth of January, 1928. For that performance, he donned a dark cowl and rope necktie. Unbeknownst to authorities, following his execution, Barker's Funeral Parlour put his body on public display. For that, his final public appearance, he wore a dark grey suit, a crisp white shirt with a stiffly starched collar, and a light grey bowtie.

Until the end, Earle vigorously maintained that each and every one of the witnesses who identified him during the identification parades had to have been mistaken because he had never been to Regina or Winnipeg until the police brought him there. "He was," he said, "a young man of the highest ideals and such crimes as he was charged with were quite impossible."

Two
Michael Angelo Vescio

Just before 10:00 in the evening on September 22, 1945, a cool cloudy Saturday only four and a half months after Germany's capitulation, ten year old Halley Richardson returned home after seeing a movie at Winnipeg's Osborne Theatre. He had reached the yard to his home on Warsaw Avenue in the city's Fort Rouge district when a slim, dark-complexioned man, who "wasn't very tall, didn't wear a hat, had a light, sand-colored raincoat on, and had black hair, well combed back," asked Halley if he would come and help him look for his stolen car.

Ever obliging, Halley escorted the man to St. Michael and All Angels Church on Hugo Street where they ran into Halley's friend, Rodney Fox. Rodney took up their cause, grew tired quickly, and departed, leaving Halley and his unknown companion to carry on alone. Weaving their way back towards Halley's home, they entered the alley between Warsaw and Jessie Avenues. Before Halley had a chance to react, the man grabbed him. He ordered Halley to lie down and remove his trousers and then sexually assaulted him. Included in Halley's description to the police was his suspicion that his attacker was probably German. The stranger spoke with a foreign accent and punctuated his conversation with remarks like "we Germans" and "you Canadian boys."

Less than two months later, at 9:45 in the evening of Monday, November 19, ten year old Ronald Quick stopped to look for his scarf on the corner of Hugo Street and McMillan Avenue, less than four blocks from where Halley's assault had occurred. As Ronald stood scouring the intersection, a man came up from behind and seized him by the collar. Forcing him into the recess between two nearby garages, he told the terrified young boy to lie down in the snow and remove his pants. Just as he had done to Halley Richardson, the man then raped him.

When questioned by police, Ronald described his assailant as "not extra tall, with black hair, brown trench coat and brown army pants," and "a medium brown suntan." He thought his attacker was German because he spoke with a German accent.

Based on Ronald's description of his assailant and the location of the assault, police had no doubt the same man was responsible for both attacks. There were, however, two significant differences between the first and second. In a noticeable departure from Halley's assault, on this occasion the rapist had pulled a gun, telling his young victim he had nothing to fear if he quietly cooperated. Secondly, during Ronald's assault the rapist appeared considerably less nervous than during his first attack, leaving police to wonder whether the gun had boosted the rapist's confidence or if he was becoming more dangerous.

While Winnipeg police were still laboring under the investigations of the first two attacks, there was a third.

Having spent the better part of Christmas Eve delivering magazines, at 10:30 that evening, eleven year old Donald Hewitt returned to his home on McMillan Avenue. He was mounting the stairs to his apartment when a man called out, asking Donald if he would come down and help him find "Belmont or Balmoral or a street with a name something like that."

Donald and the man worked their way up and down several streets and avenues before reaching the alley running behind Gertrude Avenue. Using the ruse of looking for an empty garage to rent, the man enticed Donald into the alley. There, the man drew a gun, forced Donald into an empty garage, and raped him.

Donald's description of his assailant matched those given by Halley and Ronald. He was slim, not very tall, and had longish, slightly wavy dark hair combed back from his forehead. Donald guessed the man's age at about twenty, and told police that at the time of the assault the attacker had been wearing a long, greenish-brown trench coat with epaulets on its shoulders. His long dark trousers, which appeared to be of army issue, dragged beneath his shoes, and, judging from the man's accent, was probably German.

In this most recent attack, police immediately recognized the stamp of what the papers would soon dub the "Fort Rouge Sex Maniac." As disturbed as they were to know he had struck again, what worried them more was proof he was in fact becoming more violent. During the Hewitt attack, he had again brandished a gun, but rather than calmly telling his young victim he wouldn't be hurt if he cooperated, he had ordered Donald to "shut up or I'll shoot."

* * *

By all accounts, thirteen year old Roy Ewen McGregor was a very fine lad, "one of the best," eulogized Donald Thompson, a family friend and member of the Fort Garry Horse whom Roy greatly admired. Roy did well at school and his teachers spoke of him warmly. His mother described him as a young man who "was into everything: hockey, clubs, school patrols, he loved swimming and went to the YMCA often." Determined to fill his every waking hour, Roy was also a member of the 176 Winnipeg Optimist air cadet squadron, attended Sunday school at Augustine United Church, and had a job delivering papers for the *Free Press*. Roy Ewen McGregor was, as his mother said, a young man who "enjoyed every minute of living."

On the evening of January 4, 1946, an unusually warm Friday for a city universally known as "Winterpeg," Roy debated whether to attend a meeting of his air cadet squadron, or go and see the *Vote for George* and *Early Life* double feature at the Rialto Theatre with his friend Ronnie Flowers. By ill chance or by fate, he chose the movie.

At 7:30, Roy said goodbye to his parents and sister and departed his home at 149 Clarke Street, leaving him ample time to meet Ronnie at the bus stop. Because it was Friday and there was no school the next morning, when the movie ended at 10:30, Roy and Ronnie took a streetcar to the Dutch Maid ice cream bar on Osborne Street. The boys left the ice cream bar at 11:00 and walked south on Osborne. Ten minutes later they reached the corner of Osborne and Gertrude Avenue and headed off in opposite directions.

"Goodnight Ronnie," said Roy, turning and waving goodbye as he walked east on Gertrude. "See you in the morning."

Ronnie wouldn't.

At 11:45, Roy's mother put her ironing aside and took note of the time. Surprised to discover how late it was, she began to wonder about

Roy. He should have been home by then, and it wasn't like him not to call if he expected to be late. More puzzled than concerned, she rang the Flowers's residence and learned that Ronnie was already home and could offer no logical explanation why Roy wasn't.

Growing increasingly anxious, Mrs. McGregor called around to some of Roy's other friends while her husband, Allister, and Roy's uncle, Jim Ewan, went in search of Roy, tramping up and down the streets and avenues neighboring Clarke Street. At 2:00 a.m., when Roy had yet to call or appear, his mother and father called the Rupert Street police station to report him missing.

Six hours after Mr. and Mrs. McGregor put in their call to the Rupert Street police, Roman Klibak and Paul Ross arrived for work at Moore's Coal and Wood Yard at 158 Clarke Street, directly across the street from the McGregor's. Ten minutes later, Roman went out to the yard to turn on the lights and found the body of a young boy lying face down in a coal bin.

The boy's hat had ridden up on his head and his parka was bunched up under his arms. His pants were pulled below his knees and the flap of his long underwear was open. His torso and head were caked in dry blood and droplets of blood led from the coal bin to a frozen pool of blood next to a boxcar, which was parked on a spur line running twenty-two metres to the north. The five feet one inch, one hundred and fifteen pound boy was quickly identified as Roy McGregor.

The provincial coroner's preliminary examination indicated that Roy had been shot twice, first in the stomach, then through the side of his head, just above his right ear, and both bullets had exited his body.

Map of Winnipeg streets showing Roy McGregor's final whereabouts.

Based on the body's degree of rigor, the coroner concluded that Roy had died sometime between 10:00 p.m. and midnight.

Results of the autopsy, performed later that afternoon by pathologist O. C. Trainor, confirmed the coroner's initial assessment, and added that Roy likely died the instant the second bullet entered his skull. Because the autopsy failed to produce evidence of scorch marks to Roy's body or clothing, Trainor also believed that Roy had not been shot at close range. From stains found on the outside of the flap on Roy's long underwear, Trainor further assumed a sexual assault had been attempted.

The Winnipeg police's ensuing canvass of the neighborhood produced information from three women living on Stradbrook Avenue, which helped narrow the estimated time of death. Nancy Horne of 321 Stradbrooke had been reading when she heard what she thought was a car backfiring. Startled, she checked her watch. It read 11:45 exactly. Three minutes later she heard a second loud bang. Caroline Patrician of 248 Stradbrooke thought she heard a car firing once at about 11:40 and once again a few minutes later. Her sister, Mrs. Puchniak, who lived at the same address, told police her Pomeranian, Snowball, had started barking at 11:45 and had kept it up for the next twenty minutes.

Police theorized that after bidding Ronnie farewell, Roy had walked a block east on Gertrude before cutting over to Wardlaw. He followed Wardlaw to Clarke Street where he likely encountered his murderer. Crime scene evidence suggested that Roy had been shot next to the boxcar, carried from there to the coal yard, and dragged by his feet into the coal bin. The scenario explained the pool of blood found next to the boxcar, the droplets of blood found between the boxcar and coal bin, and answered why Roy's coat had bunched up under his arms and his hat had ridden up on his head.

Though police had no idea who could commit such "a very unusual and ghastly crime," they were convinced that whoever he was, he was the same man who had sexually assaulted Halley, Ronald, and Donald in the final four months of 1945. The location of the murder, the use of a gun, and the attempted sexual assault all pointed to the same perpetrator. The murder underscored the unwelcome reality that not only did Winnipeg have a dangerous serial sexual predator on its hands, but it had a dangerous sexual predator whose propensity for violence had just leapt to a new level.

Police immediately warned all citizens to exercise extreme caution when out and about. They specifically cautioned boys to avoid going out after dark, and, if going out after dark was unavoidable, warned them to go out in groups, preferably with an adult escort. The Monday after the murder, students at five Fort Rouge schools – Fort Rouge, La Verendrye, Gladstone, Earl Grey, and Kelvin – gathered in their school auditoriums to hear Detective Sergeant Jack Reeves press upon them the importance of being on the constant alert for strange men.

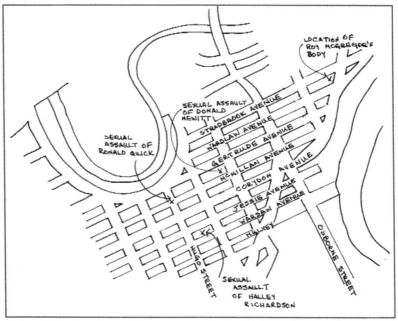

Map of the locations of the rapes and murder.

Chief Constable George Smith assigned additional men to the investigation and officers went door to door asking if anyone was housing an individual whose appearance matched that of the assailant. Authorities rounded up "scores of shady characters" and questioned all known "sexual perverts" (which at the time would have included homosexuals). They encouraged Fort Rouge residents to think back to the night of January 4 and try to recall seeing any strange men loitering about Clarke Street between ten and eleven, or leaving the area, likely dishevelled, possibly splattered with blood, sometime around midnight.

The *Free Press* published an artist's rendition of what the murderer might look like – a poor likeness which probably did more to hinder than help the investigation – and a $1000 reward was offered ($500 from the Winnipeg Board of Police Commissioners and $500 from Roy's employer, the *Free Press*).

Though their efforts failed to produce any promising leads, the reward money produced an over-abundance of amateur detectives only too happy to generate a host of implausible theories regarding the identity of the "Fort Rouge Sex Maniac."

One group came up with the idea that Ronnie Flowers was responsible. They imagined that Ronnie had somehow contrived to sneak a gun into the Rialto Theatre, and then, after stopping to enjoy milkshakes with Roy, one of his best friends, lured him to the coal yard, sexually assaulted him, and killed him. He then carried Roy's body through eighteen metres of snow, dragged him into the coal bin, and still made it home in time to take Mrs. McGregor's phone call at 11:30, bearing no signs of blood or a struggle. Chief Smith swiftly put an end to that nonsense. "Young Flowers had no more to do with this shooting than I did."

Spurred on by the *Free Press*'s bold headlines – "Police Intensify Hunt For German Suspect" – a second faction of amateur detectives believed the murderer was an escaped German prisoner-of-war (at the time concentration camps still existed in Canada). While it was a remote possibility, at the time of Roy's murder, Winnipeg police were only aware of one German escapee and it was more reasonable to assume that, rather than pausing halfway through the escape attempt to murder and rape a thirteen year old boy, the escapee would not waste any time fleeing, or attempting to flee to, his native land.

Police were not buying the whole German thing anyway. During his sexual assaults, the rapist had been so eager to be identified as German that police suspected the accent and the 'me-German-you-Canadian' references were nothing more than attempts to mislead the investigation. Furthermore, though there were no guarantees, police also believed that had the murderer been German, he was more likely to be Nordic blonde and fair-complexioned than Mediterranean dark and olive-skinned.

One final explanation for Roy's murder, and one which, according to the *Free Press*, the majority of the arm chair detectives especially favored, was that Roy had stumbled upon a crime in progress and had been killed to keep him silent. The problem with that theory was that there was absolutely no evidence to suggest a crime had been in progress anywhere near the site of Roy's murder, and it was stretch to think that a thief, or thieves, would stop to sexually assault him before making good on their escape.

Mimicking *Dragnet*'s popular 1940s gumshoe, Chief Smith responded to the unlikely theories in true Joe Friday fashion: "we want the facts, not guesses."

Chief Smith and the Winnipeg police would get those facts soon enough. On the morning of January 5, 1946, immediately after Roy's body had been removed, police began searching the area between the boxcar and the coal yard for the bullets that had passed through his body. During their search, they found one live shell and two empty cartridges, but no spent bullets. From the shell and cartridges, police knew they were looking for a 9 mm automatic, but, without a spent bullet, forensics had no way of examining the striations made by the weapon's rifling, and hopefully in time identifying the gun that had made them.

Necessity being the mother of invention, that same afternoon, Winnipeg police made history when a group of detectives gathered downtown to brainstorm ways of locating the spent bullets. Detective Inspector George Blow, who would go on to serve as Winnipeg's Chief Constable from 1965 to 1970, has been credited with suggesting they scan the crime scene with a military mine detector. Today, metal detectors are regularly used by law enforcement agencies throughout the world; in January, 1946, the concept was sheer genius.

Those officers assigned to the task, first tested the detector against an assortment of metal objects – bottle caps, nails, bits of scrap metal, bullets – until they were able to distinguish between the sound each object made. Once they had that mastered, the officers began their tedious hunt. Working at twenty minute intervals in sub-zero temperatures, for two and a half days the officers took turns sweeping the area around the coal and wood yard, their ears straining to hear the distinctive sound of the detector locating a bullet. On the third day their efforts paid off. Four inches beneath the compacted snow and ice, they found one of the bullets. Together with the shell and cartridges, the bullet was sent to the RCMP's world class forensic lab in Regina for ballistics testing.

Roy McGregor's funeral was held on January 10, six days after his death and three days after police found one of the bullets that killed him. Five-hundred people turned out to pay their respects to the McGregors and the young man with the inexhaustible joie de vivre. The funeral's focus on children – the singing of children's hymns, the presence of dozens of Roy's school-mates and friends, his fellow air cadets and newspaper carriers, and the six young boys who acted as pall bearers – made it an especially heart-wrenching occasion. Following a brief ceremony, Roy's body was interred at Elmwood cemetery, the same cemetery where Lola Cowan and Emily Patterson had been laid to rest twenty years earlier.

With no new developments or leads in the case, the public began to fear that the identity of Roy's murderer may have been interred with him.

The fear was unfounded. Winnipeg police wouldn't give up so easily.

At the end of February, after a painstaking process of elimination, Sergeant A. Mason-Rooke, Regina's firearms expert, notified Winnipeg police that the bullet found at the McGregor crime scene had come from a Browning 9 mm Fabrique Nationale GP 35 automatic pistol manufactured by the John Inglis Company of Toronto for the Canadian army and specially designed to take German ammunition.

On the chance that the man Winnipeg police were looking for had come from, or fled to, another city or country, when Chief Smith received Mason-Rooke's information, he distributed a confidential bulletin to the FBI, Scotland Yard, and various police agencies throughout Canada and the United States detailing the circumstances surrounding Roy's murder, and asking all law enforcement officers to be on the lookout for a gun matching the description of the murder weapon. He also asked the various police agencies to check their "sexual pervert" files and report back on any crimes similar to the ones they were investigating in Winnipeg.

* * *

In many respects, George Robert Smith (no relation to Chief George Smith) and Roy McGregor were alike: both were thirteen years old, both were in grade seven, both had one sibling, and both were exceedingly likeable. In other ways, the boys were dissimilar. Unlike Roy, the dark-haired, brown-eyed, and gregarious social butterfly, fair-haired and blue-eyed George was quiet and generally stayed close to home. His two favorite pastimes were playing the accordion and scouting, an organization he had joined during the winter of 1945-1946.

More than eight months had passed since Roy McGregor's murder when George left his home on Wednesday, September 18, 1946, to attend the 23rd Scout Troop's first meeting of the season. The gathering was held at the Home Street United Church in West Central Winnipeg, less than three blocks away from his house at 585 Home Street. Because it was threatening to rain, George wore his skull cap and blue raincoat.

When the meeting broke up at 9:45, George left the church with fellow scouts, Jack Brown and Bruce Leibrock. They hung around outside the church until Albert Tait, their scoutmaster, joined them. The four boys walked north on Home Street until they reached the corner of St. Matthews Avenue where Albert said goodbye and proceeded east. Even though it was raining heavily by now, Jack, Bruce, and George stood on the corner talking for another five minutes before Jack and Bruce turned and walked west.

"See you tomorrow," Bruce called to George over his shoulder.

"Maybe," George called back before continuing north on Home Street. It was just after 10:00 and he was one and a half blocks from home.

When George had not returned home by 11:00, his parents began to worry. Like Roy McGregor, it wasn't like George not to call if he expected to be late. Mr. and Mrs. Smith called the Rupert Street police station to ask if there had been an accident involving a thirteen year old boy and were told there had not been. Growing ever more anxious, Mr. Smith went out in search of his son while Mrs. Smith phoned a number of his friends. When all attempts to locate him failed, George's aunt, Helen McGregor (no relation to Roy McGregor), called police to report her nephew missing.

At 7:00 the following morning, Mrs. J. Johnson, another of George's aunts, called Reverend Whitmore, the pastor of Home Street United Church, to see if George had inadvertently been locked in the church overnight. Reverend Whitmore thought it highly unlikely, but obligingly set out to examine the church.

At the same time Reverend Whitmore was making his way to Home Street Church, Frank Zehethofer was backing his car out of his garage into the alley between Home and Arlington Streets. Checking first to his left, then to his right, he saw what appeared to be a body huddled across the lane, at the rear of 626 Home Street thirty metres to his south. Racing back to his house, Frank told his wife to call for police and a doctor and hurried back to the alley to stand guard over what he then discovered was the body of a young boy.

At 7:20 a.m., five minutes after Mrs. Zehethofer contacted the Rupert Street police, Constables Alex Jamieson and Fred Gibson arrived on the scene. Rain from the previous night, combined with the excavation of an empty lot immediately to the west of 626 Home Street, had turned the alley into a morass of mud and clay. The constables waded through the ankle-deep muck and stared down at what was undoubtedly the body of young George Smith. The boy's feet had been bound by the belt of a coat and he was naked from the waist up. From head to toe, his body was coated with mud, clay, and blood from a fatal gunshot wound.

Twelve metres north of where George's body lay, Constable Gibson discovered a torn singlet (a sleeveless undershirt), a blue raincoat, and a blue plaid shirt. The sleeves of both the raincoat and shirt were turned inside out and all the clothing was saturated with mud. Halfway between the body and the clothes, Constable Gibson found George's skull cap; two metres west of the skull cap, he spotted three or four drops of blood the size of a dime. On the west side of the lane, Constable Jamieson noticed tire tracks that had veered wide of the body, as though someone had swerved to avoid hitting it.

When the coroner arrived, he told investigators that George had been shot in the back and had suffered a crushing blow to the head. Because rigor was fixed, he estimated George's death at 10:00 the previous night.

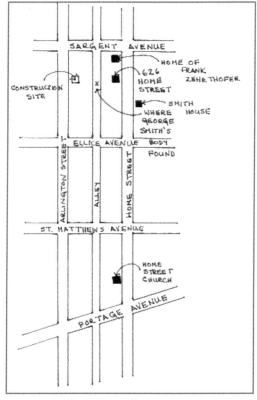

Location of the body of George Smith.

Pathologist O.C. Trainer again performed the autopsy and again confirmed the coroner's findings. The bullet that killed George had entered his back, just under his left shoulder blade, and had exited below his left breast. The blow to the head had fractured his skull above the right ear. The fracture had possibly been made by the butt of the same gun used to shoot him, probably post-mortem. As he had done in the McGregor murder case, Trainor also pointed out that there was no evidence of scorching to George's body or clothes, suggesting that George had been shot from a distance, but conceded that the previous night's rain may have washed away any gunshot residue. Trainor believed that a sexual assault had been attempted but not completed.

Based upon a careful examination of the sites where the constables found the skull cap, the pile of clothes, and the body, police believed that before he was killed, George had put up a fierce struggle. They were so convinced of George's frenzied fight, in their media release they asked people to be on the lookout for a man with bite and scratch marks to his hands and face.

Once again, a small army of officers hit the streets, interviewing West Central residents, asking them if they knew of anyone matching the assailant's description, or if they had seen a strange man loitering about Home Street or Home Street United Church. Suspecting the tire tracks found in the alley might point to a get-away car, they also asked residents if they had seen any unfamiliar vehicles parked in, or cruising, the neighborhood.

Though no one recalled seeing any suspicious characters, five people remembered hearing unusual noises at the time of the murder. Gier Thorgieson of 594 Home Street told police he had just retired to bed when he heard what could have been a shot at 10:09 exactly. Immediately after the shot, he heard a dog begin to bark and footsteps running south down the alley towards Ellice Avenue. James Wright of 592 Home Street told police his dog barked for an hour between 10:00 and 11:00. William Restall of 640 Home Street heard a car backfire about ten, and Mr. and Mrs. Zehethofer said they thought they had heard a car backfire sometime between 9:30 and 10:00. Because the reports matched the pathologist's estimated time of death, police fixed the time of George's murder at 10:10 the previous evening.

George Smith's murder launched Winnipeg into a state of hysteria. Horror-stricken citizens wanted to know what kind of man could do such a thing.

"A lone wolf," Chief Smith told them, "a dangerous and cunning killer." One who would not associate with other "perverts" and was a stranger to the boys. Deputy Chief Charles MacIver added that if and when the murderer attacked again, "this man will kill his victim whether or not the victim submits to a criminal assault. He will do so to avoid detection." And St. Boniface mayor, George MacLean, warned that the man "could be normal for months at a time – could just as easily be the sober and steady man across the street as the shadiest character in the darkest alley in town."

Because large numbers of officers were needed to follow through on the hundreds of sightings of suspicious looking men that were now pouring in, Chief Smith asked for and received additional manpower from the RCMP and the suburban police forces of Tuxedo, East and West Kildonan, St. James, St. Boniface, and Fort Garry. Using rental cars and vehicles on loan from, or chauffeured by, private citizens, police moved through the city following up the leads.

Night time sporting events, where "some boys were wearing hunting knives strapped to their waists as a means of protection," were rescheduled to daylight hours and children no longer played in the streets after school. Police once more rounded up all known "sexual perverts" and "shady characters" for questioning, and a $7000 reward, the second largest in Winnipeg history, was offered.

Because of their earlier success, police again borrowed an army mine detector to sweep the tons of mud and clay that hid the bullet that had killed George Smith. But this time they met with success faster. On the second day of their search, police heard the familiar sound of the detector scanning a bullet. Digging it out from beneath six inches of mud, they immediately dispatched it to Regina for comparison with the bullet found at the McGregor murder scene. They didn't wait long for Sergeant Mason-Rooke to confirm that the gun that killed Roy McGregor had also killed George Smith.

Keeping this new information under wraps, Chief Smith ordered that all unregistered guns be registered immediately, no small feat after the war when guns were as plentiful as children. Over the course of the next several months, police fired and compared dozens of bullets from registered 9 mm pistols. But register and compare as they would, police remained no closer to matching the bullets from the guns they tested with the bullets they had found at the crime scenes.

Though Chief Smith admitted to being completely baffled by the murders of Roy McGregor and George Smith, he remained "confident that eventually the killer of these boys will be brought to justice," and that police "will go on to a successful conclusion, even though it takes many more years."

Six hundred people, including friends, classmates, and members of the 23rd Scout Troop attended George Smith's funeral on Monday, September 23, 1946. The Greenway School safety patrol stood duty throughout the somber and emotional affair. Following the ceremony, George was interned at Winnipeg's Brookside cemetery.

* * *

After George Smith's murder, several months passed without police making any headway. Then, on June 30, 1947, seven hundred kilometres away, in the Lakehead cities of Port Arthur-Fort William (now Thunder Bay), in a seemingly unrelated incident, two masked men brandishing guns robbed the Port Arthur Palm Dairy of $380. Despite the gunmen's attempts at disguise, the three Palm Dairy employees caught in the hold-up were able to provide police with a good physical description of the thieves. Within thirty minutes of the robbery, Port Arthur police had thrown a dragnet over the cities and had guards posted at all points of departure.

At 11:30 that evening, Constable Hermann Scarnati and plain-clothesman Onni Harty spotted two men matching the robbers' descriptions loitering about the Fort William Canadian Pacific Railway Station. When Scarnati and Harty confronted them, the men gave their names as twenty-two year old Michael Angelo Vescio and eighteen year old Frank George Guarasci. They told the officers they were waiting to board the midnight train to Winnipeg. Suspicious of the two men, Harty and Scarnati asked them to accompany them to the police station for further questioning.

Shortly after midnight, by now July 1, Constables Harty and Scarnati escorted Michael and Frank back to the train depot to examine the locker holding their suitcases. Just as Constable Harty was about to open the bags, Michael Vescio inexplicably blurted out, "There's something in there that doesn't belong to me." Their curiosity piqued, inside the bags Constables Harty and Scarnati discovered the guns used in the Palm Dairy hold-up, an 8 mm pistol and a Browning 9 mm FN GP 35 automatic pistol manufactured by the John Inglis Company of Toronto for the Canadian army. The officers confiscated the weapons and returned Michael and Frank to the Port Arthur police station. Faced with the damning weapons, Vescio and Guarasci confessed to the Palm Dairy robbery.

Later that day, the guns landed on the desk of Port Arthur's Chief of Police, George Taylor. As Chief Taylor sat at his desk fingering the Browning, something triggered his memory. Reaching into a desk drawer, he pulled out a thick manila folder holding an assortment of memos and circulars. He thumbed through the contents until he found what he was looking for, a confidential bulletin issued by Winnipeg's Chief Constable George Smith several months earlier asking police to keep their eyes open for a gun matching the description of the Browning automatic Chief Taylor had sitting in front of him.

Chief Taylor contacted Winnipeg's new Chief Constable, Charles MacIver (George Smith retired to Victoria in 1947), who asked Taylor to test fire three bullets and forward them to the RCMP lab in Regina. On July 12, while Chief Taylor was waiting for the ballistics results, Michael Vescio and Frank Gaurasci pled guilty to armed robbery. Because of his age, Frank was sentenced to two years less a day at the Burwash Reformatory; Michael, the older of the two and thought to be the mastermind behind the robbery, was sent to Stony Mountain Federal Penitentiary near Winnipeg to serve out a three year sentence.

Michael Vescio had only been in prison a week when Sergeant Mason-Rooke delivered the news Winnipeg police had been waiting eighteen long months to hear. The bullets sent by Chief Taylor matched those found at the McGregor and Smith murder scenes. Detective Inspector George Blow immediately left for Port Arthur to personally take charge of the weapon and hand deliver it to Regina for another round of ballistics testing. As expected, the second set of results confirmed the first – the gun found in Michael Vescio's possession at the Fort William CPR station had been used to kill Roy McGregor and George Smith.

Sergeant Mason-Rooke would later testify that between September 23, 1946, and July 18, 1947, the forensic lab in Regina had fired bullets from forty-two different arms and compared 168 different cartridges cases before reaching that conclusion. The odds of the bullets coming from a gun other than the one found in Michael Vescio's possession "were one in millions." On August 8, two Winnipeg police officers were sent to Stony Plain Penitentiary to serve a warrant on Michael Vescio for the murders and bring him into Rupert Street headquarters for questioning.

Faced with the irrefutable scientific ballistics evidence, Michael admitted to shooting both Roy and George, but insisted he had done so by accident. Asked where he got the gun, Michael offered three different explanations. Initially he told police he had bought the gun for $25 from "a Frenchman in the army who had stolen it from a Sergeant-Major's holster at Grassmere Ditch prisoner-of-war camp." Next, he said he'd stolen it from a fellow named Joe Cushman the day an army friend, Joseph Winzoski, had taken him to Cushman's house so Cushman could show them his vast collection of guns. Finally, Michael admitted to stealing the gun when he delivered supplies to Grassmere Ditch while he was employed with the Canadian military.

Michael's preliminary hearing for the murder of George Smith began October 8, 1947. Because Joe Cushman was working out west and was unable to testify until his return, on October 14 the hearing was postponed for a week. In the interim, the court proceeded with Michael's preliminary hearing for the murder of Roy McGregor. On the second day of the fall assizes, Magistrate M. H. Garton committed Michael Vescio to trial for George Smith's murder. His trial for the murder of Roy McGregor was put off until the spring assizes, and if Vescio was found guilty of the George Smith murder charge, the second trial was unlikely to be heard.

Michael Vescio's trial lasted from November 18 to November 25. Given the pandemonium that had surrounded the murders, Vescio's arrest, and the preliminary hearings, the trial, unable to compete with the media's coverage of Princess Elizabeth's November 20 wedding to Phillip Mountbatten, Prince of Denmark and Greece and soon to be Duke of Edinburgh, received scant attention.

Michael's defense was grounded upon his insistence that he had accidentally shot George. He testified that on the night of the shooting, he had been drinking heavily. When he came across George, he asked him if he could borrow the Smith's telephone, and George responded by saying that his father would not want a drunk using his telephone. George's response so enraged him, Michael grabbed

George. During the ensuing melee, Michael slipped in the mud and his gun went off.

During his closing statements, Vescio's council, John L. Ross, argued that George's comment about his father not wanting a drunk using the telephone ought to be viewed as grounds for provocation. As a result, the shooting was unintentional. Ergo, the charge against his client could only be manslaughter.

Ross's arguments were as weak as they were futile. In his closing remarks, Crown Prosecutor, O. M. M. Kay, demanded to know if the shooting had been accidental, why was George Smith naked from the waist up. Unless there had been some ulterior motive, why had Michael drawn a gun on a thirteen year old boy who stood four-feet seven inches tall and weighed less than one hundred pounds? If the gun had gone off when Vescio grabbed George, why were there no powder burns on the victim? Why, for that matter, was Michael even carrying a gun? And why had Michael taken George to the alley in the first place?

Kay also made much of the fact that the gun's hammer had to be cocked before it could be fired, meaning that the gun's safety had to have been off at the time it went off.

Kay's painting of the crime was as different from Ross's as a da Vinci is from a Warhol. It was the prosecutor's contention that Michael had somehow lured George into the alley. When George realized what Michael's true motives were, he fought back with every morsel of strength he could muster. That explained why the clothes found at the crime scene were saturated with mud and why the singlet was torn.

Kay argued that during the struggle, George managed to break free, which explained why the sleeves of the shirt and raincoat were turned inside out. As George ran, Michael drew his pistol and fired. The bullet caught George in the back and he fell to the ground. Unsure whether George was alive or dead, Michael knelt by the fallen boy and struck his head with the butt of the gun. "That's the whole story," said Kay. "The fleeing boy had to be stopped. That's the thought and the only thought that was in Vescio's mind. It was a deliberate shot to stop the boy from getting away." At all costs, Michael had to prevent George from reaching home and calling police. There was nothing accidental about it.

On November 25, 1947, only thirty-five minutes after they retired to deliberate, the jury found Michael Angelo Vescio of the murder of George Smith. Chief Justice E. K. Williams immediately sentenced him to hang, the execution to be carried out on February 18, 1948. Michael Vescio was hustled out of the courtroom and taken to Headingly Jail to await his execution. His tireless defense managed to get him five stays of execution before he was finally hung on November 19, 1948 at 1:01 in the morning.

* * *

Unlike the vast quantities of information available about modern sexual predators, little is known of Michael Vescio. Of Italian descent, he was born in Port Arthur in 1925, the youngest of eight children. Traumatized by the death of his mother and his father's remarriage, Michael lived with his father and step-mother until 1942 when he turned seventeen and was old enough to join the army. Assigned a job driving for the Royal Canadian Army Service Corps in Manitoba, during the first two of his five-year stint in the military, he was shuffled about the province. In 1944 he was permanently assigned to the Fort Osborne Barracks in Winnipeg's Fort Rouge District. The next year, Michael stole the Browning 9 mm pistol while making the supply delivery to the Grassmere Ditch prisoner-of-war camp.

For his final three years in the army, Michael lived at Mr. and Mrs. Sidney Wright's boarding house at 115 Rose Street on what was called a sleeping-out pass. He remained with Mr. and Mrs. Wright until May 1947 when his father wrote to say there was a job waiting for him back in Port Arthur.

As so commonly happens with serial predator cases, people who knew Michael were stunned by the charges against him. His landlord and landlady remembered him as "shy and reserved, a man who seldom drank and never swore." Mrs. Wright considered him a "very handsome fellow" whose "room was very tidy . . . everything was in its place;" Sidney called him a good tenant and "no trouble at all."

Though police had interviewed the Wrights when they canvassed the Fort Rouge and West Central districts after the murders, the Wrights insisted that they would never have connected Michael to the man police were looking for because "it was impossible to think of him committing those horrible murders."

According to the Wrights, Michael always followed the same routine. He left for work at 7:00 in the morning and returned at 5:30 in the evening. When he got back he cleaned himself up before going to dinner at the Margaret Rose Tea Rooms, located not far from the Rose Street boarding house. After dinner, he frequently stopped to browse through the bookstore located next door to the tea rooms. On Saturdays he went for a haircut and shave at the Fort Rouge Hairdressers. On Sunday mornings he was often the bookstore's first customer; on Sunday evenings he shared supper with the Wrights. Unlike the rest of his evenings, which he generally spent reading or going for a walk, on Monday nights Michael invariably went to the movies. Occasionally he attended a hockey game at the Amphitheatre, sometimes he went out with friends, and on the rare occasion, went to a tavern for a couple of beer. The Wrights knew Michael had a gun, he had shown it to them around Christmas, 1945, but, since he was in the army, having a gun only seemed natural.

The clerk in the bookstore, where Michael bought his *Colliers, Liberty, Life, Newsweek* and true detective magazines, recalled him as "very much the gentleman. He wasn't the talkative type, but he was always very polite if you talked to him." The pharmacist at Brooking's Drugstore said, "I never got to know him, but he acted perfectly normal." His army buddies considered him quiet and shy, especially around girls, but thought him friendly enough. In a macabre twist of irony, they nicknamed him "Killer" precisely because they thought he wasn't. Short and small boned, at times he over-compensated for his slight build by acting the tough guy. Given his crimes, his army pals were convinced he was a twentieth century reincarnation of Dr. Jekyll and Mr. Hyde.

If acquaintances and coworkers expressed shock at Michael's arrest, his family was dumbfounded. When his brother and sister, Frank Vescio and Frances Bernardi came out from Port Arthur to arrange for Michael's defense, Frances told police that "Mike is too kind and gentle to do such a thing." It was her firm belief that if Michael had confessed to the crimes it was only because he was being "forced to cover for someone else," or because Winnipeg police had "forced it out of him."

All in all, the general consensus was that Michael Vescio was the "last person one would suspect of the two bestial crimes."

Yet, after Michael's arrest, friends and family admitted, perhaps unwittingly, to symptoms of trouble. He was different from the other lads said Mr. Wright. He kept to himself and never bothered with girls. Sergeant Thomas Moir, Michael's military superior, and whose idea of a good soldier was "one who dresses neatly and acts smartly and does not come in at eight instead of six am," said Michael wasn't his idea of a good soldier. One of Michael's army co-workers called him sly, another said he was immature, a third remembered him as a "bit of a gun nut."

Even Michael's sister Frances, who had been so vehemently convinced of her brother's innocence, admitted that after their mother's death "Mike did get into some minor trouble with the law," and added that "after mother's death, Michael was not happy at home. He spent more time at my place than at his home. Mike found himself a kind of vagabond. We tried to help him but he didn't tell all his troubles at home." Frances also admitted that after her brother's return to Port Arthur in May 1947, "he seemed quieter than usual." His long absence from home had made him "strange," and he must have "got into bad company at Winnipeg."

All those involved with Vescio's capture and conviction received accolades. Constables Onni and Scarnati were given cash bonuses, Port Arthur's Chief Taylor was hailed as brilliant, and letters of thanks poured into Winnipeg police headquarters.

The accolades were not misplaced.

If Winnipeg police had not come up with the idea of using a mine detector to locate the bullets used to kill Roy McGregor and George Smith, if two Port Arthur constables had not spotted two suspicious characters thought to be involved in the Port Arthur Palm Dairy heist hanging about the Fort William train station, and if Chief Taylor had not linked the gun used in the robbery back to the two Winnipeg murders, Michael Vescio would certainly have claimed more victims. As criminal behaviorists now know, it is exceedingly rare – almost unheard of – for serial predators to stop committing their crimes unless they are caught, incarcerated for a different crime, hospitalized, or dead.

Michael Vescio's arrest and conviction were justifiably held out as a crowning example of dedicated police perseverance and a first-rate scientific achievement.

Three
Robert Raymond Cook

"[I] must admit my knees buckled when I heard that foreman say guilty. I used to think it was up to the Crown to prove a person guilty. After that I believe differnt. Mr. Main I know that they cannot prove me guilty, for in all truth, I am not. I've been guessed into a death sentence . . . If I hang, murder will be committed in the name of the law."

Robert Raymond Cook

Unexpectedly embraced by the capricious hand of good fortune, Robert Raymond Cook and one hundred non-violent offenders at Saskatchewan Penitentiary in Prince Albert received amnesty in honor of Queen Elizabeth and Prince Phillip's royal visit to Canada in 1959. Of the one hundred people released, sixty were released the same day as Robert, Tuesday, June 23.

On the day Saskatchewan Penitentiary opened its doors and released Robert to freedom, he was three weeks shy of his twenty second birthday and a little better than two and a half years into a three year sentence for breaking and entering and car theft.

Robert managed to savor his freedom for four and a half days before being re-arrested initially on suspicion of fraud, less than twenty-four hours later, for murder.

* * *

Robert's father, Raymond Albert Cook of Sunnynook, Alberta, married Robert's mother, Josephine Grover of Hanna, Alberta, on November 7, 1936. Raymond was twenty-eight and Josephine eighteen. Eight months later, the *Hanna Herald* was pleased to report that, "to Mr. and Mrs. Ray Cook, July 15, a son," Robert Raymond was born. Despite the marriage's promising beginning, and the arrival of a much welcomed son, the Cook relationship quickly slipped into a union of querulousness and recriminations, in part because Josephine believed Raymond's wandering eye did more than just wander, in part because Josephine's weak heart and other chronic ailments placed undue stress on the union. Yet, for all its ups and downs, Raymond and Josephine's marriage survived until September 16, 1946, when Josephine unexpectedly died during a routine operation to repair a twisted bowel.

With Josephine's sudden death, Robert became the focus of his father's attention, a position he held unrivaled until Raymond began courting Daisy May Gaspar, Robert's grade three and four teacher. On July 7, 1949, a week before Robert's twelfth birthday, Raymond and Daisy wed. One year later, the Cook family, now expanded to four with the February, 1950 arrival of Gerald, gathered its belongings and moved to Stettler, a farm community of 3600 situated half way between Edmonton and Calgary. Whether it was the move, the marriage, the addition of a new brother vying for his father's affections, or, as is more likely, a combination of all three, it was then Robert forged his career path as car thief, petty crook, and multiple murderer.

Only in notoriety was Robert Cook ever a big person. At the time of his arrest for his father's murder, Robert stood five-feet-seven and weighed between 150 and 155 pounds, shorter but huskier than Raymond. Though he was small in stature, men viewed him as a man's man – tough, quiet, would not back down from a fight, a loyal friend, a guy who rallied behind the underdog. Women found him attractive – raw and masculine, a handsome face set upon a square jaw and bull-dog-thick neck.

Considered clever with his hands, boxing experts like fight promoter Alex Turk and Alex Wilson, who had helped train Robert while Robert was doing a stint in Stony Mountain Penitentiary, regarded him as a natural welterweight who could have made a name for himself as a professional boxer had he been so inclined.

Given his obvious talents, it is regrettable that Robert's clever hands proved too clever by far. By all accounts there was no one to rival him when it came to hot wiring cars, a hobby he claimed to enjoy "for the excitement and adventure more than for devilness." By the time Robert turned fourteen, authorities surrendered all hope he would outgrow his addiction for "wiring up" cars and "taking a ride," and packed him off to Bowden Reformatory, the first of the many stops he would make down his dead-end street.

From Bowden it was but a short hike to Lethbridge Provincial Jail, and for the remainder of his brief life Robert merely relocated from one penal institution to another. By the time he was released from Saskatchewan Penitentiary in June of 1959, Robert's criminal record catalogued nineteen offenses, all but one for theft, breaking and entering, and car theft, and he had become, as Alan Hustak writes in *They Were Hanged*, "fully institutionalized."

On the day of their release from jail, Robert and his fellow amnesty recipients rode the prison bus from Prince Albert to Saskatoon. In Saskatoon, Robert and his pal Jimmy Myhaluk proceeded to get drunk, lurching from bar to bar, celebrating their good luck well into Wednesday morning when they caught a Greyhound to Edmonton. Upon their arrival in Edmonton, Jimmy went home to his parents and Robert sought out the Commercial Hotel to catch a few hours of sleep. At 1:00 p.m., presumably refreshed and sober, Robert appeared at Hood Motors where he and salesman Carl Thalbing discussed the possibility of Robert trading in a 1958 station wagon on one of Hood Motors's showpieces – a sparkling new, white Impala convertible with red leather upholstery.

If one believes Robert's story, after leaving Hood Motors he hot-wired a car from a used car lot on the south side of Edmonton and drove to the outskirts of Bowden, two hours south, to dig up a $4300 stash of money he had cached there in 1957. Though Robert's Bowden trip is cloaked in uncertainty, there is no question that by 6:00 p.m. he was in Edmonton sharing dinner with Jimmy Myhaluk and Jimmy's parents.

Robert left the Myhaluks in search of a good time at 8:00 in the evening. He quickly ran down half a dozen prison pals holed up in the tavern of the Selkirk Hotel. The small fraternity partied until early Thursday morning when Robert decided it was high time he went home to visit the family he had not seen in well over two years. Borrowing a truck from Eddie Read, Robert asked Walter Berezowski to drive him to Stettler. Walter dropped Robert off on the outskirts of Stettler at 1:00 in the afternoon, but rather than going home, Robert rambled about town until 9:00 in the evening.

* * *

Raymond and Daisy knew Robert was to be released from Saskatchewan Penitentiary on June 23; Daisy had even sent him a new white shirt, a red tie, and a pair of yellow socks to mark the occasion. They patiently waited for Robert to arrive on Tuesday, again on Wednesday, and by Thursday, when he had still failed to appear, may have begun wondering if he would ever show up.

Tragically, he did.

At 7:00 Thursday evening, while out riding his bicycle, Robert's half-brother Gerald, accidentally came across his older brother. The siblings enjoyed an affectionate tousle and Robert told Gerald he would be home shortly.

Shortly came and went, and, at 7:30 p.m., Raymond and Daisy's friends, Jim and Leona Hoskins, dropped by the Cook house for a visit. Over coffee, Raymond agreed to help Jim move furniture on Saturday and Daisy and Leona arranged a Sunday family picnic. At 9:00, after Jim and Leona departed, Raymond went out in search of his missing, but hopefully prodigal, son. Shortly thereafter, Arnold Filipenko saw Raymond pick Robert up from Main Street.

Other than Robert, no one saw any of the Cooks alive again.

* * *

At 8:00 on Friday morning, Robert showed up at Edmonton's South Park Motors driving Raymond's station wagon and spoke to salesman Arthur Pilling about trading the station wagon for a different vehicle. Unable to reach an agreement, Robert left South Park Motors and went to collect Jimmy Myhaluk. At 11:30, he and Jimmy reappeared at Hood Motors where Robert again broached the possibility of trading the station wagon for the Impala. His mind made up, Robert gave salesman Len Amoroso a $40 down payment and said he would be back at five to sign the papers. Robert and Jimmy then "bummed around" until Robert went to collect his new automobile.

For the next thirty hours, Robert drove the Impala harder than an over-taxed dray horse. Leaving Edmonton, he drove to Camrose, one hour south. Unsuccessful in his bid to find a friend whom he thought lived there, Robert fell in with three teenagers, Ricky Feth, Homer Teeple, and Lorraine Beasely, and drove to Whitecourt, 175 kilometres northwest of Edmonton. After leaving Whitecourt, Robert drove Ricky, Homer, and Lorraine back to Camrose and headed for home. By then, it was 4:00 p.m., Saturday, June 27.

Having broken in the Impala to the tune of 720 hard-driven kilometres, Robert arrived in Stettler at 7:00 p.m., three hours after leaving Camrose for what should have been less than a sixty minute drive. He spent an hour at home before driving downtown, unaware it would be the last time he would flaunt his shiny new wheels. While cruising Main Street, Constable Allan Braden of the Stettler RCMP stopped Robert to tell him that Sergeant Tom Roach wished a word with him at the detachment offices.

While Robert had been out touring Alberta, Hood Motors had been in touch with the Stettler RCMP. One of the car dealership's new customers, Raymond Cook, had just purchased a new Impala convertible. It was likely nothing more than an oversight, but Mr. Cook had forgotten to sign the necessary documents. Putting two and two together, Sergeant Roach realized it had not been Raymond who had bought the Impala, it had been Raymond's son Robert posing as his father. Before assuming the worst, Sergeant Roach attempted to contact Raymond to hear his side of the story, but had not been able to find him.

When Sergeant Roach questioned Robert at the detachment offices that Saturday night, Robert told the Sergeant that the reason he had been unable to contact Raymond was because Raymond was out of town. He and the rest of his family had gone to British Columbia to scout out a suitable garage to buy. While they were gone, Robert was to trade the station wagon in on the Impala. Because he had none of his own, Robert was to use Raymond's identification to complete the transaction. Robert told Sergeant Roach not to worry. When his father returned he would clear everything up.

Coming from a young man who had made a career from hot-wiring and stealing cars, Sergeant Roach was hardly mollified by Robert telling him not to worry. He placed Robert in a holding cell pending false pretenses charges and drove to the Cook residence, a short two blocks away. Sergeant Roach noticed nothing unusual during his visit, but his gut instinct told him something was wrong.

Nagged by his persistent sense of unease, at 12:30 a.m., Sunday, June 28, Sergeant Roach returned to the Cook house, taking Constable Al Morrison with him. Using nothing but the beams from their flashlights to guide them, Sergeant Roach and Constable Morrison ventured into the small, four room bungalow and took a hasty look around. Though there was nothing about the search to suggest that Robert was not telling the truth about his family having gone to British Columbia, Sergeant Roach and Constable Morrison puzzled over why the five youngest Cook children would leave their sneakers tucked under their beds and why the entire family would strip their beds and take their bedclothes to British Columbia.

At 11:00 that morning, five RCMP officers, including a photograph and fingerprint expert, revisited the Cook residence. Even though it had been some presentiment of evil that had brought them there in the first place, the officers could not have imagined they would find the scene of violence they actually found: walls, pillows, and mattresses covered with blood, bone matter, and bits of human tissue, the shattered remains of a shotgun crusted with bits of blood, brain, and human hair.

Half an hour later two officers entered the attached garage at the rear of the Cook house. Peeling back a couple of flattened cardboard boxes that covered a section of the garage floor, the officers discovered a row of wooden planks lying over a grease pit and caught the pungent whiff of decay. One by one the officers lifted away the planks, gagging from the ever-growing stench and recoiling at the spectacle that awaited them.

Robert Cook's family lay rotting in the two-foot wide, four and a half foot long, five foot deep grease pit in the floor of the Cook's garage. Robert's thirty-seven year old step-mother, Daisy, and his fifty-one year old father, Raymond lay nearest the top. The "contents of Daisy's skull were removed by the blast" of a shotgun. Raymond had been killed by a shotgun wound to the chest, before, or maybe after, his face had been pounded by the butt of the rifle. The process of putrefaction was already turning him a greenish-blue.

Beneath Raymond and Daisy lay Robert's five half-brothers and sisters – nine year old Gerald Ray, eight year old Patrick William, seven year old Christopher Frederick, five year old Kathy Verne, and three year old Linda Mae – their arms, legs, and torsos knotted into a monstrous sculpture. The children had been bludgeoned to death by the butt of the same gun used to shoot their parents, all but one were unrecognizable. All five children had died of their head fractures; all seven bodies were dressed in their night clothes.

The blood and bits of human tissue found on the walls, floors, ceilings, and furniture told an appalling story of human depravity. From the blood on their mattresses police deduced that Daisy, Raymond, Gerald, Patrick, and Christopher had been killed in their beds, while an absence of blood on Kathy and Linda's mattresses told police the two girls had not. Based on blood evidence found in the living room, police speculated that Kathy and Linda, who had shared a room with Raymond and Daisy, had fled into the living room as their parents were being murdered. It was there they had been hunted down and slaughtered.

Logic said that the killer murdered Daisy and Raymond first. Once the adults had been disposed of, the murderer stalked through the house killing Gerald, Patrick, Christopher, Kathy, and Linda, raining down blow after blow on their skulls. When the last of his victims was dead, the killer scooped up the bodies and tossed them into the pit, interspersing their corpses with a jungle of debris – clothing, bedding, tires, chains, hubcaps, newspapers, and garbage. The killer then covered his massacre with the wooden planks and covered the planks with the flattened pieces of cardboard.

Fixing a time of death would not prove easy. Pathologist Peter Davey was unable to be more precise than saying the murders had probably occurred twenty-four to seventy-two hours before the bodies were discovered, placing the time of death between noon on Thursday, June 25, and noon on Saturday, June 27.

Jim and Leona Hoskins visited with Raymond and Daisy until just before 9:00 on Thursday night. Shortly after they left, Arnold Filipenko saw Raymond pick up Robert. On Friday the children failed to show up for school and Raymond failed to show up for work. The blood stained mattresses and the night clothes the bodies were dressed in indicated the Cook's had been in bed when they were attacked. It was therefore reasonable to assume the family had been murdered some time after Jim and Leona left Thursday evening and sometime before the Cooks would have generally risen to get ready for work and school, narrowing the time of death to sometime between 9:00 Thursday night and 6:00 or 7:00 Friday morning.

From the moment they discovered the bodies, police viewed the murders as a cut and dried case. Robert Raymond Cook, already in jail pending fraud charges, became the only suspect. He was charged with his father's murder and at 10:00 Monday morning, June 29, appeared before Magistrate Fred Biggs, who remanded him to a thirty day psychiatric evaluation at the Ponoka Mental Hospital.

On July 2, while Robert was in Ponoka undergoing his psychiatric assessment, the seven dead members of his family were laid to rest in a common grave at the cemetery in Hanna, a farm community 120 kilometres south east of Stettler. Authorities denied Robert's request to attend his family's funeral.

On Saturday, July 11, Albertans awoke to a gloriously sunny day, an update on Queen Elizabeth and Prince Phillip's tour of Lake Louise, speculation that the Calgary Stampede was on the verge of breaking attendance records, and the terrifying news that Robert Cook, the alleged butcher of seven innocent people, and who the police considered "extremely dangerous," had escaped from the Ponoka Mental Hospital just before midnight the previous night.

"Possibly the biggest and certainly the most important" manhunt in Alberta's history was underway. Seventy-five officers, two tracking dogs, and a light spotter aircraft combed the Ponoka countryside. Motorists were warned not to pick up hitchhikers.

On Saturday, investigators trying to best guess which direction their quarry had fled caught their first break when they received reports that an automobile believed to have been stolen by Robert at Ponoka was found overturned near Nevis, and the Nevis Hall had been broken into.

By Sunday the search had intensified. Heavily armed RCMP, whose numbers had expanded to one hundred, patrolled the area between Nevis and Alix. Dozens of police cruisers roared up and down the dusty back roads, and a second light aircraft had joined in the aerial sweep of the country.

On Monday, the same day a second automobile believed to have been stolen by Robert was discovered abandoned near the outskirts of Bashaw, sixty members of the Canadian Army Provost Corps, manning helicopters and jeeps loaded with machine guns, joined the hunt. From the location of the second abandoned vehicle, police believed that Robert had traveled southeast towards Stettler then shifted north. Police and military personnel cordoned off the eastern, western, and southern portions of the district, exposing only the north as a means of escape.

Just after 3:00, Tuesday afternoon police received a call from Mrs. Dufva, a farmer living three kilometres south of Bashaw. Mrs. Dufva told them that only moments before she had seen a suspicious looking man out behind her barn. Though police had taken dozens of similar calls from well-meaning citizens over the course of the previous three and a half days, two squad cars rushed to the Dufva farm. When they arrived, Mrs. Dufva's husband Norman took the officers to the spot where his wife had seen the stranger. As Norman and the officers stood talking, the stranger stepped out from behind the barn and came towards them.

Hungry, tired, and exhausted, at 4:00 in the afternoon on Tuesday July 14, seventy-four hours after his escape, and one day before his twenty-second birthday, Robert Cook gave himself up. He was taken to Bashaw where police saw to it that he was fed and given a new set of clothes before whisking him away to the Fort Saskatchewan Jail, north of Edmonton.

Robert's preliminary hearing for the murder of his father ran from August 24 to August 28. Its conclusion delivered no surprises. Magistrate G. W. Graves announced there was sufficient evidence for the case to proceed to trial. The trial, heard in Red Deer under Justice Peter Greschuk, began November 30 and ran to December 10.

Before they retired to deliberate, Judge Greschuk told the six person, all male jury they were not to concern themselves with penalty or punishment. "Each of you," said Greschuk, "is to banish all questions of penalty from your mind." Because the prosecution's case was built exclusively on circumstantial evidence, Greschuk also told jurors that with circumstantial evidence cases, "the facts must be consistent with the guilt of the accused and inconsistent with any other rational explanation." Carrying Greschuk's words of advice with them, the jurors deliberated an hour and a half before finding Robert guilty. As the criminal code at the time dictated, Justice Greschuk sentenced the defendant to death. Robert was returned to Fort Saskatchewan jail to await his execution, scheduled for April 15, 1960, Good Friday.

Genuinely surprised by the verdict, Robert's defense team immediately launched an appeal to the Appellate Division of the Supreme Court of Alberta. When the Appellate Court granted Robert another trial, his new senior lawyer, Frank Dunne, and Dunne's co-counsel, Dave McNaughton, who had served as junior counsel at both trials, asked for and received a change of venue.

Justice Harry Riley presided over the second trial held in Edmonton, beginning on June 20. The evidence presented at the second trial was essentially the same as that presented at the first, as was the outcome. The jury deliberated a brief thirty minutes before finding Robert Cook guilty. Just as Judge Greschuk had done seven months earlier, on June 28, precisely one year after the bodies of the Cook family were found, Justice Riley sentenced Robert to hang, the execution to take place on October 11.

When Alberta's Appellate Court rejected Robert's appeal for a third trial, Dunne and McNaughton appealed to the Appellate Division of the Supreme Court of Canada which upheld the decision of the lower court. It was a bitter blow, but Robert's defense team had yet to concede defeat. In order to give them time to mount a campaign to have their client's hanging commuted to a life sentence, Dunne and McNaughton asked for a postponement of the execution. They won their fight for the postponement, but lost the bigger battle.

Stoically maintaining his innocence to the end, Robert Raymond Cook went to Fort Saskatchewan's gallows just after midnight on November 15, 1960, the first person in Alberta to do so since 1952 when Caspar Gorczak was hung for the murder of his wife. Robert was pronounced dead at 12:18 in the morning. He was twenty-three years old and the last man hung in Alberta. He donated his body to the University of Edmonton for medical research and two eye bank recipients received his "cold, cold eyes."

Death may have obliterated the name Robert Raymond Cook as readily as he obliterated his family if not for the swell of people who either believed in his innocence, or believed his trials and legal representation were, to put it kindly, substandard. In his book *The Trials of Robert Raymond Cook*, Jack Pecover not only lays before the reader the shortcomings of Robert's legal counsel, but he also questions the integrity of the evidence, the investigation, and the preliminary hearing and trials. By the end of the book, the reader acknowledges that, while there may have yet been opportunity to do so, crucial pieces of evidence were, shall we say, left hanging.

But as compelling as many of Jack Pecover's arguments are, and as correct as he may be in many of his assessments, in the end Pecover offers nothing to censure either jury's decision or fear that in hanging Robert Cook the courts committed an unpardonable blunder.

Aside from the obvious – the Cook family was likely murdered sometime between 9:00 p.m. on Thursday, June 25 and 7:00 a.m. on Friday, June 26, within hours of Robert's return to Stettler, and when he readily allowed being in the house for at least part of that time – there is an avalanche of circumstantial evidence to snow Robert under in guilt.

Following his arrest and during his hearing and trials, Robert stuck to the same story. His father picked him up about 9:00 Thursday evening. They went to the bar to celebrate Robert's early prison release, to raise a glass to the first time father and son were able to enjoy a beer in a bar since Robert had reached the legal age of twenty-one, and, most importantly, to discuss buying the garage Raymond and Robert had so often dreamed of buying, their own little shop where they could work side by side in a harmonious Norman Rockwell setting. It is too late to ever know the absolute truth, but Robert claimed that after he and Raymond finished their beers, "Wed decided then we should talk it over with Mom and left for home." At home they put the proposition to Daisy, who, given Robert's version of events, must have fallen in with the plan wholeheartedly.

Having convinced Daisy of the merit of their scheme, Robert and Raymond set about putting their plan into play. Robert gave Raymond $4100 from the money he'd dug up at Bowden to use as a down payment on the garage, keeping back $200 for his personal use. Before departing, Robert also gave Raymond his blue, prison-issue suit. In exchange for the suit and the $4100, Raymond gave Robert the family station wagon, his car keys, his wallet, and the documents necessary for Robert to trade the station wagon for the Impala. When Robert left at 10:30, Raymond and Daisy and Robert's five half-brothers and sisters were alive and well and preparing to leave for British Columbia.

After he had completed the automobile trade, Robert was to return to Stettler to take Raymond's call telling him where and when he was to pick up his family. He arrived back in Stettler at 7:00 Saturday evening and spent an hour at home before going downtown where he was taken into custody. End of story.

Though the essence of Robert's story never altered, the details frequently did. At various times Robert told police his family was going to British Columbia via train or bus, departing from Calgary or Edmonton. He expected his family to leave on Friday or Saturday, and he was to be back in Stettler to take Raymond's call on Monday, Tuesday, or Wednesday.

Robert's memory for details fared no better when attempting to recall the amounts of money he had cached away, given his father, and kept for himself. At one point he said he had hidden $4100, given $4000 to Raymond and kept $100 for himself. He later revised those figures to $4300 and $100. A second revision had him hiding $4300 and keeping $200, the figures he finally settled on.

One could concede that details were not as strong a suit for Robert as, say, his ability to "wire up" cars, or that under the circumstances, details were the least of Robert's worries, but the suspicious timing of Robert's recollection of other details further undermined his credibility.

Prior to the discovery of the bodies, Robert told Sergeant Roach he did not know exactly where his family intended to go, just "somewhere in British Columbia." After the discovery of the bodies, when it was no longer important that police be handicapped in their attempts to track the Cook family to British Columbia, Robert conveniently remembered they had planned to go to Vancouver.

As suspect as Robert's sudden recollection was, it was less suspect than his sudden recollection of his alibi. Though his life hung in the balance, not until three months after his incarceration at Fort Saskatchewan, and with his first trial little more than a month away, did Robert think to remember that during the critical late Thursday-early Friday time period he and prison pal, Sonny Wilson, had been occupied with breaking into Edmonton's Cosmo Cleaners.

According to Robert, after leaving Stettler at 10:30 that fateful Thursday night, he drove to Edmonton. His first port of call was Frankie's Café where, at about 1:00, he ran into Jack Mitchell, a fellow prison graduate, whose memory for details seemed as unimpeachable as Robert's. Jack testified that he had indeed met Robert, probably that night, maybe at 1:00, possibly at Frankie's Café. Robert swore that after leaving Jack he bumped into his friend, Sonny Wilson, another prison graduate, who was engaged to rob Cosmo Cleaners that night. According to Robert, when Sonny's intended partner in crime reneged on his agreement, Robert stepped in to fill the vacancy.

As flawed as the alibi was, Sonny Wilson *did* rob Cosmo Cleaners that night, though there is nothing but Sonny and Robert's word to substantiate that Robert was there with him. Indeed, in addition to the belatedness of Robert's recollection of the break-in, there is ample evidence to discredit the story. First, answers to why Robert chose not apprise his lawyers of the break-in until after his and Sonny's incarceration at Fort Saskatchewan overlapped are highly suspect. Second, Robert's description of how he and Sonny broke into Charm Cleaners did not match the description given by Sonny. Third, it is impossible to believe Sonny's claim that he could find nothing suitable to pry open the shaft on the roof of Cosmo Cleaners when a tool box Robert claimed to have had in the back of the station wagon at the time of the robbery contained a wide assortment of wrenches, files, chisels, pliers, and more than a dozen screwdrivers. And finally, it is incredulous to think that Robert, who described himself as "well versed in crime and is not an idiot," would plan a robbery but neglect to bring.

With little more than his word going for him, Robert's word was doing little to help his cause. The likely trumped up alibi did as much to weaken Robert's credibility as his insistence that his family had intended to leave for British Columbia the weekend their bodies were discovered. Crown Prosecutor Wallace Anderson easily toppled that story by asking three critical questions. Why it was that no one other than Robert knew of Raymond and Daisy's plans to go to British Columbia? Why did Robert's story contradict what Jim and Leona Hoskins knew about Raymond and Daisy's plans for the weekend? And why, if Raymond and Daisy had talked about buying a garage and moving for months, had they been struck by such a sudden and overwhelming sense of urgency they felt compelled to leave immediately?

Robert could no more provide persuasive answers to those questions than he could explain away a number of other points of dispute. How, for example, would Raymond hope to buy a garage without identification as important as his driver's license? Why would Raymond and Daisy drag five small children aimlessly about British Columbia? If the family was planning on being away for the weekend, why would Daisy buy $5 worth of milk tokens Thursday morning? And why would Daisy, from all accounts a shrewd money manager, choose to spend money unnecessarily on bus and/or train fare for two adults and five children when the family had a perfectly good car?

The best Robert's lawyers could do to staunch the flow of damage was show that it was common knowledge that Raymond one day hoped to buy his own garage, and to verify that the Cooks had every intention of leaving Stettler because their house was for sale.

Robert fared no better with other parts of his story. Though there was nothing to prove or disprove his tale of stealing the car from the Edmonton used car lot, Crown Prosecutor Anderson easily dismissed it with one simple, but shrewd question. After Robert testified that he had returned the car to the same lot from which he had stolen it, thereby greatly increasing his risk of capture, Anderson asked, "You could have left the car a couple of blocks away and have been much better off, would you not?"

Had there been nothing more to condemn him than specious stories and dubious alibis, Robert may have stood a chance of acquittal, but the damning evidence didn't stop there. After the massacre, the killer attempted to wash away blood. While answers to how and when may be engaging, the critical question is why someone other than Robert would bother?

The absence of the $4100 Robert reportedly gave to his father swings both for and against him. Though police doubted it ever existed, $4100, even the belief in its existence (a la Truman Capote's *In Cold Blood*, Robert frequently mentioned his cache while he was in jail) could have provided motive for an outsider, say a recently released con with no money or job prospects.

Slim at best, there nevertheless exists the possibility that someone released from Saskatchewan Penitentiary the same day as Robert
trailed him to Stettler with the intention of stealing his reputed
money cache. That the individual knew Robert had been to Bowden
and dug it up, either through some sixth sense or because he had
tracked Robert from the Commercial Hotel to Hood Motors to the used
car lot on the south side of Edmonton to Bowden is a bit of a stretch.
But it is no less a stretch than believing that out of all the gin joints,
in all the towns, in all the world, an unknown thief would choose the
Cook's chipped and peeling, clapboard-sided, modest home as the
ideal house to plunder for hidden wealth, or that with all the isolated
ranch and farm homes within shouting distance of Stettler, a thief
would settle on a house two blocks from the Stettler police station.

When taken in conjunction with a pile of clothes police found
heaped upon Raymond and Daisy's bed, the improbability of the
released-prisoner-or-unknown-thief-cum-mass-murderer multiplies.
Because the clothes were set on top of the bloodstains, police knew
they were put there after Raymond and Daisy's bodies were removed.
Why the clothes were put there is less easy to answer, but the logical
explanation is that they were tossed onto the bed as the killer was
rummaging through the closet or chest of drawers next to the bed,
looking for something. The next question necessarily becomes, what
was it the killer was looking for? A change of clothes? Jewellery or
other valuables? The real or fictitious $4100?

Because there was no evidence of ransacking in any other part of
the house, if the clothes were tossed on the bed by someone looking for
something, the implication is that whoever was doing the looking
either knew that whatever they were looking for was in the closet or
chest of drawers, or they were inordinately lucky and found what they
were looking for in the first place they looked.

Perhaps a small metal strong box police found in the trunk of the
Impala when Robert was first taken into custody was linked to the
pile of clothes on the bed. The strong box held the kinds of things one
might expect to find in a box of that sort: bills, receipts, birth certifi-
cates, a marriage certificate, tax notices, letters from Robert, and
maybe, whatever the murderer was looking for.

If the many possible explanations for the pile of clothes are
complicated, the issue of Robert's clothing is tortuous. When he was
released from Saskatchewan Prison, Robert was wearing a prison
issue blue suit, a new white shirt, and was either wearing or had in
his possession the red tie sent him from Daisy. When police searched
the Cook house the Sunday the bodies were discovered, beneath the
mattress on Raymond and Daisy's double bed, they found Robert's red
tie, his blue suit, and a filthy white shirt. All bore traces of blood.

Because there was never any doubt where the suit and tie came from, rather than attempt to deny they were Robert's, the question Robert and his defense raised was – had Robert been wearing them at the time of the murders. Not without merit, Robert asked:

> Is it reasonable to belive I would hide all signs of the crime . . . and then leave my own suite under such an obvous place as the blood stained mattress? . . . And the suit being found in such an obious place and no attempts to destroy it or hide the owners identity. The evedence that the accused is well versed in crime and is not an idiot.

Robert's theory was that the real murderer put on the suit to avoid getting blood on his own clothes. Though feasible, surely the real killer would not also put on the tie. The rebuttal to that was of course that the tie may have been slung over the footboard and had been splattered with blood during the killings.

While it may be possible to shrug off the tie as doing nothing more sinister than accessorizing the footboard, it is infinitely harder to shrug off the suit. Robert told police he had given the suit to his father, that Raymond had been wearing it when Robert left the house at 10:30. The problem is, had Raymond been wearing the suit when Robert left, he had taken it off when he got ready for bed that night, presumably in the bedroom. How then did the real murderer reach the suit while Raymond and Daisy were in bed? An equally important question asks why a stranger would bother to hide the suit in the first place.

To complicate the suit matter further, after its discovery, police found a small, pill-sized box in the suit jacket pocket. Inside the box were a metal washer and a single key, the key to a 1952 truck parked at the side of the house, perhaps a vehicle intended as a homecoming gift for Robert. According to Robert, Raymond, while wearing the blue suit, took out his key case and gave it to Robert. Robert gave the key case back to his father so Raymond could slip off the truck key. Raymond then put the truck key into the pill box, dropped the pill box into the suit pocket, and gave the key case back to Robert.

The contortions necessary to get the key into the small box, the small box into the suit pocket, and the suit onto Raymond seem unnecessarily complicated when held against the much simpler theory that Raymond slipped the truck key off the key case and gave it to Robert. It was Robert who then put the key into the small box and put the box into the pocket of his blue, prison issue suit, the suit he was still wearing.

To make matters worse, Robert had difficulty keeping track of who was wearing the suit and who had the key when. He told the court that while he and his father were outside, standing beside the station wagon immediately before he left for Edmonton, "I still had the keys for the station wagon in my pocket, since like leaving the hotel (where Robert and Raymond had gone for their beer), and he (Raymond) asked me for the keys back to get the key for the half-ton truck out of the key case."

Because Robert had been wearing the suit at the time he and his father left the hotel, if he had had the keys in his pocket "since like leaving the hotel," he had to have been wearing the suit while standing outside with his father. Conversely, it was impossible for Robert to have had the keys for the station wagon in his pocket "since like leaving the hotel" because Raymond would have needed them to drive home.

Like so many things in the Robert Cook case, questions concerning the suit and the tie, the truck key and the small pill box, were no better resolved than the issue of the two suitcases police found in the trunk of the Impala at the same time they found the small metal strong box. Inside the suitcases were an eclectic collection of children's pajamas, bed sheets, razors and photographs. When asked why he put the suitcases into the trunk, Robert told police that he had found them in the kitchen, thought they had been inadvertently left behind when Raymond and Daisy and the children left for British Columbia, and had planned to take them with him when he drove out to pick up his family. The question becomes why the Cooks might need sheets, four razors, and family portraits during their return trip from British Columbia.

If one supports Robert Cook's innocence, the answer is that Robert did not know what was in the suitcases; if one supports Robert Cook's guilt, the answer is that Robert intended to get rid of them to bolster his family-gone-to-British Columbia story and what they contained was entirely irrelevant.

The grease pit in which the Cook family was found also looms large against Robert's protestations of innocence. Photographs show that unless someone had former knowledge of its existence, it would have been almost impossible to know the grease pit was there. When covered with the wooden planks and pieces of cardboard, it merely looked as though someone had laid cardboard on the garage floor to protect it from oil and grease spatters.

Robert's failure to go to Stettler until two days after his release from Saskatchewan Penitentiary, compounded by his failure to go directly home after Walter Berezowski dropped him off on the outskirts of town at 1:00 p.m. on Thursday, June 25, do nothing to redeem his character. Nor should they. If actions speak louder than words, Robert's delays in going home serve as silent testimony to his true attitude towards his family.

As damning as much of the evidence is, there is also evidence that supports Robert's claims of innocence. Apart from pre-pubescent outbursts of anger, there is nothing to indicate that Robert had a predilection for violence. While his criminal career is certainly checkered, it is checkered with non-violent crimes, car theft and breaking and entering, and not, for example, assault or armed robbery.

Robert's post-Stettler behavior is also at odds with someone who had just finished annihilating their family. From the time he appeared in Edmonton on Friday morning until he was detained by the police on Saturday evening, Robert exhibited no signs that he had murdered seven people and left their bodies decaying in a grease pit back home. His companions during the Camrose-Whitecourt-Camrose trip described him as pleasant, gentlemanly, and a great guy. Furthermore, when arrested, nothing about Robert's demeanor suggested to police that only two days earlier he'd committed the worst multiple murder in Alberta's history (second worst if one includes Swift Runner's murder of nine members of his family during the winter of 1878-1879, twenty-six years before Alberta became a province).

Cook supporters have also made much of the white shirt found with the blue suit and red tie under Raymond and Daisy's mattress. On the day he left prison and during the evening he shared dinner with the Myhaluks, Robert wore a new white shirt, either bought by the prison or Daisy or prison made. But the bloody white shirt found under the mattress was both filthy and bore a laundry stamp with the name ROSS.

As valuable as it is to Robert's defense, the shirt does not come without its own set of problems. Just as there is no way to prove it had come into the Cook house via Robert, there is no way to prove it had not. There *was* a salesman named Don Ervin Hughes Ross staying at the Commercial Hotel at the same time as Robert, and while Robert testified that it was beneath his criminal dignity to steal something as mundane as a shirt, he openly admitted he was not above planting evidence at the scenes of his crimes. "I always . . . carried match books from Calgary," he told one police officer. "I'd always tear them off from the left side so then they would think we were left-handed and from Calgary."

But the greatest problem with the dirty-white-Ross-shirt evidence is the plethora of white shirts in the Cook case. There were so many white shirts – the two white shirts Robert had when he was released from Saskatchewan Penitentiary, a white shirt that police found hanging out of the chest of drawers next to Raymond and Daisy's bed, a number of white shirts inter-mixed with the pile of clothes found on Raymond and Daisy's bed, white shirts in a garment bag driven around by Robert in the Impala – it is impossible to keep

track of where they all came from. Sadly, police only further complicated an already complicated matter with their careless handling of
the clothes found on Raymond and Daisy's mattress.

White shirts aside, the strongest piece of exculpatory of evidence
is what a writer of murder mysteries might call "The Case of the
Missing Friday Newspaper." Raymond and Daisy subscribed to the
Calgary Herald. It was delivered to their door each evening at 6:30.
When police arrived at the Cook house on Sunday, the Saturday
Herald lay on the floor inside the door to the front porch where the
paperboy always left it. Wednesday's and Thursday's and possibly
Friday's papers (not all the dates on the papers were legible) were in
the pit with the bodies. But regardless of whether Friday's paper was
missing or in the pit with the bodies, it could not have been removed
or put in the pit before 6:30 p.m. on Friday, after which time Robert
has an irrefutable alibi until 4:00 p.m. Saturday afternoon.

The Cook case is rife with other pieces of evidence that only
muddy the waters further. The murder weapon itself – a half century
old, double barreled shotgun, prophetically called a Demon – was over
a metre long, and certainly was not being trotted around by Robert as
he roamed about Stettler on Thursday afternoon and early Thursday
evening. In the end, nobody could say where it came from or how it
came to be in the house.

Fingerprints, or more accurately, a lack thereof, were equally
problematic. When police descended upon the Cook house that
Sunday, the entire house was dusted for prints, begging the question
why police lifted a mere ten prints (which ultimately proved of no
evidentiary value) from a house that should have produced prints
from five children, two adults, a boarder who had only moved out the
previous week, Jim and Leona Hoskins, a paper boy who had opened
the porch door Friday and Saturday evenings, a parade of policemen,
and Robert of course.

Though the prosecution attempted to attribute the absence of
prints to Robert, suggesting he had wiped the house clean, one is
again faced with Robert's completely logical question.

> Is it reasonable to belive I would hide all signs of the crime
> and wipe all the fingerprints up and then leave my own
> suite under such an obious place as the blood stained
> mattress? The following evedence is both inconsistent with
> the accuseds guilt and consistent with his innocence: The
> evidence that finger prints were carfully wiped up and all
> obvious signs of violence covered and the suit being found in
> such an obious place and no attempts to destroy it or hide
> the owners identity. The evidence that the accused is well
> versed in crime and is not an idiot.

The lack of identifiable prints is especially frustrating in light of other items that held such evidentiary promise. Robert told police that when he and Raymond arrived home Thursday night they sat down and talked with Daisy over coffee. In the police photograph of the kitchen, there are coffee cups stacked by the sink, but unclear how many. Had police been able to lift them, fingerprints may have been able to determine whether the cups had been used by Daisy, Raymond, Jim, and Leona, or by Daisy, Raymond and Robert. If police had been able to determine the cups had been used by Raymond, Daisy, Leona, and Jim, and not Robert, it would have strengthened their case against him. Viewed from the flip side, if the cups had been wiped clean, there was no reason for anyone to have cleaned them, save Robert.

The inability to trace the gun's ownership and the lack of fingerprints are merely two of an endless list of unanswered mysteries concerning the Cook case. When Hood Motors's salesman Len Amoroso picked up the Impala from Stettler the Monday after Robert's arrest, why did its odometer read eight hundred miles when it should have only read five or six hundred? Why did it take Robert three hours to drive from Camrose to Stettler on Saturday night? If Robert left Saskatchewan Penitentiary with little more than $30 in his pocket, where did he get the money to pay for his partying in Saskatoon, his bus trip from Saskatoon to Edmonton, the liquor for the party in Edmonton on Wednesday night, his room at the Commercial Hotel, the $40 down payment made on the Impala, the beer he bought for Ricky, Homer, Lorraine, and himself, his lawyer's $40 retainer, the gas for his road trips, and still have $90 in his wallet when he was detained on Saturday night? And why, given the fact he was on trial for his life, would Robert maintain his "usual jaunty" behavior throughout?

If, at the end of the day, one concludes that Robert was guilty of butchering his family, one must then face the not inconsequential "M" word – motive – and ask themselves why.

Doctor Harry Maynard of the Tisdale Associate Clinic, the clinic that oversaw the medical needs of inmates at Saskatchewan Penitentiary, offered the theory that Robert suffered from epileptic automation, an epileptic seizure that operates much like a blackout and leaves the individual unable to remember what he or she did during the black out.

In *The Work of Justice*, Jack Pecover wonders if it were possible for Robert to be guilty, but to also be able to successfully "relegate (the murders) to some dark corner of the subconscious where they no longer existed because they never happened."

There are numerous possible theories, but the most logical one agrees in principle with Crown Prosecutor Wallace Anderson's opinion that Robert murdered his family in a fit of rage. What triggered the rage is anybody's guess. Perhaps Daisy vetoed the garage-buying venture. Perhaps she or Raymond told Robert he was no longer a welcome member of the Cook family. Perhaps they told him they were weary of his incorrigible ways and were casting him aside. Perhaps they told him he could not trade the station wagon in on the Impala.

While it is likely that it was some inner rage that sparked the massacre, it could not have been a spontaneous reaction, otherwise Robert would not have been armed with the Demon and Raymond and Daisy would not have been in bed.

One is then left with the uncomfortable idea that the murders were colder and more calculated and intentional than that. Robert probably stewed about something Raymond and/or Daisy said to him. Unable to subdue his anger he chose to avenge himself for the real or imagined wrong by waiting until everyone was in bed before systematically going through the house killing his family.

That degree of premeditation implies the work of a cold-blooded, sociopath and compels one to ask whether Robert was remorseless enough to kill his five brothers and sisters, his step-mother, and his father, and then drive to Edmonton to reward himself for the spoils of his labors with the Impala.

Such a theory flies in the face of how the majority of people remembered Robert. Almost everyone who came into contact with him – prison chaplains, prison guards, psychiatrists, psychologists, lawyers, fellow inmates, foster parents, boxing instructors, friends, neighbors, employers – liked Robert, really liked Robert. He has been variously described as gentle, kind, courteous, pleasant, polite, down-to-earth, unable to do such a thing, soft-spoken, mild-mannered, quiet, outstanding, gentlemanly, good-natured, courageous, popular, wholesome, without a mean streak in his body, and exceedingly likeable. Moreover, Robert appeared genuinely distraught at the news of his father's murder (but not Daisy's or the children's).

Even Doctor J. P. S. Cathcart, a forensic psychiatrist sent to interview Robert while he was incarcerated at Fort Saskatchewan Jail, jotted down in his notes, "It's getting harder and harder to see this guy as a wholesale murderer of his own folks." If Robert was as cold as the crimes suggest, not only was he a sociopath, he was a sociopath brilliant enough to beguile everyone around him – almost.

Doctor D. J Krause, who interviewed Robert as part of his thirty day psychiatric evaluation at Ponoka, reported that "in the realm of interpersonal relationships, the subject tends towards social isolation, withdrawing in a cold, schizoid way." (Meaning Robert showed an emotional coldness, an aura of detachment or a flattened affectivity.) Dr. J. M. Byers, assistant medical superintendent at the same institu-

tion felt that Robert's response to the murders was "perhaps inadequate in view of the tragedy having to do with his family." And boxing
instructor Gordon Russell, recalling Robert at the age of eleven or
twelve, said: "he seemed to me to be troubled; emotionally there was
something wrong with Bobby. He was beating up on kids thirteen and
fourteen; when he got them down he would take the boots to them. He
was a mean, small kid."

Robert's father's sister, Mae Ramesbottom, remembered her
nephew as cold and asserted that Daisy not only agreed that Robert
was cold, but was actually afraid of him. Mae and Daisy were not
alone. According to author Frank Anderson, one police officer who had
arrested the then eighteen year old Robert found "a coldness on the
part of the young criminal . . . that actually frightened him."

When examining Robert for sociopathic signs, it is interesting to
note that best-selling true crime writer Ann Rule, who knew Ted
Bundy better that anyone seems to have known Robert Cook, called
Ted "her trusted friend" and described him from personal recollection,
and the recollections of others, as brilliant, handsome, sensitive,
exceptionally well-mannered, popular, shy as a boy, a lovable rascal,
patient, caring, void of anger, and a "knight in shining armor."

In his book *Mind Hunter*, even famed criminal profiler John
Douglas, who served as the model for Jack Crawford in *The Silence of
the Lambs*, and who has been said to know, "more about serial killers
than anybody in the world," confesses to coming close to being duped
by a sociopath. Recounting his first impression of three time murderer William Heirens, the 1940s Lipstick Murderer, Douglas writes, "no
matter what we asked him, he had an answer, insisted he had an alibi
and wasn't even close to any of the murder scenes. He was so convinc-
ing and I was so concerned there might have been a massive miscar-
riage of justice that when we got back to Quantico, I dug out all the
case files." Like Robert Cook, sociopaths can appear convincingly
innocent.

Robert's advocates will be outraged at the suggestion that he was
a sociopath, but outrage does not make it any less a possibility.
Drawing on the expert works of Hervey Cleckley, William and Joan
McCord, Robert Hare, and Lee Robins, Henry Gleitman writes that
sociopaths show a lack of genuine love or loyalty to anyone other than
themselves. They are irresponsible, impulsive, selfish, lacking in
judgment, unable to feel guilt, emotionally shallow, unable to learn
from experience, and lacking in moral values. Undercontrolled, they
"readily yield to the fleeting impulse of the moment" to achieve
instant gratification. Sociopaths show a lack of concern for future
consequences, are comparatively fearless, socially adept, frequently
charming, and emotionally cold.

In *The Mask of Sanity*, Cleckley writes that sociopaths are noted for "their extraordinary poise, their smooth sense of physical being, and their relative serenity under conditions that would produce agitation in most of us." In an issue of *Journal of Abnormal of Psychology*, Hare states sociopaths are underaroused and, because they are underaroused, they "court thrills and danger to rouse themselves to some optimal level of stimulation." And in "Deviant Children Grown Up: A Sociological and Psychiatric Study of Sociopathic Personality," Robins writes that "inconsistent discipline in childhood or no discipline at all correlates with sociopathy in adults."

Close examination of Robert Raymond Cook shows that signs of sociopathy are present: the inconsistent or lack of discipline in his childhood, his inability to learn from his mistakes, his constant need for stimulation, his inability to grieve for his family, his ingratitude, fearlessness, irresponsibility, and charm, and his "extraordinary poise and relative serenity under conditions that would produce agitation in most of us."

It is impossible to ignore the fact that from one side of his mouth Robert, a self-confessed and consummate liar, spoke of his regrets, his intentions of going straight, his plans to mend his ways, while simultaneously saying from the other side of his mouth that one reason he had his heart set on the Impala was because "no one, especially the police would suspect anyone driving a new car like a Chev convertible of pulling any jobs?"

Like Lipstick Killer William Heirens, Robert had an answer for almost everything. When challenged about the discrepancies between his explanation of how he broke into Charm Cleaners and the explanations given by Sonny Wilson, Robert merely discounted them by saying he may have been mistaken because it was dark on the night of the robbery and he had not paid much attention.

When asked why his parents would want to trade the station wagon, a vehicle far better suited to a family of five children, for the Impala, Robert said it was because the station wagon was underpowered for the mountains. When Crown Prosecutor Anderson pointed out that the station wagon did not appear to be too underpowered to drive to Edmonton, Robert explained that that was because "it rolls nicely once it gets going."

On those occasions when Robert could not come up with a reasonable explanation, he would fall back on his last line of defense and claim he was confused, could not remember, or admit to lying – a far cry better than owning he had butchered his family.

When Robert traded his father's station wagon for the Impala, he told Hood Motors's salesman Len Amoroso he was a diesel mechanic with steady employment with John Grover in Red Deer. When Crown

Prosecutor Anderson asked why, if Robert had Raymond's permission to trade the station wagon, he would lie to the salesman, Robert said he didn't know. When asked to account for the $4300 he had stashed at Bowden, Robert could account for no more than $1100 and couldn't remember how he'd managed to accumulate the remainder.

As absorbing as an examination of the evidence in the Cook case is, the sad irony is that, in the end, the evidence doesn't matter. If one strips away each piece of evidence – the blue suits, white shirts, small metal boxes, suitcases, pill boxes, unidentifiable shotguns – the one thing left standing is the emotional fury of the murders themselves. The Cook's murderer held the gun close enough to take away the top of Daisy's head; he crushed the skulls of five defenseless children including a three year old toddler. At some point during his brutal attack, the killer swung the Demon with enough force to bend its steel barrels.

Each fragment of bone and each spatter of blood bespeak of the murders as crimes of passion, crimes personal in nature one would be unlikely to find in an assault by an unknown assailant. Crimes that are at once inexplicable and violent and exhibit an unleashing of rage. Who then, other than Robert, could have been consumed with enough latent anger to be capable of murdering with that degree of brutality?

Thankfully for Canadian juries, the burden of finding defendants guilty in capital punishment cases has been lifted. In 1962, twenty-nine year old Ronald Turpin and fifty-four year old American, Arthur Lucas, were the last men executed in Canada. Turpin had been found guilty of shooting and killing Toronto police officer Frederick Nash; Lucas had been found guilty of murdering Carolyn Anne Newman, a working girl caught with the wrong person at the wrong time, and Therland Carter, an FBI informant who was scheduled to testify against American drug lord Gus Saunders. Amidst much public opposition, Turpin and Lucas were hanged together at Toronto's Don Mills Jail on December 11 at 12:02 in the morning.

After the Lucas and Turpin executions, for all intents and purposes, Canada abolished capital punishment. Though still on the books, it was never again used. In 1966, excepting those cases involving police officers and prison guards, and cases outlined in Canada's National Defense Act (cowardice, desertion, unlawful surrender, and spying for the enemy), Canada officially removed capital punishment from the Criminal Code. In 1998, Canada expunged it completely.

Four
Victor Ernest Hoffman

"Phantom fighting is the art of fighting without the use of the flesh body, but with the phantom body, or you could call it the soul, or still yet the astral body. The battles can be experienced by those who have a sensitive mind to pick up on it. The fighting is invisible, not to be seen by the naked eye of the flesh. Fighters will do that before they fight their adversary, to feel him out, to find his weaknesses. A fighter is capable of fighting in the flesh as he also fights like he does soul wise.

"How is it done? It is done by astral projection of the inner invisible body. It is very simple and very easy to develop. For fighters that all comes natural. In closed places like prisons like Oakridge everybody does it and there are hundreds of fights that go on daily. It is like being on a battle field at the time. It's an art that should not be allowed, but to control such behaviors the system would need special trained men, to enforce peace and control over such evil art."

Victor E. Hoffman

from Peter Tadman's Shell Lake Massacre

In January 1967, about the time of his twenty-first birthday, Victor Ernest Hoffman's fragile mental state began to crumble. Already painfully shy, he grew increasingly insular, confining himself to the farm where he and his younger brother Allan still lived with their mother and father, Stella and Robert, halfway between the villages of Leask and Kilwinning, seventy-two kilometres north of Saskatoon, Saskatchewan.

Victor's conversations became more unintelligible and rambling, his behavior more agitated. At times he erupted into senseless laughter, at others he flew into an inexplicable rage. His condition continued to deteriorate until the end of May when he carried a loaded shotgun into a hay field and opened fire on the devil.

Confused and alarmed by thoughts and behaviors over which he had no control, Victor told his parents he wished to speak to a minister. No less confused and alarmed than their son, Robert and Stella arranged for him to speak to Pastor Edward Post, a Lutheran minister from Shellbrook, a neighboring town thirty-two kilometres to the east. Anxious to offer whatever help he could, Pastor Post drove out to the Hoffman farm and spoke to Victor in private. When he and Victor finished talking, Pastor Post stressed upon Robert and Stella the importance of taking Victor to a doctor.

Taking Pastor Post at his word, on May 28, Robert drove Victor the eighty kilometres to the Prince Albert hospital. Upon completing his examination, the attending doctor advised Robert and Victor that Victor needed to see a psychiatrist. The following day, Robert and Victor once again made the eighty kilometre trip to Prince Albert. Gravely concerned by Victor's condition, Rathana Nakintara, the psychiatrist who examined Robert at the Prince Albert Mental Health Clinic, made arrangements for his immediate admittance to North Battleford's Saskatchewan Hospital for the Insane.

Saskatchewan Hospital, an imposing stone structure, sits authoritatively at the southern edge of North Battleford, on a hill overlooking the North Saskatchewan River. Opened in February 1914 as the first mental health hospital in Saskatchewan, at that time it was considered "one of the most modern on the American continent."

Built to accommodate eight hundred patients, by the end of the 1920s the hospital was housing one thousand, by the mid-1950s, between fifteen and nineteen hundred. To add to the facility's critical overcrowding, hospital personnel were alarmingly over-worked and often lacked proper training. By the time Victor was admitted in 1967, the number of patients had dramatically dropped to eight hundred and fifty, lending weight to criticisms that the hospital was "being overly eager to get rid of patients."

When Victor was admitted to Saskatchewan Hospital, Stanislaw Jedlicki, the doctor who would oversee Victor's treatment and monitor his progress during his hospital stay, diagnosed Victor with "undifferentiated" schizophrenia, the most common of the schizophrenia subtypes.

Schizophrenics generally go through what mental health professionals call a prodromal or premorbid stage, an interval of time which precedes the onset of the actual disease. Abrupt psychosis, or an absence of a premorbid stage, appears in about twenty-five percent of schizophrenics. The average age for the onset of schizophrenia in males is between fifteen and twenty-five and, often, the earlier the symptoms appear, the worse the prognosis will be.

Symptoms of undifferentiated schizophrenic include eccentric ideas, erratic behavior, loss of interest or motivation, persecutory thoughts, poor hygiene, social withdrawal and impaired social functioning. The behaviors worsen until the patient begins to show signs of psychotic symptoms. Psychotic symptoms include delusions and hallucinations and may lead to what is called an acute psychotic episode. According to mental health professionals, any individual, but especially a male, rarely returns to normal after a psychotic episode. Further, once an individual has experienced a psychotic episode, the possibility of a psychotic recurrence is likely.

Because of Victor's condition, and because Doctor Jedlicki had warned that Victor could be in the hospital for "a long time, maybe even one year," Robert and Stella were as bewildered as they were delighted when two months after Victor's confinement they received a letter from Battleford Hospital telling them that their son was ready to come home. Victor, it seems, had responded extraordinarily well to his electric shock treatment and anti-hallucinatory medications.

Prior to the mid-1950s, health care workers employed by mental health facilities such as Saskatchewan Hospital acted more like guardians than health care professionals. Often their duties included little more than "cleaning rooms, changing beds, and shuffling patients from one room to another." The mid-1950s heralded the emergence and use of psychotropic drugs and revolutionized mental health care. Mental health care facilities were now able to "emphasize rehabilitation rather than custodial care." Able to keep their symptoms under control through drug therapy, more and more patients were discharged.

As promising as those medical advances were, they didn't come without drawbacks. Many of the pschotropic medications that were prescribed carried unpleasant side effects – drowsiness, nausea, severe weight gain, headaches, involuntary twitching, muscle spasms, watery eyes – making patients less eager to ingest them.

On July 26, when Robert drove to Saskatchewan Hospital, North Battleford to collect Victor and bring him home, Victor was given a month's supply of anti-psychotic pills. Told nothing more than to take them twice daily, when those pills ran out he would have to renew the prescription.

After Victor's return, the Hoffmans got on with the daily rigors of farming. Heedless of Victor's mental health, there were cows to be milked, chickens to be fed, eggs to be collected, hay to be baled, machinery to be repaired, and fields to be tended. Sometimes Victor took his medication, sometimes, when he found the unpleasant side-effects particularly distasteful, he didn't. Through it all, Victor had his good and bad days.

Tuesday, August 15, 1967, would be his worst.

Victor woke that morning sometime between 3:00 and 4:00. Unable to get back to sleep, he went out to the garage and tinkered with a motorcycle he was putting together. Around 5:00 he wearied of that and decided to do something else. He briefly considered killing his parents, but the devil told him to hop in behind the wheel of his grey, 1950 Plymouth Chrysler, and go for a drive.

Victor's route took him east along Highway 40, and north along Highway 694, winding him up and over the rolling hills, past the poplar groves circling the town of Kilwinning, beyond the thickets of spruce trees, the fields of golden wheat, and the small pools of cerulean blue where all variety of prairie water fowl gathered. An hour after leaving home, he reached the crossroads of Highway 694 and Highway 3. Turning west, onto the paved surface of Highway 3, Victor drove past the small clusters of farm buildings huddling to his left and his right. Six and a half kilometres beyond Shell Lake's soaring elevator spire, he drove through a gate on the south side of the highway.

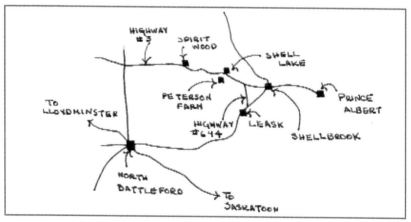

* * *

Jim Peterson grew up on a farm twenty-four kilometres south east of Shell Lake. During the Second World War he served overseas in France, Belgium, Holland, and Germany as a driver with the Royal Canadian Armored Service Corps. Under the Soldier Settlement Scheme, when Jim returned to Canada, he bought a half section of land six and a half kilometres west of Shell Lake. The land abutted a quarter section his father had bought for back taxes in the 1930s.

Jim also married Evelyn Finlayson of Shell Lake and in 1947, Katherine, the first of their nine children was born. When Jim's mother and father retired from farming, they gave the land they owned to their son.

In addition to their ever-expanding brood of children, by 1967 Jim and Evelyn raised twenty-five head of dairy and beef cows, kept a handful of pigs and chickens, and cultivated oats and wheat on their four hundred and eighty acres of land. They and their children lived on the farm in a small, four-room, two-bedroom house about two hundred metres south of Highway 3.

The summer of 1967 had promised to be a memorable one for the Petersons. On July 7, Jim and Evelyn's eldest child, Kathleen married Lee Hill, the son of another district farmer and moved to British Columbia. At the end of August, Jim and Evelyn's second oldest, Jean, a runner, hoped to attend the week-long Dundurn track and field camp. If they could afford it, the rest of the Peterson clan planned to drive to Dundurn and visit Jean for a couple of days.

Five weeks after Kathleen's wedding, Wildrew Lang, the thirty-five year old bachelor who farmed the property adjoining the Peterson farm, spent the evening of August 14 visiting his neighbors. Over coffee, he and Jim made plans for the following day. Early the next morning the two men would empty fifty bushels of wheat from the Peterson feed bins and haul it to the Shell Lake grain elevator. The proceeds from their labors would fund Jean's Dundurn track and field trip and the family's corollary visit.

The sun was just squinting over the horizon when Jim and Evelyn rose the morning of August 15. If the warm air and absence of clouds were any indication, it was going to be a glorious day. Evelyn sat on the edge of the bed in the bedroom off the living room feeding her one-and-a-half year old son Larry. Jim sat beside her preparing to dress when they heard a car pull into the yard. The car door slammed and footsteps approached the house. Jim checked the time. Even for prairie farmers, accustomed to being up at the crack of dawn, daybreak was early for callers. Suspecting it might be Wildrew, Jim called out:

"Who is it? Who's there?"

When nobody answered, Jim called again:

"Who is it? Who's there?"

The visitor opened the door, raised a .22 calibre Browning pump-action rifle and responded. Jim leapt from the bed, and lunged towards him and the stranger fired again, pumping four shots into Jim's stomach.

Having exhausted his ammunition, the intruder returned to his car and reloaded. His killing spree had only begun.

Moving quickly and relentlessly, the gunman returned to the house, stopping inside the door long enough to pump another three bullets into Jim. Stepping across the body, the intruder came face-to-face with eleven year old Dorothy who slept on a small cot in the living room. Paralyzed by fear, she shut her eyes and screamed. The gunman levelled his gun to her head and squeezed the trigger. Dorothy's blood splattered the walls and the ceiling.

In the bedroom off the living room, six more of the Peterson children cowered in horror. Showing no mercy, the gunman entered the room and fired. Mary, Pearl, Jean, William, and Colin lay either dead or dying. In the bedroom off the kitchen, Evelyn clasped Larry close to her chest and made a desperate scramble out the window. Hearing her movements, the intruder leapt from the children's bedroom window and captured Evelyn in his sights. Four shots rang out in rapid succession and Evelyn crumpled to the ground. Stalking back to the house, the gunman finished off anyone yet clinging to life before circling back to where Larry stood clutching his mother. Taking aim, the intruder pulled the trigger.

Twenty-seven bullets the gunman fired had found their mark. Having accomplished what he set out to do, he retraced his steps, pocketed seventeen shell casings and two wallets containing a total of $7, and departed.

It had taken Jim and Evelyn Peterson twenty-two years to carve out their modest but comfortable life; it took the killer less than twenty-two minutes to destroy it.

* * *

Unaware of the tragedy he was about to discover, Wildrew drove to the Peterson farm early that morning. Without waiting for Jim, Wildrew began transferring the grain from the feed bins to the bed of his truck. By 9:00, with the job half finished and Jim still nowhere in sight, Wildrew began to grow impatient. Setting his shovel aside, he set off on foot to find Jim and give him an earful for sleeping so late.

As Wildrew approached the Peterson farmhouse, he sensed something wrong. The Peterson farmyard was eerily quiet and empty, and Skippy, the Peterson's dog, acted oddly restrained when he came out to meet him. Wildrew knocked on the porch door, shouted a greeting, and gently pushed the door ajar. Spotting Jim's body lying in a puddle of blood, Wildrew ventured no further. Spinning around, he raced for the Peterson's station wagon and sped the six and a half kilometres to Shell Lake to contact the Spiritwood police.

Corporal Barry Richards was the first person to enter the Peterson house following Wildrew's discovery. What he found inside completely unnerved him. Jim Peterson lay immediately inside the door, his body riddled with bullets. Dorothy lay on a cot in the living room, her pajamas and bedclothes soaked in blood. In the bedroom off the living room, Corporal Richards discovered Jean, Mary, Pearl, William, and Colin. The children lay incongruously beneath their glossy, blood-splattered magazine pictures of Mick Jagger, Elizabeth Taylor, the Animals, and the cast of *Bonanza*. The bodies of Jean and Pearl lay in one of the two beds, the bodies of Mary, William, and Colin in the other. All five children had been shot in the head, and, judging from the powder burns, all at close range.

Standing amidst the carnage, Corporal Richards struggled to take it all. Suddenly his heart skipped a beat. Unless his eyes were playing tricks, one of the blood-stained bed sheets had moved. Stepping cautiously towards it, Corporal Richards drew back the covers and stared down in disbelief. Huddled between the corpses of her older sisters was four year old Phyllis. Though covered in blood and trembling with fear, she was alive. For reasons which have never been satisfactorily explained, the gunman had spared her.

Carefully gathering her into his arms, Corporal Richards carried the terrified child out of the house and entrusted her to the care of the Simonars, the Petersons' neighbors to the north. Leaving Wildrew to guard the house, Corporal Richards then raced to Shell Lake to call for medical and police assistance.

Doctor Micaud of Spritwood reached the Peterson farm before officers from Battleford's RCMP detachment arrived. He was met by Richards, who proceeded with him towards the house. Before reaching it, they spotted what appeared to be a pile of clothes heaped on the grass near the rear of the building. Upon closer inspection they discovered the bodies of Evelyn and Larry.

Grateful for any diversion, friends and family attended to necessary farm chores while police began sifting their way through the crime scene. Amidst the bodies and blood, they found cartridge cases from a .22 calibre rifle and two distinctive footprints stamped onto the blood-stained linoleum. A diamond shaped pattern imprinted the sole and a "V" imprinted on the heel.

Over the course of the next couple of days, ballistics experts at Regina's RCMP forensics laboratory narrowed the number of possible gun manufacturers to three while other forensic investigators determined the bloody footprints had been made by a pair of red-soled, red-trimmed, made-in-Taiwan, black rubber boots distributed by a Prince Albert company – one of a possible eighteen hundred pairs.

Using the Peterson farm as their focal point, seventy-five RCMP officers, armed with mine detectors or accompanied by tracking dogs, spiralled out from the farmhouse, scouring the countryside in a "bush-to-bush" search for clues. Police threw up roadblocks and followed through on any reports of strange cars seen in the area. They investigated tips about an Alberta oilfields worker, a Saskatchewan farm laborer, possible links to a nine year old, unsolved Vancouver homicide, and a two year old San Bernadino, California murder. They ultimately ruled every lead out.

While police were occupied with their search, district residents began to debate whether the crimes had been committed by one individual or two. Those who favored the single man theory insisted that the murders could not have been committed by two men because the possibility of two cold-blooded murderers coming together to annihilate a family was far too remote. Those who favored the two men theory argued it was impossible for one person to have killed his victims so quickly that half of them did not have time to jump out of bed. That theory led to the particularly frightening idea that the reason the Peterson children had not fled from their beds was because they had known their murderer.

But whether there were one or two intruders, what especially disturbed area residents was their fear that if the murderer or murderers could do what they had done to he Petersons, there was nothing to prevent them from doing it to somebody else. The night following the discovery of the murders, during what the *Regina Leader Post* called the "Night of Fear," lights in the district burned continuously and no one retired to bed without a rifle tucked in beside them.

While area residents continued to debate the question of who could be depraved enough to commit such a crime, the bigger question became why. Because no murder weapon had been found at the crime scene, police immediately ruled out the possibility of a murder-suicide. Given the Peterson's financial position, robbery hardly seemed a probable motive, and because there was no evidence of a sexual assault, police discounted the possibility of an attempted rape gone bad. It was also impossible to imagine any member of the quiet, God-fearing Peterson clan to have wronged someone seriously enough to inspire such an awful vengeance. And even if Jim had somehow managed to acquire an enemy bent on revenge, what could he have possibly done that was momentous enough to warrant the killing of his children?

"The shocking thing about this," said lead investigator, Inspector Brian Sawyer, "is that we haven't been able to determine a motive."

Struck by the senselessness of the slayings, it was Inspector Sawyer's opinion that the murders were the work of a lunatic. Police also suspected that the crimes had been committed by someone who lived in the district. "It is hard to fathom," said Staff-Sergeant Ronald Sondergaard, "a stranger coming into an area, picking a farm, and wiping out a family. We have not ruled out the possibility that it was someone in the area."

In short, Inspector Sawyer and Staff-Sergeant Sondergaard believed the person they were seeking was a local madman. As it so happened, a farmer from a small community to the south knew just such a person.

On August 17, two days after the murders, Corporal Charles Nolan of the Shellbrook RCMP detachment, received a tip about a twenty-one year old young man from Leask who had been released from the Battleford asylum only three weeks earlier. Accompanied by five fellow officers, the following day Corporal Nolan drove to the farm of Robert and Stella Hoffman and asked to speak to their son Victor. Within moments of their arrival, Corporal Nolan knew they had their man. On the back seat of a grey, 1950 Plymouth Chrysler parked in the farmyard, police found a .22 calibre rifle. On the stoop at the entrance to the Hoffman house, they spotted a pair of red-soled, red-trimmed, black rubber boots with a diamond shape pattern imprinted on the soles and and a "V" shape pattern imprinted on their heels.

Corporal Nolan confiscated the gun and the boots and dispatched them to Regina for testing. Less than than twenty-four hours later, forensics identified the boots as the ones that had left the bloody prints at the Peterson farmhouse and confirmed the rifle was the one used in the murders.

On August 19, two hours after 1500 people watched eight coffins (Larry was buried with his mother), containing nine members of the Peterson family, being lowered into a mass grave at God's Acre, the Shell Lake cemetery, Sergeant Gerry Fraser and Corporal Gus Gawthrop apprehended Victor Hoffman on suspicion of murder. That evening police announced that an arrest had been made. The following day they released the suspect's name.

Tying Victor Hoffman to the Peterson murders was easy. Ballistics had confirmed that the rifle taken from the backseat of his 1950 Plymouth was the murder weapon. His jeans, handkerchief, boots and gloves had produced evidence of blood. He had been found in possession of two billfolds, one bearing the name of Evelyn Peterson, the other Jean Peterson. And if the rifle, boots, blood, and billfolds weren't arsenal enough, police also had Victor's confession.

"Okay, I killed them. I tried to change the rifling on it. I should have burned the house, then you would not have found those cartridges. I stopped at the gate. I don't know what made me do it. I collected seventeen cartridges. I didn't want to shoot anymore. The one I left didn't see me . . . after it got just about daylight, the sun was just starting to come up, I saw this house on the left side of the road. I just drove in there and started shooting."

On August 21, two days after his arrest, Victor was formally charged with the murder of James Peterson, a capital offense, and sent to the University Hospital in Saskatoon, Saskatchewan for a psychiatric evaluation. The head of the University's psychiatric department, Doctor Donald McKerracher, interviewed Victor on August 23 and 24 and concluded that Victor was fit to stand trial.

If found guilty, Victor would be sentenced to hang, the mandatory penalty in a capital murder case. If hung, Victor would become the first person executed in Saskatchewan since Jack Loran was hanged in February, 1946 for the June, 1945 murder of Gustav Angerman.

Until 1961, the sentence for capital crimes in Canada – murder, rape, treason – was death. In 1961 the Criminal Code subdivided murder charges into capital and non-capital murder. A charge of capital murder was reserved for a premeditated murder or for the killing of an on-duty police officer or prison guard. In December of 1966, against the better judgment of Canada's official hangman who believed putting an end to the death penalty "was all foolishness," the Criminal Code was again modified, and a charge of capital murder could only apply to the murder of an on-duty police officer or a prison guard. Today Canada's Criminal Code divides murder charges into three classifications: first degree murder, punishable by a life sentence with no chance of parole for twenty-five years; second degree murder, punishable by a life sentence with no chance of parole for a minimum of ten years, and manslaughter, punishable by a life sentence with no chance of parole for seven years.

Because the amendments to Canada's Criminal Code went into effect at the same time Victor was about to stand trial for murder, Victor's capital murder charge for the death of Jim Peterson was reduced to two non-capital murder charges, one for the murder of Jim Peterson, the other for Evelyn. To Victor's good fortune, the changes meant that at worst, even if found guilty, he could only be sentenced to life imprisonment, and not hanging.

Victor's trial, which commenced on Monday, January 8, 1968, was as poignant and brief as the massacre itself. There was never any question who had committed the crimes, the question was whether or not he was guilty. On April 8 and April 9, jurors listened to sixteen crown witnesses recount the events of August 15, including Victor's own account given in his taped confession. As compelling as the testimony was, the most critical statements came on January 10 when the defense called to the stand psychiatric Doctors Donald McKerracher, Abram Hoffer, and Stanislaw Jedlicki, to present their views on Victor's mental state at the time of the murders.

Doctor McKerracher testified that Victor, who wept and "showed great remorse over the killings, was acting on a divine injunction by shooting the family." It was the doctor's opinion that "when [Victor] was participating in the killings . . . He didn't appreciate the implications of what he was doing until he was halfway through the killings."

Prior to that, "he was in a world of unreality." Doctor McKerracher went on to say that Victor "told me that for ten years he had been having a struggle with the devil," who appeared as a large black pig, over six feet tall and weighing three hundred pounds. For all those years, "the devil was trying to make him bow down."

Doctor Abram Hoffer, also from Saskatchewan University Hospital, agreed with his colleague. "A robot programmed to kill and not get caught could have done what Hoffman did . . . an appreciation of right or wrong was not involved. I don't think Mr. Hoffman clearly separated in his mind the difference between killing birds, cattle, or people. He thought he was killing pigs. . . . His victims looked rotten and pig-like," and God approved of their murders.

Doctor Jedlicki added nothing more to Doctor McKerracher and Doctor Hoffer's remarks except to say that the devil had pleaded with Victor to "sell your soul to me or suffer a million times" at the same time God was telling him "He would look after him."

Essentially, all three doctors were arguing the same thing. At the time of the murders, Victor was experiencing an acute schizophrenic attack and could not be held responsible for his actions. "He was legally insane" and was "entitled to a verdict of not guilty."

Even Crown Prosecutor Serge Kujawas seemed inclined to agree. "There is no doubt in this case that the accused caused the death of Jim and Evelyn Peterson," said Kujawas. What the jury had to decide was "whether [Victor] knew he was shooting people and knew what he was doing was wrong."

As favorable as the testimonies were to Victor's plea of insanity, the chances of being found not guilty by reason of insanity are as remote as being able to pick the Paul Bernardo's of the world out of a crowd.

In his final address to the jury on January 11, Justice Sandy MacPherson told jurors there was no need for them to decide whether or not Victor had committed the murders, that he had pulled the trigger, over and over again, was a given. What the jurors had to decide was whether or not Victor appreciated the nature and quality of his acts at the time of the shootings, whether he was capable of distinguishing between their rightness or wrongness.

Three and a half hours after they had retired, the jury found Victor Hoffman not guilty by reason of insanity.

In his book, *Shell Lake Massacre*, author Peter Tadman cites a number of quotes describing the mixed reactions the verdict received.

"I think it was the only possible verdict and I thought so from the time I took a look at the facts," said Victor's attorney, Ted Noble. "Victor just had to be insane. It went the way it should have."

Others were less sympathetic. "If the guy had nine lives," said one gentleman, "I'd take every one of them. He sure got off easy."

Many people expressed a mixture of dismay and astonishment.

"No, I didn't think they'd say he was insane. That would be admitting they shouldn't have let him out, wouldn't it?"

"After he was in the hospital such a short time before, the government might as well admit they killed the family if they found him insane."

"I'm sure the government would never say he was insane. People would expect an inquiry, or do you think so? I know they made a mistake, but I know damn well they wouldn't ever admit it. Can you imagine what people would think?"

"If he's not guilty somebody is. I think it's a coverup for the government, the hospital, and the doctors. Everybody I've talked to is so mad and so disgusted. The doctors at North Battleford must have known he was dangerous. Why didn't they know?"

Perhaps the two most extraordinary responses, voiced twenty five years after the fact, came from the two least likely sources.

"I was upset that he was let out. I thought the man was sick which he was," said Kathy Hill Peterson, Jim and Evelyn's daughter who had been married five weeks before her family's massacre. "I felt sorry for his parents and his younger brother who had to deal with all that. They probably felt as bad as he did but they were not the criminals."

"I don't really blame him either," said Phyllis Peterson, the sole survivor of the murders, echoing her sister's remarkable compassion. "It was him who did the actual action but as a person I don't think he had what it took upstairs to be able to lay the blame on him. I don't think his mind was there and you can't blame somebody who doesn't have a mind for doing something. Kathy and I are not holding grudges. If we're not – the rest of the world shouldn't."

After his trial, Victor was held at the Prince Albert Penitentiary while Saskatchewan's provincial government waited for results of an assessment of North Battleford Hospital, conducted to determine whether the facility could adequately house him. In the end, the assessment concluded the hospital could not. In March, 1968, seven months after the murders, Victor Hoffman was transferred to Oak Ridge, the maximum security division of the Mental Health Centre for the criminally insane at Penetanguishene, Ontario, to be detained for an indefinite period. Penetanguishene remained Victor's home until he passed away at the age of fifty-eight on May 21, 2004, a victim of cancer.

As tragic as the Peterson murders were, they publicly exposed serious flaws with Saskatchewan's existing mental health care system, sadly, problems the Saskatchewan Mental Health Association was already aware of. In a 1966 report presented to Saskatchewan's provincial government, Saskatchewan's Mental Health Association informed the provincial government that "the re-admission rate for all units (Saskatchewan Hospital, North Battleford, Saskatchewan Hospital, Weyburn, University Hospital in Saskatoon) is very high and many patients are released from hospital who appear to be quite ill."

Partly because of that report and partly because of the Peterson family murders, Doctors Shervert Frazier and Alex Pokorny of Houston's Baylor University were contracted to conduct a survey of Saskatchewan's existing psychiatric services. Their survey paid particular attention to the: admission and discharge criteria of in-patient facilities, the quality of psychiatric treatment, and the adequacy of out-patient facilities and care with particular reference to the follow-up of discharged patients.

Results of the survey showed that the early discharge at North Battleford "is based on unrealistic criteria and not based on improvement from psychotic symptoms," and that the hospital "seemed overly eager to get rid of patients." The report also uncovered reports of "inadequate or even no communication between hospital and follow-up programs." The survey further found that the "personnel situation [was] of crisis proportions and [had to be] given top priority," and that the North Battleford Hospital "received more criticisms than any other in-patient unit concerning lack of communication."

Based on their findings, Doctors Frazier and Pokorny made four major recommendations: first, that the practice of discharge not be "determined by bed counts, statistics, or attempts to satisfy institutional goals, but by the needs of the patient, his family, and his community"; second, "a simple form letter, containing admission dates, diagnosis, and recommended treatment (including drug dosage) should be completed and handed to each patient at discharge"; third, "that no heroic efforts be made at this time to reduce the in-patient population"; fourth, that "prompt steps be taken to increase the numbers of community supervisory workers, and also to increase their level of skill."

Five
Dale Merle Nelson

"I have no doubt that each of you has been shocked and horrified by some of the things you have heard in this courtroom. But you must not allow the emotional reaction to your shock and horror to affect your good judgment."

Justice John Somerset Aikins
Trial Judge

Thirty-one year old Dale Nelson spent much of September 4, 1970 attending to the needs of his two favorite pastimes: drinking and hunting, both of which he was very good at. At 3:00 that Friday afternoon he bought a six-pack of beer and a mickey of vodka at the Creston, British Columbia liquor store. Next, he stopped for coffee at the Kootenay Hotel Café before wandering into the hotel's tavern where he knocked back ten beer and bought a second six-pack. At 5:30, two of his drinking pals drove him home to West Creston, a small, sparsely populated farming enclave separated from Creston proper by the Kootenay River.

At 6:00, and 1970 hunting season only six hours away, Dale drove to the West Creston home of his wife's sister, Maureen McKay, to retrieve a seven-millimetre, bolt-action Mauser rifle he'd lent her for protection against prowlers a couple of weeks earlier. When he arrived, he discovered that Maureen's thirty year old aunt, Shirley Wasyk, was there visiting too. Pleased to see her, Dale spent a few minutes talking to both women before taking his rifle and departing.

An hour later, Dale was back in Creston, making his way to Brennan's Garage to gas up his car and buy a box of seven-millimetre rifle shells. From Brennan's he drove to Armand Chauleur's auto shop in Erickson, a three-hundred person community three kilometres east of Creston. He and Armand shared a drink and a bit of convivial conversation before Dale disappeared behind the shop to take target practice, first testing his rifle's unsighted accuracy, then its accuracy enhanced by its nine-power scope sight.

At 8:00, he showed up at Swanson's Sporting Goods to buy back the press and die he had sold to the Swansons when he was strapped for cash the previous month. Before leaving the store, he purchased a second box of seven-millimetre bullets. Half an hour later he was back at the Creston liquor store buying a bottle of wine and a mickey of brandy. At 9:00 he migrated to the King George Hotel tavern where he enjoyed another three beers before he and his friends, John McKay and Rex Smith, retired to Smith's room at the hotel to party a little longer.

By midnight he was ready.

Ten minutes into hunting season Dale once again steered his light blue, 1966 Chevrolet, towards Maureen McKay's cabin. Leaving the car on the dirt road leading up to her cabin, he tramped as far as the front porch and halted. A second car in the driveway announced that Maureen already had a late night guest, so he turned and retreated.

Inside the cabin, Maureen and an old school friend, Frank Chauleur, heard Dale's footsteps approach the house, stop, and mysteriously withdraw. Thinking perhaps it was one of the late-night prowlers Maureen had been so anxious about, Frank stepped out onto the porch in time to see the tail lights from Dale Nelson's blue Chevrolet flickering through the trees in the distance. The car was moving in a south by south east direction.

At the same time Frank Chauleur was standing on Maureen's porch, peering into the darkness, Shirley Wasyk was at home with three of her four daughters: seven year old Candace Tracey Jean, eight year old Alexis Sharlene, and twelve year old Debbie. Shirley's husband, Alex, was away for the night at his logging camp and had taken their fourth daughter, ten year old Laurie, with him.

At quarter past midnight, Shirley heard the crunch of tires in her driveway. Rising from bed, she pulled her curtains aside and spotted the familiar, curly blonde-hair of her niece Annette's husband. From the way he was staggering, Shirley suspected he'd been drinking. As churlish as Dale could sometimes be when he was drinking, what concerned Shirley more was the rifle he carried. Throwing a housecoat over her nightgown, Shirley hurriedly dialed Maureen to tell her that Dale had pulled up to the house and, for some unknown reason, had brought his gun with him.

All too familiar with her brother-in-law's unpredictable behavior, especially when he'd been drinking, Maureen asked Frank to drive to the Wasyk home to check on her aunt and her aunt's children. Happy to oblige, Frank drove the two hundred metres separating the Wasyk home from Maureen's cabin and pulled into the driveway behind Dale's blue Chevrolet. When Shirley answered his knock, Frank squinted into the dark interior and asked Shirley if her husband was there.

"No," said Shirley. "Alex isn't home."

Catching sight of Dale's silhouette pressed into the living room shadows, and sensing he was unwanted, Frank said goodnight and drove back to Maureen's. Nothing, he told her when he returned, seemed untoward.

At 12:15, Debbie Wasyk had also heard the sound of a car in her driveway. Moments later she heard her cousin Dale and her mother speaking "in either the living room or her mom's bedroom." Because their voices were low, she couldn't hear much of what was being said, but she thought her mother was trying to get Dale to drink some coffee.

Before Dale had a chance to say yes or no, Debbie heard a second car and a second knock at the door. Straining her ears, she heard her mother say to whoever it was, "No, Alex isn't home."

Other than the sound of the second car driving away, Debbie heard nothing until she heard her mother cry out, "No, Dale. Don't!"

More confused than alarmed, Debbie snuck out of her bedroom and tiptoed into the darkened kitchen. From there she heard strange sounds – "sort of like snoring, kind of gurgling" – coming from her mother's bedroom. The next thing she heard were footsteps coming her way. Squeezing herself into a recess between the refrigerator and the kitchen wall, she silently watched Dale herd her sister Tracey into the kitchen. Debbie thought about "jumping out to scare them," but something about Dale's demeanor changed her mind. Hugging the wall and holding her breath, she heard Dale order Tracey to find him a sharp knife. Although it was dark, there was enough light from the porch light for Debbie to see Tracey pull from a drawer an elk-handled carving knife with a ten inch steel blade from a drawer. Once Dale and her sister were gone, and she thought the coast was clear, Debbie slipped out of her hiding space. Removing her sandals, she crept into her mother's bedroom and locked the door tightly behind her.

* * *

No more than fifteen minutes after they heard the first set of footsteps approach the porch and retreat, Maureen and Frank heard a second set of footsteps coming their way. Unlike those they'd heard earlier, these were lighter and moving faster and were followed by a desperate pummeling of the door. Flinging it open, Frank found Debbie Wasyk standing in front of him. Dressed in nothing but her nightgown, she was pale and shaking and barely coherent. Cousin

Dale was in her house, she cried. He "wasn't right." He had hit her mother in the head with a fire extinguisher. There was blood everywhere. He had a gun. He had a knife. He had her sisters.

At 12:30 a.m., July 5, Constable Earl Moker of the Creston RCMP detachment received a frantic telephone call from Maureen McKay. Something was terribly wrong, she said. Her brother-in-law, Dale Nelson, had snapped and assaulted her aunt. One of her aunt's daughters had safely escaped the house, but two of her aunt's other daughters were still trapped in the house with him. Maureen also informed him that Dale's mother-in-law, Iris Herrick, his wife, Annette, and his three small children all lived within shouting distance of the Wasyk residence.

Constable Moker wasted no time dispatching Constable Gary McLaughlin to West Creston. As he raced west, McLaughlin reached the bridge spanning the Kootenay River and noticed a car speeding towards him. When the vehicles drew closer together, Constable McLaughlin saw that the driver of the other car was feverishly waving his arms, trying to flag him down. Constable McLaughlin stopped and cautiously approached the other vehicle. Inside he found Frank Chauleur, Maureen McKay, and Maureen's four year old daughter, all rushing Debbie Wasyk to the Creston Valley Hospital.

Unfamiliar with the bewildering network of roads that crisscrossed West Creston, Constable McLaughlin asked Frank to lead him back to the Wasyk residence. With no hesitation, Frank made a U-turn and raced back in the direction from which he'd just come. Constable McLaughlin followed at a close distance, his lights flashing, his sirens screaming.

Inside the Wasyk house, Dale heard the sound of the sirens heading his way. Grabbing eight year old Sharlene, he bolted out the door, and made for cover behind the thick brush at the rear of the property. By the grace of God or good fortune, as Dale crashed through the tangle of bushes, Sharlene became inextricably snared in the branches, so he abandoned her.

Moments later, Frank Chauleur and Constable McLaughlin reached the entrance to the Wasyk property. Upon seeing Dale's blue Chevrolet parked in the driveway, rather than taking any unnecessary risks, Constable McLaughlin waited for back up from Constables Gus Slomba and Moker before proceeding forward. When the backup arrived, the officers ordered Frank to maintain a safe distance while they investigated the Wasyk house. Moving forward, they unexpectedly came upon Sharlene standing inside the picket fence surrounding the property. Constable Moker lifted the terrified child into his arms and gestured for Frank to drive forward. Frank advanced far enough for Constable Moker to transfer Sharlene to the car before speeding off for the Creston Valley Hospital.

Once Frank and his passengers were safely away, Constable Slomba stood cover while Constables McLaughlin and Moker entered the Wasyk house. Though the officers found no sign of Dale, they found plenty of evidence he'd been there. Shirley Wasyk's lifeless body lay on the bed in the master bedroom. Her head had been repeatedly battered by a fire-extinguisher that lay on the floor beneath the shattered bedroom window through which Debbie had fled.

Stepping across the small hallway, Constables Moker and McLaughlin entered a second bedroom and found Tracey. The seven year old lay on top of her child-sized cot, her body and bedclothes soaked in blood. A hideous gash ran through her mouth, carving her face into a macabre, ear-to-ear grin. A second gash tore through her body, slicing her small torso from chest to vagina and exposing her internal organs. A bloody, elk-handled knife lay tucked in beside her.

One look at Tracey's mutilated body warned Constables Moker and McLaughlin that if Dale Nelson was capable of inflicting that kind of savagery on a defenseless child, there was no telling what else he might do. Shifting their immediate priority to the safety of the living, they left the Wasyk home to evacuate Dale's wife, his three small children, and his mother-in-law to safety.

From his hiding place on the edge of the Wasyk property, Dale "watched the police officers go in and out, and . . . seriously thought about shooting them." Thinking better of it, he remained motionless as they jumped into Constable McLaughlin's cruiser and sped away. When he saw the cruiser's tail lights fade into the blackness, he scrambled out of the bushes and disappeared into the Wasyk house. Five minutes later he reappeared carrying a bloody bundle.

Once they had removed Dale's family to safety, Constables McLaughlin, Moker, and Slomba returned to the Wasyk residence. To their disbelief and horror, when they arrived they discovered that Dale's blue Chevrolet was gone and fresh blood smeared the previously unmarked porch steps.

Worse, Tracey's body was missing.

* * *

Six people occupied the small wooden house at the end of Corn Creek Road: forty-two year old Raymond John Phipps and his twenty-six year old common-law-wife, Isabelle Alice St. Amand, Isabelle's ten year old son, Paul Roger St. Amand, her eight year old daughter, Catherine Rose St. Amand, her seven year old son, Bryan Ross St. Amand, and Raymond and Isabelle's eighteen month old son, Roy Kenneth Phipps.

Just before 1:00 in the morning on September 5, Elizabeth McKay, another of Maureen McKay's sister-in-laws, and the nearest neighbor to the Phipps-St. Amands, heard a car speeding west on Corn Creek Road. Elizabeth couldn't imagine why a car was out on Corn Creek Road at that time of night, nor could she imagine why it was traveling so fast.

Five minutes after Elizabeth heard the speeding car, Corporal Harvey Finch of the Creston RCMP took a call from a terrified woman. Speaking in a barely audible whisper, the woman identified herself as Isabelle St. Amand and told Corporal Finch there was a man with a gun in her house. Before Corporal Finch had a chance to make further inquiries, the telephone went dead. When his frantic efforts to return the call met with an ominous silence, he and Constable Dennis Schwartz raced for the Phipps-St. Amand's.

Back at her home on Corn Creek Road at "exactly 1:00 a.m.," immediately after Isabelle St. Amand rang Corporal Finch to report an armed intruder, Elizabeth McKay heard a loud shot followed by "a pause, then another loud shot, a further pause, then a group of shots" ring out in rapid succession. Elizabeth was certain they were rifle shots and that they had come from the direction of the Phipps-St. Amand's.

For almost a quarter of an hour, Corporal Finch and Constable Schwartz hunted desperately through West Creston's web of roads, searching for the Phipps-St. Amand residence. It was nearly one-thirty before they spied the small, two room building tucked into a clearing among the trees at the end of Corn Creek Road. Detecting no sign of movement and hearing nothing but the wind in the trees, Constable Schwartz stood cover while Corporal Finch entered.

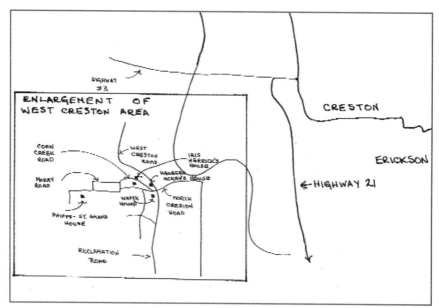

On the floor immediately inside the door, Corporal Finch found the body of Raymond Phipps, killed by a single gunshot to the front of his head. The body of Isabelle St. Amand lay a few metres from her husband. She too had been killed by a single shot, hers to the back of her head. Advancing into the cabin's cramped sleeping quarters, Corporal Finch found the bodies of the two eldest boys, Paul and Brian St. Amand, and the body of their younger brother, Roy Phipps. Paul lay in a single bed, Roy in his crib, and Brian in the upper tier of a bunk bed. All three boys had died of gunshot wounds that had blown away parts of their heads.

Reeling from his initial discoveries, Corporal Finch gazed down at the lower bunk and was seized by an additional horror. Though the lower tier of the bed was empty, the disarrayed bedclothes indicated that someone had been sleeping there. A double-check of the members of the Phipps-St. Amand household confirmed that eight year old Cathy St. Amand was missing. As horrified as Corporal Finch was by his discovery, an absence of blood offered hope that Cathy had been taken alive.

Over the next six hours, forty RCMP officers from Nelson, Cranbrook, Castlegar, Kimberely, and Vancouver arrived to reinforce Creston's ten-man detachment which was ill-equipped to handle a case of such magnitude. Under the command of Staff-Sergeant Miles McLeod and Superintendent Terrance Stewart, RCMP officers established road blocks throughout the entire East Kootenay district, cordoned off the West Creston area, and organized armed foot patrols.

By daybreak, the citizens of Creston and West Creston began waking up to discover that their communities were under siege. The RCMP had issued an all-points bulletin against Dale Merle Nelson and there were armed police "all over the place." Warned that the fugitive was armed and extremely dangerous, Creston and West Creston citizens didn't have to be told that Dale Nelson was one of their best marksmen.

As daylight continued to trickle in, fifty armed police and a military helicopter combed the area adjacent to the Phipps-St. Amand residence, seeking any clues that might hint at the direction Dale Nelson was headed. Faced with the prospect of hunting their quarry through the thousands of acres of uninhabited and heavily wooded forestry lands to the north, south, and west, which, to add to their problems, were presently covered in fog, police desperately needed something to help them reduce the scope of their manhunt into something more tenable.

Police caught their first break at 6:00 a.m. when they spotted a set of fresh tire tracks veering off into a section of broken fence 275 metres west of the Phipps-St. Amand cabin. But morning gave way to afternoon without searchers any closer to finding Dale. Confronted by his twelve hour head start and the difficult terrain they were hunting through, police brought in tracking dogs and a private Piper Cub spotter plane, directing the pilot to focus his search on the forestry access roads leading to Ezekiel Creek. At 3:30 p.m., the Piper Cub's pilot leaned out of his cockpit and signaled to ground searchers that he had spotted Dale's blue Chevrolet stuck in a ditch on the right-hand side of the Corn Creek logging road just to the east of Ezekiel Creek Bridge.

Moving in from all directions, police wondered whether the fugitive would greet them with a hail of bullets, or whether they might find his body slumped over his steering wheel after taking his own life. They met neither. Upon reaching the Chevrolet, they found blood on the car's floorboards, blood on its passenger seat and door, and a hammer clotted with strands of bloody hair.

What they didn't find was Dale, Cathy, or Tracey.

Fanning out into the surrounding brush, police resumed their hunt, and at 4:30 made the first of their grisly discoveries. Twelve metres from the blue Chevrolet they found a child's arm, crudely severed at the shoulder. Moments later they made an even grislier discovery. Six metres from the tiny arm lay a child's head. Another seven metres and they stumbled upon a child's leg; a mere three metres from the Chevrolet they discovered a child's torso with one arm and one leg still attached. In bits and pieces, police had finally located Tracey Wasyk, but Cathy St. Amand remained missing.

Because the lands they were scouring were laborious to search even under ideal conditions, and because Dale was armed and obviously unhinged, when darkness fell, rather than exposing themselves to risk, police called off the search, leaving a small number of officers to patrol West Creston during the night.

* * *

Police resumed their search at daybreak, and at 10:30 a.m. on September 6, more than thirty-four hours after Dale's rampage had begun, a search party working the area south of the forestry access road found a child's pajama leg floating in the shallow waters of Ezekiel Creek. Concentrating their search on the vicinity where the pajama leg was discovered, police soon happened upon a more disturbing find. A rope discovered amongst the trees suggested it was likely there where Dale had rested for at least a portion of the previous night. It also suggested that, while he'd been resting, Dale had tied something, or someone, to the tree.

As alarming as the discovery was, it momentarily restored hopes that Cathy St. Amand might yet be alive and encouraged police to resume their search with renewed vigour. But six long hours of peering into bushes and under deadfall, of scouring Ezekiel Creek and its creek beds, and of tramping through dense brush and forest, uncovered nothing. And as each hour dissolved into the next, expectations of finding Cathy St. Amand alive dwindled.

While one contingent of police continued searching the area south of Ezekiel Bridge, a second contingent began systematically checking and re-checking homes and empty buildings in West Creston. Two hours before dinner time, a routine check of the Nelson residence produced evidence that someone had slit open a plastic window covering and broken into the house. Staff Sergeant McLeod and Superintendent Stewart quickly dispatched forensic fingerprint specialist Corporal Alan Marcotte, brought in from Cranbrook to work the Wasyk and Phipps-St. Armand murder sites, to the Nelson house.

After examining the window and confirming that someone had indeed cut the plastic and entered the house, Corporal Marcotte proceeded to circle the building, looking for signs of the fugitive's escape route. Thirty-six metres from the back of the house he spotted fresh footprints leading into the bush. He followed the trail for about twenty-seven metres and was brought up short. Dale Nelson lay dozing less than thirteen metres in front of him.

Rather than jeopardize his own safety or the fugitive's successful capture, Corporal Marcotte took stock of the situation and quietly retreated. Hastening back to the house, he told Superintendent Stewart what he had found. Dale Nelson was on the far side of a small clearing no more than seventy metres from the rear of the house. He was lying on the ground, his back to a log, his hands folded over his chest, his rifle resting in the crook of a tree an arms length away. Close at hand were a dozen rounds of ammunition, and his position provided him an unobstructed view of the house. Police later learned that Dale had chosen the site "to settle and fight." Determined to "die in this spot," if circumstances so willed it, Dale would end his rampage with a "suicide by cop."

Police and police dogs circled the clearing and assumed their positions. Superintendent Stewart then issued a warning. "Dale Merle Nelson, this is the RCMP. You are surrounded. Stand up, put your hands in the air and walk towards the cabin. All units hold your fire." When the warning failed to draw a response, it was repeated. But Dale remained motionless. When a third warning still failed to draw a response, Constable Glen Madsen and his police dog Count, moved in. When Dale rose to meet the dog, Count pounced and knocked him over.

At 5:00 in the afternoon of Sunday, September 6, Dale Nelson was taken into custody. The only words he spoke were "keep the press the hell away from me."

Superintendent Stewart and Staff-Sergeant McLeod herded Dale into a waiting police car where they addressed their most pressing concern: was Cathy St. Amand alive? Dale shook his head, confirming what police had suspected. Staff-Sergeant McLeod then asked Dale to draw a map and indicate the location of her body. An hour after he marked his crude map with an X, police recovered the body of Cathy St. Amand "lying face down in a semi-prone position, and she was wearing just a t-shirt."

Police took Dale to the Creston RCMP detachment house, where he was stripped of his clothes, locked in a cell, and held for the murder of Shirley Wasyk. The following day, Doctor J. V. Murray attempted to interview the prisoner but found him "mentally depressed" and unwilling to talk. On Tuesday, provincial Judge, Harold Langston, remanded Dale for thirty days without plea, for a psychiatric examination at Oakalla Jail.

Dale Nelson's preliminary hearing began in Cranbrook on February 1, 1971. Following three days of testimony, Judge David Lunn determined there was sufficient evidence for Dale to stand trial on eight counts of non-capital murder. As had happened in the Robert Cook and Victor Hoffman cases, in an effort to simplify the trial the Crown chose to proceed on only two counts of murder – one for Cathy St. Amand, the other for Tracey Wasyk.

Because Dale's attorney, Michael E. Moran, intended to base his client's defense on an insanity plea, he felt it was critical to his position that jurors hear an unabridged version of the totality of his client's crimes. Moran therefore agreed to the Crown's proposal provided the Crown agreed to address the more grisly details of the crimes.

Address them the Crown did.

On the first day of Dale's trial, which began in Cranbrook on Monday, March 22, 1971, only three days after his thirty-second birthday, the sixty spectators jammed into the forty-eight seat courtroom learned that after murdering her mother, Dale had sexually assaulted eight year old Sharlene Wasyk, subjecting her to an act of cunnilingus.

They also learned that not only had Dale manually choked Tracey until she was unconscious before slicing her open, he had also placed his face into her gaping abdominal cavity and eaten undigested cereal from her stomach. But the horrors didn't stop there. That same day, the spectators heard that Tracey's heart and external genitalia were missing (and never recovered), prompting speculation as to their means of disposal.

On the sixth day of the trial, pathologist, Doctor Otto Brych, detailed the results of his autopsy on Catherine St. Amand. Although it was common knowledge that she had been stabbed in the back and that her skull had been fractured, not until Doctor Brych's testimony did the public learn that Cathy's abdomen had been sliced open in a manner similar to Tracey, and that Cathy's bowels had been protruding when her body was recovered.

There was more.

"I examined the anus and found it abnormally dilated," Doctor Brych told the court, adding that there were, "small tears in the skin around the entrance to the anal canal."

"Were you able to reach any opinion as to whether the condition of the anus was caused before or after death?" asked Crown prosecutor, T. G. Bowen-Colthurst.

"The absence of bleeding suggested that the child was dead at the time, or close to it."

"In your professional opinion and experience, are you able to state whether the dilated condition of the anus, and the tears, are consistent to an act of buggery being performed after or close to death?"

"Yes," said Brych, stunning the courtroom. "That was my impression."

Following six days of testimony, the questions of who, how, and when had been sufficiently answered, leaving only the question of why. As expected, to answer that question, the Crown and the Defense squared off from opposite corners.

It was the Crown's contention that Dale had committed his crimes because he was a "sexual pervert." And just "because a sexual pervert, in gratifying his perversions, commits an act that is wholly repugnant to normal persons, that does not make him insane. . . . Is a person to be found not guilty by reason of insanity purely on the shocking nature of his act?" asked Bowen-Colthurst.

In contrast, the Defense's position was that there was no definitive answer to the question of why. Dale had committed his crimes without motive while in some kind of psychotic state. Only a moment of temporary insanity could possibly explain why the father of three small children would slice open the body of a seven year old child, a cousin through marriage, eat undigested food from her abdomen, dismember her body, and, if the rumors concerning the whereabouts of the child's heart and external genitals were true, consume the unimaginable. Only some form of acute psychosis could explain why that same father would stab and sexually assault an eight year old girl before crushing her skull. And finally, insanity was the only possible reason why that same man, during an hour long homicidal frenzy, would savagely murder eight people, six whom he barely knew, two with who he was on very good terms.

Doctor Robert Halliday, testifying for the defense, talked of Dale's history of depression, a condition Dale had been repeatedly hospitalization for. He talked of Dale's sense of rejection, his female relationship problem, and his "strong feelings of hatred towards women." Halliday went on to say that Dale felt inadequate financially, vocationally, socially, and maritally. He felt persecuted and rejected by his parents, his family, and his wife's family. And he felt sexually impotent, believing he made a better sexual partner after he'd been drinking.

Doctor Halliday pointed out that in the year leading up to Dale's rampage, Dale had attempted suicide, resulting in a two week stay at the Coquitlam's Riverview Mental Hospital the previous January. He had been unable to find steady employment, further exacerbating his precarious mental state. He had attempted to drown his sense of low worth in alcohol, or to take his frustrations out on his wife who had recently charged him with assault and "asked him to leave the home again."

In his impassioned closing address, Dale's defense attorney conceded that "Dale Merle Nelson cannot go free," but pleaded with the jury to "jail him, but jail him as the truth indicates, as a sick, sick, sick man."

The jury didn't buy it.

On Thursday, April 1, 1971, after deliberating for less than an hour and a half, the eight man, four woman jury found Dale Merle Nelson guilty of two counts of non-capital murder. Trial judge, John S. Aikins, sentenced him to life in prison without the possibility of parole for ten years. In the end, those Creston and West Creston residents who had wished for a stiffer sentence got their wish.

After twenty-eight years behind bars at Agassiz's Kent Penitentiary, in February 1999, Dale Merle Nelson died of undisclosed causes. He was fifty-nine.

Six
Clifford Robert Olson

"[When selecting victims] a lot are just encountered by serial killer who is hunting for the victim he needs. As for how they are stalked, approached, attacked, and trapped, each serial killers has his own personal mode and manner or form of current style and fashion . . . the serial killer kills strangers 95 per cent of the time because as the safest target in terms of avoiding detection . . . Children, young boys and girls are frequently desirable victims by the serial killer for sex. . . . Most serial killers have selected there murder scenes by the place they take there victims to: as for the relevant geographic areas selected by the offender this depends on the seasons, and were the serial killer is killing. In fact most of their victims are strangers although at times family members and acquaintances are slain."

Clifford Olson

Cecilia Anne Christine Weller was a spunky, dark-haired, blue-eyed, twelve year old tomboy who looked her age. A neighbor once described her as a "cute little gaffer." On a cold and wet Monday in November 1980, Christine left her home at the Bonanza Motel on the King George Highway in Surrey, British Columbia to hang out with friends at the Surrey Place Mall and never came back.

Alex Walker simply wanted to get back his son's red Universal, ten-speed bicycle. It had been missing since November 19, 1980, the day his son had lent it to Christine Weller to ride home from the Surrey Place Mall. Since that day neither the bike nor Christine had been seen. Determined to recover the missing ten-speed, Alex approached police to file a missing persons report. Police told Alex to contact the human resources emergency services in New Westminster who in turn told him they were not sure how they could help.

Christine was a runaway and a "low priority" case. "They would wait for the girl to get in touch with them."

Christine never did.

On December 25, exactly one month after Christine was officially reported missing, a man walking his dog near a dike behind the 22 000 block of River Road in Richmond stumbled upon a nude corpse partially buried in Fraser River silt. At the time of the discovery, police could neither give a cause of death, nor speculate how long the body had been there. They could only say that the body was that of a female between the ages of fourteen and twenty.

Five days later, police announced that the girl had died from multiple stab wounds and that death had likely occurred about a month before her body was found. Though police had strong suspicions regarding the girl's identity, until dental chart comparisons were completed, a formal announcement would have to wait.

* * *

The new year barely had time to open its eyes before a short stocky man with brown eyes and wavy dark hair was offering Kim Werbecky a job cleaning carpets with Hale & Olson Construction in January 1981. Flashing one of his impressive, red with gold-lettered, 3-D business cards, he coaxed the pretty sixteen year old into his vehicle and plied her with liquor. In a presage of things to come, he then drove her to Squamish and repeatedly sexually assaulted her. Held against her will, Kim finally managed to escape when her assailant stopped for gas on the drive back to Vancouver. She immediately reported her frightening ordeal to authorities.

While Squamish police were occupied with investigating Kim's allegations, Surrey police had located Alex Walker's son's bicycle behind a cluster of bushes at the rear of an animal clinic on King George Highway and Richmond police had identified the body of the girl found near River Road as twelve year old Christine Weller. Christine had been choked with a belt and stabbed ten times in her abdomen and chest, including punctures to her liver and heart.

On January 7, Kim Werbecky identified her assailant from the hundreds of photographs in the Witness Suspect Viewing System as Clifford Robert Olson, a career criminal with a rap sheet dating back twenty-five years. Armed with charges of rape, buggery, gross indecency, and a weapons violation, Squamish RCMP Constable, Jim Hunter, arrested the forty-one year old Olson at his Surrey Village apartment on King George Highway, and packed him off to Burnaby's antiquated Oakalla Jail.

While Olson was biding his time in jail, Nova Scotia police, on a nation-wide hunt for the man who had sexually assaulted a seven

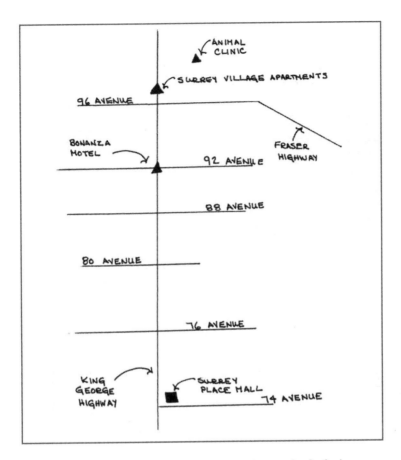

year old Sydney girl on August 3, 1978, tracked their quarry to Oakalla jail. They were as surprised as they were pleased to discover that the man they had been hunting for two and a half years was already in jail on a litany of other charges – rape, buggery, gross indecency, and two weapons violations – some stemming from his sexual assault of a young girl named Kim Werbecky, others stemming from his alleged February 10, 1980 assault of a fourteen year old Vancouver Island boy. With so many charges against him, Nova Scotia police had every confidence their man, one Clifford Robert Olson, would receive just punishment in British Columbia and stayed their charges.

* * *

By the beginning of April, the black cloud that had been darkening Clifford Olson's future began to lift. Unable to keep up with the rent on their Surrey Village apartment during his incarceration, his pregnant, common-law wife, Joan Berryman-Hale, who he'd met at the Cariboo Hotel's Lougheed Village Pub in February, 1980, had found them more affordable accommodations in a Coquitlam apartment complex managed by Olson's mother and father, just east of North Road on Whiting Way.

On April 2, South Fraser Regional Crown Council, Al Hoem, stayed the indecent assault and buggery charges relating to Olson's February, 1980 alleged assault of the fourteen year old Vancouver Island boy, citing problems with the victim's identification of his assailant. Less than a week later, amidst a storm of opposition, especially from Squamish RCMP Constable Jim Hunter and Staff-Sergeant Fred Zaharia, District Crown Council lawyers, Don Celle and Robert McNair, and Senior Crown Attorney, Alan Filmer, believing that Kim, a one-time child prostitute, would make an unsympathetic witness, stayed the Werbecky sex charges as well. As a result, when Clifford Olson walked out of Oakalla Jail on April 8, he did so with nothing more than a pair of weapons charges (one from Squamish, one from New Westminster) shadowing his head.

* * *

Thirteen year old Colleen Marian Bridgette Daignault lived with her grandmother, Julie White, on Old Yale Road in Surrey. Unlike gregarious and precocious Christine Weller, Colleen was quiet and shy. But like Christine, Colleen could hardly be mistaken for older than she was. Barely five feet tall, she weighed less than one hundred pounds, and her silky brown, shoulder-length hair, worn swept back from her face, framed her sparkling brown eyes and winsome front teeth that protruded just enough to lend her an air of childlike innocence.

On April 15, a week after Olson's release from prison and five days after his son, Clifford Stephen, was born, Colleen took advantage of spring break from school by spending the night at a friend's house in North Delta. At 1:00 the following afternoon, a warm and bright Easter Sunday, Colleen bade her friend goodbye, allowing herself plenty of time to reach home by 4:00, the time she had told her grandmother to expect her.

While Colleen stood waiting for her bus, a short stocky man with brown eyes and wavy dark hair pulled up to her bus stop. He was cheerful and friendly and wanted to know if Colleen would like a lift into Surrey. He was going that way anyway.

The following day, Julie made a long distance call to her son Art, Colleen's father, to say that Colleen hadn't returned from visiting her friend. Thinking perhaps that Colleen had chosen to extend her visit, Julie and Art waited another four days before reporting her missing. After dutifully taking Colleen's description, Surrey police assured Julie there was no cause for undue concern. "There is some indication," police said in a public statement issued four months later,

"Colleen might be traveling to Regina to visit her father, or attempting to locate her mother in Vancouver whose address is unknown." Either way, "foul play is not suspected."

* * *

Though they were almost buried beneath his shaggy, straw-colored hair, Daryn Todd Johnsrude's dark, almond shaped eyes, his sensual mouth, and his masculine, yet delicate oval face must have melted the young girls' hearts.

For Daryn, April 1981 was to have been a month full of promise. It was the month he would turn sixteen, which in teenage parlance translated into a driver's license and cars. It was the month he would enjoy a break from school, which meant a respite, however temporary, from homework and studying, and best of all, it was the month he would fly from Saskatchewan to British Columbia to visit his mother, Sharon Rosenfeldt, his step-father, Gary Rosenfeldt, and his two younger brothers, Daryl and Jan. If April ended on as high a note as it began, he might even find a job in British Columbia and never have to return to Saskatchewan at all.

On April 21, two days after his arrival at his mother and step-father's home in Coquitlam, and seventeen days after his birthday, Sharon asked Daryn to run down to buy cigarettes at the drug store in the Burquitlam Plaza, two blocks away. The easy-going young man consented. Because the weather was cool, Daryn slipped on his mother's beige ski-jacket, and at 11:00 that morning Sharon watched Daryn leave, awed by how quickly her son had grown, amused by the thought he had grown big enough to borrow her clothes.

As he was leaving the drug store, Daryn ran into a man he thought he recognized. He was short and stocky, had brown eyes and wavy dark hair, and lived in the same apartment complex as his mother and step-father. After speaking to him for a minute or two, the man generously offered Daryn a job. At that moment Daryn likely felt like the luckiest sixteen year old in the world. Odd cleaning jobs with Hale & Olson Construction at $10 an hour!

When Daryn hadn't returned by 9:00 that evening, Sharon was frantic with worry. Teenagers, she knew, were apt to lose track of the time, but surely they didn't lose it for ten hours.

Just as Surrey police had done with Julie White, Coquitlam police told Sharon and Gary not to jump to any hasty conclusions. Daryn hadn't wanted to return to Saskatchewan had he? Ten to one he had run away to avoid going back. If they wanted, Sharon and Gary could always check out Vancouver's Granville Street where the runaways congregated. Either that or be patient and wait. Daryn would show up in due course.

While Sharon and Gary were hunting for Daryn in downtown Vancouver, Clifford Olson and Joan Berryman-Hale were moving again. With the April arrival of their son, the new parents could no longer remain in the adults-only apartment building where they were presently living. Luckily Olson's parents had found them another apartment on Foster Avenue, right round the corner from their previous address, so they wouldn't have to move far.

* * *

On May 2, a sweltering hot Saturday, Mission police found the nude body of a teenage boy near the town of Deroche, sixteen kilometres east of Mission. The pathologist's report gave the cause of death as a skull fracture inflicted by repeated blows to the head from a blunt instrument, but was unable to say whether the boy had been sexually assaulted. The lack of personal belongings as well as the extent of the injuries, compounded by the degree of decomposition, which had rendered the body "unrecognizable as a human being," hampered identification. It took police almost a week to identify him as Daryn Johnsrude.

Sandra Lynn Wolfsteiner's father described his daughter as "a motoring little girl." Like thousands of other sixteen year olds, Sandra was always coming from or going to somewhere, stopping at home just long enough to eat, change her clothes, and wash her curly brown hair. At 11:00 a.m. on May 19, four days after Clifford Olson married Joan Berryman-Hale at the People's Full Gospel Church in Surrey, the tiny, hazel-eyed and pixie-faced Sandra was motoring from Langley to Surrey to treat her long-time boyfriend to lunch. When Sandra arrived at his parent's rural Surrey farmhouse she learned her boyfriend had been called into work. Disappointed but undeterred, Sandra decided to motor on over to the auto body shop where he worked and take him to lunch from there. From the front of her farmhouse, Sandra's boyfriend's mother watched Sandra walk out to the Fraser highway and hitch a ride from a man driving a grey, two-door sedan.

Sandra was instantly charmed by the driver. First he had picked her up and taken her into Langley so she could withdraw money from her bank. Then he had been kind enough to offer her a job — washing windows for his construction company at $10 an hour.

When Sandra's boyfriend reported her missing the following day, police dismissed her as a runaway. "At the early stages," read an RCMP briefing document written two and a half months after Sandra's disappearance, "it was felt she was simply a missing youth and there was no suspicion of foul play." Though Sandra's father could see no reason why his daughter would run away, he much preferred that explanation to the alternative.

* * *

On May 26, a gloriously warm Tuesday, a short stocky man with brown eyes and wavy dark hair stopped to pick up a tiny, blonde fifteen year old female hitchhiker in front of the Mac's store on the corner of North Road and Cottonwood Avenue. Like Colleen Daignault, Daryn Johnsrude, and Sandra Wolfsteiner, the teenager immediately thought she had struck pay dirt. Not only had the man been good enough to give her a lift, he had also offered her a job doing odd cleaning work for Hale & Olson Construction at $10 an hour. He had even gone so far as to ask if she wanted to start right away.

She certainly did.

Before proceeding to one of Hale and Olson's many construction sites, the driver stopped at the Turf Hotel in Surrey to buy a case of beer in celebration of his newest employee's new job. He and his passenger drank a couple of beer as they drove east; at Langley the driver dug through his pockets and produced four small green pills. Handing them to his new employee, he told her the pills would prevent her from getting drunk. The teenager popped three into her mouth and pocketed the fourth (later analyzed and found to contain chloral hydrate). Soon after swallowing the pills she began to feel groggy.

Just outside of Chilliwack, the driver turned his vehicle around and started driving back west. Reaching out, he stroked his young passenger's face and hair and lost control of his vehicle. Before he was able to regain control, the car hit the ditch and flipped. Moments later, a three-vehicle convoy of Highway Department trucks came upon the accident. The crew heaved a universal sigh of relief when they saw the occupants crawl out of the upturned car, shaken, but otherwise unhurt. Under the circumstances, the Highway Crew was delighted to take the driver and his passenger into Agassiz where arrangements could be made to have the vehicle towed.

When Corporal Darryll Kettles of the Agassiz RCMP went out to investigate the incident, he didn't like what he found. The driver of the station wagon, one Clifford Olson, had bolted like a skittish colt when Corporal Kettles confronted him; Olson's under-age passenger was too drunk or stoned or both to flee. Kettles radioed in an APB on the fleet-footed driver, and transported Olson's fifteen year old passenger to the Agassiz cells to sleep off whatever it was that had rendered her insensible.

Later that day, Sergeant Dwight Gash, also of the Agassiz detachment, stopped a taxi travelling Highway seven, west of Harrison Hot Springs. The cabbie's fare matched the description of the man Corporal Kettles had issued an APB for. After confirming he had the right man, Sergeant Gash took the cabbie's passenger into custody, pending charges for impaired driving and contributing to juvenile delinquency. At the Agassiz detachment, Gash handed Olson over to Corporal Kettles.

During his interrogation of the prisoner, Corporal Kettles learned that Olson had picked up his young female passenger near the corner of Cottonwood Avenue and North Road in Coquitlam. When Corporal Kettles asked himself why Cottonwood Avenue and North Road sounded so familiar, his answer gave him reason to pause. The junction of Cottonwood Avenue and North Road was but a hop, skip, and jump from the Burquitlam Plaza, and the Burquitlam Plaza was the last place Daryn Johnsrude had been seen. Struck by the proximity, Corporal Kettles began to wonder if it was it more than coincidence that Clifford Olson lived a mere three blocks south of the shopping mall.

One of the fundamental axioms criminal profilers use when investigating serial offenders is that these individuals generally commit their crimes in the same areas that they live, work, and play – those areas where they feel most comfortable.

Based on that assumption, Doctor of Criminology, Kim Rossmo, pioneered geographic profiling and patented the Criminal Geographic Targeting model. "For any crime to occur," says Rossmo, "there must have been an intersection in both time and place between the victim and the offender." Though geographic profiling can't catch criminals, it is "an investigative methodology that uses the locations of a connected series of crimes to determine the most probable area of offender residence." Its primary purpose is to help narrow the list of suspects in a criminal inquiry into something more manageable.

Combining gut instinct with an unsophisticated form of geographic profiling, Corporal Kettles felt Clifford Olson warranted further investigation. Digging into Olson's past, Kettle learned that he had recently wheedled his way out of two sexual assault charges, one involving a sixteen year old girl named Kim Werbecky, the other involving a fourteen year old Vancouver Island boy. That information more than satisfied Corporal Kettles's nagging suspicions: he had Daryn Johnsrude's killer behind bars. All he had to do now was bring his findings to the attention of the Mission detectives who had jurisdictional control of the Johnsrude case.

Convinced of Olson's involvement in Daryn's murder, Corporal Kettles was flabbergasted when Mission detectives were "unable to see what to (him) was as plain as the nose on (his) face," and he was compelled to release him.

* * *

Given the chance, thirteen year old Ada Anita Court would have made a wonderful mother. She was friendly and kind, especially to children. She adored her brother and sister-in-law's two baby girls, jokingly referred to as "Ada's Babies," and they adored her. Every Saturday night for the past two years, she had played surrogate mother to them at their parent's Coquitlam apartment. Saturday, June 20, was not any different.

On Sunday morning, Ada kissed her nieces goodbye and cheerfully departed. She had every reason to be cheerful. It was a glorious day, she had just spent the night with two of her favorite people, and she was now on her way home to Burnaby to meet with her boyfriend. Wearing her lovely warm smile, Ada headed for the bus stop at the corner of North Road and Cottonwood Avenue.

As she waited for her bus to appear, a short stocky man with brown eyes and wavy dark hair drove up and asked her which way she was heading. Ada told him she was going to Burnaby. The man told her that was a remarkable coincidence, he was going there too.

Back in Burnaby, Ada's boyfriend waited for over an hour at the corner of Boundary Road and Lougheed Avenue before calling her

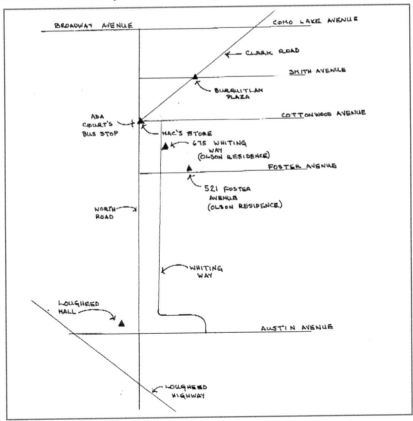

Map of abduction sites and Olson's residences

mother and sister and asking if they knew what was taking Ada so long.

Ada Court's disappearance marked a turning point in what was soon to be called the Case of Missing Lower Mainland Children. No matter what police may have thought about Christine and Colleen and Daryn and Sandra's disappearances, they couldn't dismiss Ada's disappearance as the behavior of a runaway. There was nothing in her home, school, or social life to warrant it. Like it or not, her disappearance had to be taken seriously.

* * *

Had he had the opportunity, nine year old Simon Patrick James Partington may have grown up to be an astronaut or an astronomer. He loved science and the study of the planets. Or maybe he would have been a priest. He was passionate about his Catholic faith. Then again, he may have become a soccer or hockey player. He was equally enthusiastic about both.

But the four-foot-two, eighty pound boy with the shiny blonde hair and choir-boy face would never grow up to become an astronaut or astronomer or priest or soccer or hockey player. On July 2, at 10:30 a.m., Simon left his Surrey home, only a short distance from where Christine Weller had last been seen, to pedal over to his buddy Stevie Jones's house and vanished. The only two things the ensuing search produced were Simon's bicycle, leaning placidly against the wall of the Toronto Dominion Bank at the Cedar Hills Shopping Centre, and public outrage.

All the fear and hostility that had been simmering beneath the surface of the Lower Mainland boiled over into panic and anger. Five children had disappeared during the previous seven months and two had turned up dead. Now a sixth child was missing, the second in only eleven days. A serial killer was stalking British Columbia's Lower Mainland, and residents demanded to know what police were going to do about it.

Partly because they were anxious to downplay anything that might further inflame the growing public hysteria, and partly because they honestly believed what they were saying, police responded phlegmatically. There was not a crumb of evidence to justify talk of a serial killer. Other than Christine Weeler and Daryn Johnsrude, there were no bodies, and for reasons they couldn't disclose, the murder of Christine Weller could in no way be connected to the Johnsrude homicide. Colleen Daignault and Sandra Wolfsteiner were most certainly runaways, and yes, Ada Court was missing, but there was nothing as yet to suggest she had met with foul play.

As much as police may have preferred otherwise, Simon Partington's disappearance focused the public's attention on the six missing and dead Lower Mainland children and exerted new pressure on the police investigation.

* * *

On July 3, the day after Simon's disappearance, Clifford Olson offered a sixteen year old girl a job with Hale & Olson Construction. If she was interested, she could start at 3:00 p.m. on Monday. For the next three days, the teenager bubbled over with excitement. On Monday, as previously arranged, Olson picked her up outside the Lectro Fun Arcade at the Lougheed Mall and headed for Surrey, the location of one of Hale and Olson's building sites. Enroute, the young girl thoroughly enjoyed herself; she and her new employer shared a few drinks and laughs, and just as the young girl was thinking she'd scored the perfect boss, Olson left the main road, drove into a secluded spot in the bushes, and attempted to rape her.

Furious with his new employee for resisting him, Olson drove her back to the mall and fired her. Unaware of how close she had come to losing something more valuable than her job, the young girl immediately flagged down a passing RCMP cruiser and told the officer what had happened.

Barely a month after Agassiz's Darryll Kettles had put out his APB on Clifford Olson, Burnaby RCMP were issuing a second one. Immediately after the bulletin went out, Constable Ewart spotted Olson leaving the Lougheed Mall parking lot and arrested him.While processing the arrest at the Burnaby detachment, Corporal Les Forsythe grew uneasy with the circumstances surrounding Olson's arrest. Just as Corporal Kettles had done, Corporal Forsythe decided Olson's antecedents merited a closer examination.

What Corporal Forsythe uncovered dumbfounded him. Olson had picked up the girl who had just reported him and dropped her off at the Lougheed Mall, a stone's throw away from Burquitlam Plaza, the place Daryn Johnsrude had last been seen. Olson had managed to beat two sexual assault charges, one involving a fourteen year old Vancouver Island boy, the second a Whalley girl named Kim Werbecky. If that wasn't damning enough, Corporal Forsythe also discovered that on May 26, Clifford and an underage female had been involved in a suspicious automobile accident near Aggasiz, not far from where Daryn Johnsrude's body had been found. In that incident, the teenage girl had been picked up at a Mac's store only two blocks south of Burquitlam Plaza.

Corporal Forsythe already knew that Ada Court had disappeared from the bus stop directly across from the Mac's store and that Olson lived three blocks south of Burquitlam Plaza, five blocks north east of the Lougheed Mall, and one block east of the Mac's store and Ada Court's bus stop. Further, Corporal Forsythe knew that Daryn

Johnsrude, Kim Werbecky, the girl involved in the May 26 incident, and now this girl, had all been looking for work, and that Olson had been "hiring."

With the exception of one significant detail, Corporal Forsythe came to the same conclusion as Corporal Darryll Kettles. Corporal Forsythe believed the man he had in detention, pending more drunk driving and indecent assault charges, was the murderer of Daryn Johnsrude *and* Ada Court.

Despite a mountain of circumstantial evidence, senior investigators argued there was no hard evidence linking Olson to either Daryn Johnsrude's murder or Ada Court's disappearance. There was also some doubt concerning the credibility of the girl involved in this latest assault, so investigators chose not to lay the sexual assault charges. Just as Corporal Kettles had been compelled to do, Corporal Forsythe was forced to release Olson.

At 11:00 a.m., Thursday, July 9, Clifford Olson picked up a young acquaintance of his, eighteen year old Randy Ludlow. The two men drove around drinking until Olson spotted a pretty, dark-haired girl he claimed to know from the New Westminster McDonalds. When she stepped out of the phone booth she was using, Olson pulled up to the curb and offered her a lift to Richmond.

Shortly before 11:00 that morning, fourteen year old Judy Kozma had left her New Westminster home to go for a job interview. Before catching her bus to Richmond, Judy used a pay phone to arrange to meet a friend later. Judy stepped out of the phone booth in time to see someone she thought she knew. She didn't know his name but she recognized his short stocky frame and wavy dark hair as a regular at the McDonalds where she cashiered. Judy thought he must have recognized her too because he smiled and waved and pulled his car over. Sticking his head out the window, he asked her where she was going.

"Richmond," said Judy. "I have a job interview at Wendy's."

"Hop in. We'll take you there."

Judy knew better than to accept rides with people she didn't know, but this man was not really a stranger. Besides, catching a ride saved her a long, hot, and arduous bus trip through greater Vancouver. She gratefully accepted the offer and slid into the back seat behind another passenger, a boy named Randy Ludlow.

Judy and her companions reached Richmond with plenty of time to spare before Judy's 1:00 appointment. They picked up some beer and drove around drinking. Around noon, at the driver's behest, Randy mixed Judy a drink laced with small, emerald-green pills. Shortly after that, the driver dropped Randy off at the Lougheed Mall and assured him he would get Judy to her interview safely.

But Judy failed to make her appointment. She failed to make her meeting with her friend. And she failed to make it home.

* * *

So convinced was Corporal Les Forsythe of Olson's complicity in the Case of the Missing Lower Mainland Children, on July 15, he invited officers from various Lower Mainland police forces with a "common interest in missing children" to a brainstorming session at the Burnaby RCMP detachment.

By the time the meeting wrapped up, Coquitlam police announced that, "Olson remains the strongest suspect in the Johnsrude murder." Vancouver Serious Crime Investigators agreed that Olson was a strong candidate for the Johnsrude murder, but wanted to keep an open mind about other possible suspects. Needless to say, Burnaby police considered Olson *the* prime suspect in Ada Court's disappearance, and, had they known she was missing, New Westminster police *may* have singled Olson out as a person of interest in the disappearance of Judy Kozma.

Richmond police affirmed that, "Olson could be a possible suspect in the murder of twelve year old Christine Weller," but they already had a stronger suspect. And if that suspect did not pan out, there was the possibility that Christine's murder could be linked to the 1978 and 1979 abduction and slayings of Monica Jack and Susan Duff, two twelve year old girls who, like Christine, had been kidnapped while out riding their bicycles. While not everyone present was as unequivocally convinced of Olson's guilt as Corporal Forsythe, everyone agreed that Burnaby should watch him carefully.

Burnaby's first priority was to put Olson under surveillance. Though it was a positive step, it took almost two weeks of wading through the RCMP's bureaucratic quagmire to set the surveillance in place. The two weeks proved a costly delay. In the interim, one young German tourist and two more Lower Mainland children went missing.

* * *

During the summer of 1981, nothing was more important to Raymond Lawrence King than finding a job. At 1:00 in the afternoon of July 23, Raymond rode his bike from his New Westminster home to the Canada Manpower Youth Employment Offices hoping that Thursday would be the day he would find the perfect summer job. Raymond was chaining his bike to a post outside the employment centre offices when a short stocky man with brown eyes and wavy dark hair approached him. The man told Raymond he worked for Manpower and could get Raymond a job washing windows at $10 an hour – would he be interested?

Interested! Raymond was beside himself with excitement. Ten dollars an hour! That was nearly twice as much as a fifteen year old could make at most other summer jobs.

Two days after Raymond's disappearance, police found skeletal human remains near Weaver Lake in Agassiz, nineteen kilometres from where Daryn Johnsrude's body had been recovered at the beginning of May. From the advanced degree of decomposition it was easy to dismiss them as the missing Raymond King. Four days later, dental charts identified them as those of Judy Kozma. The nineteen stab wounds to her head and upper body made it clear she had been killed in some kind of murderous frenzy. As with Daryn Johnsrude, her nude body was too badly decomposed for police to determine whether she had been the victim of a sexual assault.

While Agassiz police were grappling with their most recent discovery, Sigrun Charlotte Elizabeth Arnd, an eighteen year old foreign student from Weiner, Germany, in Canada studying English and visiting an aunt, was sitting in the Caribou Hotel Pub drinking beer and chatting with a short stocky man with brown eyes and wavy dark hair. Sigrun thought the man was as friendly and charming as all the Canadians she had met during her travels. And exceedingly hospitable. So hospitable he offered to take her out and show her some of his company's construction sites.

On July 27, at 8:00 a.m., almost nine hours before the Joint Forces Organization (JFO) began their surveillance of Olson, fifteen year old Terri Lyn Carson left her home at the Surrey Village Apartments to apply for a job at the Fin 'N' Feathers pet shop at the Guilford Town Centre Mall. But before she arrived, Terri received a better offer – a cleaning job with Hale & Olson Construction at $10 an hour.

When Terry Carson reported her daughter missing the following day, Surrey police took Terri's description – five feet tall, one hundred and five pounds, thick-lensed glasses with enormous salmon-colored frames – and immediately pegged her as a runaway. She had been fighting with her mother over her pot-smoking and curfew, and, according to Sergeant Bill Stephens of the Surrey RCMP, her "case had the classic profile of a runaway." The RCMP's position "that there [was] no foul play involved" was bolstered by someone who reported seeing Terri drinking at Surrey's Turf Hotel on August 1.

Terri's mother saw things differently. Though she and Terri had their disagreements, her daughter had never run away before. Besides, if Terri had been planning to run away, why would she have been applying for a new job?

Though surveillance of Olson went into effect at noon on July 27, he was not actually located until 4:00 p.m., long after he'd driven Terri

Lyn Carson to one of his job sites in Agassiz, and then on to Hope where he cashed $200 worth of travellers' cheques payable to Sigrun Arnd.

At noon the following day, a little better than twenty-four hours after surveillance officially began, the JFO, suspecting that Olson knew he was being followed, temporarily shut down their operation. At 10:00 that evening, Olson met Delta police officer Dennis Tarr at a White Spot restaurant to discuss his chances of becoming a police informant at a salary of $3000 a month. Olson was particularly interested in helping the police with their investigation into the missing Lower Mainland children. Detective Tarr arranged to meet with Olson the next morning to discuss the matter further, and Olson departed. The moment he left the JFO recommenced its surveillance. Concerned about the safety of two female hitchhikers that Olson, Randy Ludlow, and another man picked up shortly after Olson left the restaurant, at midnight the JFO team broke cover. Olson's drinking companions were questioned and released, but Olson was detained on yet another count of contributing to juvenile delinquency.

The question of what to do next led to a division in the ranks. One group of RCMP officers wanted Olson released, so he could keep his morning meeting with Detective Tarr and hopefully implicate himself in the Case of the Missing Lower Mainland Children. Another group of officers, including members of the JFO, wanted him kept in custody. The JFO was livid when Olson was ultimately released at 3:30 in the morning of July 29. Five and a half hours later, they quit. According to Leslie Holmes, author of *Where Shadows Linger*, the JFO's rational was that, "If Olson was as dangerous as some believed, [the JFO surveillance team] felt they could not condone a situation where they could not take immediate action if Olson enticed a young person into his vehicle and . . . eluded surveillance with disastrous consequences."

The consequences of that decision proved equally disastrous.

On Thursday evening, July 30, while police were preoccupied with their acrimonious arguing, Louise Marie Chartrand failed to show up for her 8:00 waitressing shift at Bino's restaurant in Maple Ridge. The petite seventeen year old, whose dainty features and diminutive size made her look younger than she actually was, was last seen hitchhiking to work at 6:45 at Dewdney Trunk Road and 224 Street, dressed in a tan shirt and blue pants.

In a definitive move, later that same evening, Bill Neill of the RCMP's Criminal Investigation Branch placed the Case of the Missing Lower Mainland Children in the hands of RCMP Superintendent Bruce Northorp. Not only did the move centralize an investigation that had been scattered amongst Surrey RCMP, Burnaby RCMP, Agassiz RCMP, Whistler RCMP, Squamish RCMP, Coquitlam RCMP, Richmond RCMP, Langley RCMP, Maple Ridge

RCMP, the Vancouver Serious Crimes Section, and the municipal police forces of New Westminster and Delta, the move also assigned command of the investigation to someone with the authority to make unilateral decisions. One of Superintendent Northorp's first priorities was to renew surveillance of Olson. But before he managed to set it in place, Olson disappeared on a family trip to Calgary.

* * *

On August 5, a Burnaby hiker found a tan shirt and the tattered remains of a pair of blue plants near Green Lake, five kilometres north of Whistler. In color and size, the clothing matched that described as the clothing Louise Chartrand had last been seen wearing. Police searched the surrounding area and sent divers into the Lake, but produced no other signs of the missing girl.

That same day, a couple out walking a side road one kilometre north of where Judy Kozma's body had been found, reported a foul odor. Responding to the complaint, police employing police dogs, found the decomposed remains of a nude male body, slight and sandy-haired and later identified as Raymond King. He had been beaten and stabbed, and someone had driven a three inch spike through his head.

* * *

At this point in the Case of the Missing Lower Mainland Children lead investigators had yet to tie Christine Weeler's murder to the murders of Daryn Johnsrude, Judy Kozma and now Raymond King. Terri Carson and Colleen Daignault were still considered runaways and no one even knew Sigrun Arnd was missing. While police were willing to admit that Simon Partington was likely the victim of foul play, his age and sex prevented his disappearance from being linked to the disappearances of Louise Chartrand, Sandra Wolfsteiner, and Ada Court.

Though talk of a serial killer continued, there was at least one letter to the editor of the *Vancouver Sun* in which the anonymous author took other members of the public to task for their "loose talk comparing the situation with the murders of black children in Atlanta."

Inspector Larry Proke, in charge of the RCMP's Serious Crimes Section, seemed to agree. He warned the public against assuming one person was responsible for the murders and disappearances, pointing out the "sharp differences between the methods of killing, the two boys had been bludgeoned and the girl stabbed." Basing his opinion on recent major cases, Inspector Proke also pointed out that those cases had involved only one sex which was "why I'm repeatedly telling our investigators not to get tunnel vision, not to concentrate on there only being one person, or two connected persons in this."

Despite Inspector Proke's position, when Olson returned from Alberta on August 6, surveillance resumed in earnest. This time it was not the JFO but the Special O Surveillance Unit conducting the operation and it would tail Olson twenty-four seven. On August 7 and again on August 12, Special O officers sat and watched from a distance as Olson burglarized two Burnaby senior citizens' residences. Later on August 12, after a week's surveillance had failed to produce any leads in the Missing Children investigation, Olson unexpectedly ferried to Vancouver Island. After receiving permission from Vancouver Island RCMP to enter their jurisdiction, the Special O team members followed Olson's rented Acadian from the Swartz Bay ferry terminal to Victoria where they once again watched unobtrusively as he burglarized two suburban homes. From Victoria the Special O team trailed him to Nanaimo and maintained a nervous distance after he picked up two female hitchhikers and headed for the west side of the Island.

Nervousness grew to anxiety after Olson drove the hitchhikers into a secluded area of bush off the Pacific Rim Highway, half way between Tofino and Ucluelet. Unwilling to allow the girls to be put to further risk, the Special O team moved in. Spotting their approach, Olson made a run for his car and tried to outrace them. Prepared for just such a maneuver, back-up police provided by Vancouver Island RCMP, snared him in a roadblock. Olson was arrested and taken to the Ucluelet detachment where he was charged with impaired driving. A search of his impounded vehicle produced an address book; a search of the address book produced Judy Kozma's name and number.

Following the arrest, police again found themselves in a quandary. Should they hold him in custody or release him and place him under surveillance again?

After carefully weighing his options, Superintendent Northorp discounted the possibility of releasing Olson and renewing surveillance. To date, Northrop reasoned, surveillance had done nothing more than confirm Olson's penchant for picking up teenagers. Furthermore, now that police had swooped down on him for a second time, unless he was completely dim-witted, Olson would know he was being followed.

Because Canada's Criminal Code makes it illegal to keep someone in custody longer than twenty-four hours without laying charges, police charged Olson with the two breaking and entering counts relating to the August 7 and 12 Burnaby robberies. Hoping to shake him into a confession, the next day they publicly announced that a suspect was being held in Judy Kozma's murder. It was a risky tactic. Police knew they needed a good deal more than a name in an address book if they hoped to get an indictment for Judy's murder. And even if they were fortunate enough to get an indictment, the best they could hope for was a charge of second-degree murder.

On August 18, police spoke to Randy Ludlow and were subsequently able to link Olson to Judy Kozma on the day she disappeared. Though Ludlow's information provided police with another piece of sorely needed ammunition against their prisoner, their case against him was weak.

Painfully aware that their evidence against Olson remained judiciously feeble, police trusted to chance and gambled that a murder charge would pressure him into a confession. On August 20, they charged him with Judy Kozma's murder.

The gamble paid off.

Later that day, Clifford Olson immortalized himself with the thirty chilling words that have come to define him – "I'll give you all the evidence. The things only the killer would know. I'll give you eleven bodies for $100 000. The first one will be a freebie."

It was a sick and callous offer and placed police at the heart of an unprecedented dilemma.

Olson was holding a platter of proof that would jail him forever. Without his confession, what did police have? Judy Kozma's name in an address book, the testimony of Randy Ludlow, a street-wise petty thief who had been involuntarily admitted to Riverview Hospital for a psychiatric assessment, and a host of geographical connections.

Christine Weller and Terri Lyn Carson had both lived in the Surrey Village Apartments at the same time Olson had lived there, and had known one another vaguely. Olson was still living in Surrey when Christine disappeared from the Surrey Place Mall. The bicycle she had borrowed from Alex Walker's son was found across the street from his home on the King George Highway. Olson had also been living in Surrey when he picked up Kim Werbecky in Whalley, a small Surrey community.

By the time Daryn Johnsrude and Ada Court had disappeared from North Road, Olson had moved to the Coquitlam apartments half a dozen blocks from both the Burquitlam Plaza and the Lougheed Mall. The girl involved in the May 26 motor vehicle accident had been picked up from the Mac's store one block south of Lougheed Mall, and the girl involved in the July 6 attempted rape, had been picked up from the arcade at the Lougheed Mall.

Olson frequented the Macdonald's where Judy Kozma worked, while Randy and the address book could further tie him to Judy, and Sigrun Arnd had been seen drinking with Olson at the Cariboo Hotel Pub the day she disappeared.

Kim Werbecky, Daryn Johnsrude, the girl involved in the attempted rape, Judy Kozma, Raymond King, Terri Carson, and the teenage girl involved in the May 26 automobile accident, had all been looking for work and Olson had been actively seeking employees.

Unfortunately, the connections were as circumstantial as they were suggestive and any competent defense attorney would tear them to shreds. Though police had conducted the most massive investigation in British Columbia's history – helicopter aerial searches, underwater diving team searches, land searches aided by one hundred and forty eight full-time staff and police tracking dogs from Chilliwack, Coquitlam, Burnaby, and Surrey, the installation of a new, state-of-the-art, data-processing computer system, and offers of $36 000 in reward monies – they had been unable to produce a weapon, a drop of blood, a follicle of hair, or a sliver of fibre – not one piece of forensic evidence that tied Olson to the crimes.

What they had was his offer.

The cash-for-bodies proposal gave rise to a bitter verbal tug of war:

"A criminal can not benefit his crimes. The idea of paying Olson for his testimony runs counter to the very fibre of Canadian law."

"Olson isn't benefiting, his wife and son are."

"Two or three months in prison with the skinner (child molester) haters and he'll be singing like a canary. And it won't cost us one bloody cent."

"Forking out $100 000 is a decidedly more cost-efficient way of uncovering evidence than having police attempt to locate it on their own."

"The only evidence we have against him is circumstantial. Can we be sure of getting a conviction?"

"People have been convicted on less. Besides, we have enough outstanding charges to keep him in prison for a long, long time."

"If they ever find out, the media and the public will crucify us."

"They'll crucify us worse if they find out we had the opportunity to put Olson away for good and didn't take advantage of that opportunity."

"The deal is repugnant."

"It's practical."

"It's distasteful."

"NOT locating the children's bodies is more distasteful."

* * *

Under a veil of secrecy, the RCMP and the Attorney General's office, approved the deal. On August 26, a trust deed, setting out the terms and conditions of the agreement, was signed by RCMP Staff-Sergeant Arnie Nyland and E. James McNeney, Barrister & Solicitor for Joan Berrymore-Hale-Olson. The trust deed included the following disbursements:

(i) For information leading to the recovery of the body of Louise Mary Chartrand – $10 000.

(ii) For information leading to the recovery of the body of Colleen Daignault – $10 000.

(iii) For information leading to the recovery of the body of Terri Lyn Carson – $10 000.

(iv) For information leading to the recovery of the body of Ada Court – $10 000.

(v) For information leading to the recovery of the body of Sandra Wolfsteiner – $10 000.

(vi) For information leading to the recovery of the body of Simon Partington – $10 000.

(vii) For information leading to the recovery of the body of an unidentified female – $10 000.

(viii) For information leading to the recovery of evidence relative to the identification of the recovered body of Elizabeth Judy Kosma (sic) and descriptions of the conditions of bodies assisting in the identification of Johnsrude, King, Weller – $30 000.

That same afternoon, following Olson's instructions, police uncovered the remains of Louise Chartrand from a shallow grave in a gravel pit north of Whistler. She had been killed by repeated hammer blows. The next day, Simon Partington's mummified remains were found in a Richmond peat bog, one and a half kilometres west of where Christine Weller's body had been found eight months earlier. He had been strangled. Terri Lyn Carson's body was located near Agassiz, six and a half kilometres east of the Rosedale turnoff. She too had been strangled. And finally, Ada Court's body, identified through dental charts, was found at Agassiz, further up the road from where Raymond King's body was found. She had been killed by repeated hammer blows.

Two days later, police announced that some personal effects had been found, "items which could be established as belonging to each of the four victims whose bodies had been found without Olson's assistance, thus establishing he was the killer. Only the killer would have knowledge of where these articles had been hidden." Police also exhumed Sigrun Arnd's body from a ditch that ran through the tall bottomland grasses north of River Road in Richmond. Her body lay

120 metres from where Simon's Parington's body was found. Until August 24, no one had even known she was missing.

On September 1, 1981 police found human remains off Chilliwack Lake Road. While Olson maintained they were the remains of Sandra Wolfsteiner, it would take another nine months before a Simon Fraser anthropologist positively identified them. The last body located was that of Colleen Daignault. On September 17, police found Colleen's skull and skeletal remains east of 144 Street, near 26 Avenue in a south Surrey forest that skirted the American border. Like Louise Chartrand and Ada Court, she had been battered to death by a hammer.

* * *

Clifford Olson went to trial on January 11, 1982 charged with ten counts of first-degree murder. Because Sandra Wolfsteiner's remains had not yet been positively identified, he was not charged with her murder. Olson pleaded not guilty to each of the charges and Canadians steeled themselves for a long and grisly ordeal. What they got was something quite different. On the third day of the trial, January 14, shortly after he was charged with the first degree murder of Sandra Wolfsteiner, Olson reversed his plea. The trial which had been expected to last for months was over in two and half days.

After insuring that Olson understood the consequences of changing his plea, Judge Harry McKay sentenced him to twenty-five years without the possibility of parole, the stiffest sentence possible under Canadian law.

* * *

As a serial killer, Clifford Robert Olson – sometimes incorrectly identified as Canada's first serial-killer – is somewhat of an enigma. On one hand, he shares several characteristics common to what behaviorists call "organized" sexual predators. At the time of his murders, he was in a steady, but abusive relationship with his wife Joan; he carefully orchestrated the murder of his "targeted strangers;" he used the ruse of employment to entice his victims into his vehicle; he hid the bodies of his victims and removed their personal effects to delay their identification and destroy any forensic evidence that could possibly be traced back to himself; he drove his own car, or several rental cars; he attempted to inject himself into the police investigation by offering his services as an informer; he had a lengthy criminal record; he thought himself superior to everyone around him; reveled in the notoriety his crimes afforded him.

On the other hand, there is nothing about Olson's formative years to suggest he would evolve from petty thief and juvenile delinquent to a psychopathic child serial killer. There is no evidence of the *homicidal triad* – fire setting, bed wetting, and cruelty to animals – found in the childhood of 75% of other serial killers. Nor is there evidence to show he was nurtured by a dysfunctional family. Indeed, his early childhood seems to scream middle-class. His family lived in east Vancouver near the Pacific National Exhibition (PNE) grounds until after the war when they moved into Gilmore Crescent in Richmond. Before he retired, Olson's father, Clifford senior, had been a milk man, and since his retirement had done nothing more sinister than call bingo in Vancouver's Fraserview and work as the maintenance man for the apartment complex Olson's mother, Leona, managed. Olson's younger siblings, brothers, Richard and Dennis, and sister, Sharon, matured into normal, law-abiding citizens.

Furthermore, serial sexual predators *generally* begin to live out their perverse fantasies during their twenties. Yet Olson didn't commit his first sexual offense – the 1974 alleged rape of a fellow prison inmate – until he was thirty-four, although the sheer amount of time he was incarcerated and "unavailable" could explain the delay. In *Final Payoff: The True Price of Convicting Clifford Robert Olson*, author Ian Mugrew states that, Olson "had been free for exactly 1501 days from the time he was seventeen, until he was incarcerated for the Lower Mainland murders."

There is also the possibility that Olson committed crimes for which he was never caught. Still, one of Olson's numerous parole officers is quoted as saying, "Clifford was seen as a thief, a false-pretense artist, a garrulous, extroverted, egotistical kind of person, but not as a sexual offender."

Enigma or not, Clifford Olson is an exceedingly dangerous serial offender. During his August 1997 judicial review, court-appointed psychiatrist Doctor Tony Marcus said, "he is still as devious and animated as he was when convicted in 1982, and he shows no sign of burnout."

Forensic psychiatrist, Doctor Stanley Semrau offered much the same opinion. "[Olson is] the most extreme sexual deviant, the most disturbed, the most pathological personality I have ever encountered. [He is] completely untreatable."

Olson became eligible for parole in July 2006. As frightening as that sounds, parole was denied. Clifford Olson will most certainly end his days in his cell in the special housing unit at Quebec's Saint Anne's des Plaines Prison.

Seven
David William Shearing

"I wish my grandma were here to teach me how to bake a pie. I wish my grandpa were here to tell me stories of the war and how he fell in love with my grandma. I want my aunt and uncle to tease me, and my cousins to talk to me about the stuff that cousins talk about. I'm sure I would have been a flower girl at their weddings and helped with their baby showers. So much they missed out on, so much I missed out on not knowing them."

George and Edith Bentley's granddaughter
from Michael Eastman's *The Seventh Shadow*

Late one August night in 1980 on the Wells Gray Highway, two men were driving home from a party when they crested a hill.

Dave Carter was stumbling drunkenly along the Wells Gray Highway when he was momentarily blinded by the headlights of a car coming straight at him.

The car lurched and Dave Carter died instantly.

The fatality was never solved.

* * *

The Johnsons of Kelowna, British Columbia were a typical, middle-class Canadian family. Forty-four year old Robert was a steady and reliable worker, and a devoted husband and father, who worked hard to provide a comfortable home for his two daughters and his wife of twenty-one years. Like hundreds of other Canadian men, during winter, Robert delighted in snowmobiling and hockey; in summer, he turned his attentions to motorcycling.

Robert's forty-one year old wife, Jackie, had left her job at a plywood mill to stay home and tend to her family full-time. With both her daughters in school, Jackie had taken up photography as a new hobby. Robert and Jackie's two daughters, thirteen year old Janet and eleven year old Karen, were cheerful, well-adjusted girls who filled their time away from school playing the piano, attending Girl Guide meetings, and participating in sports.

Though each member of the tight-knit Johnson family took pleasure in their own special interests, the one thing they shared in common was their passion for camping.

On August 2, 1982, Robert, Jackie, Janet, and Karen set out from their Kelowna home to pay a short visit to friends in Red Deer, Alberta. From there they were heading back to British Columbia to spend a week camping with Jackie's mother and father, George and Edith Bentley, in Wells Gray Provincial Park, a five hundred and forty thousand hectare wilderness of alpine meadows, cascading mountain streams, and isolated campsites tucked into the towering peaks of the Monashee and Columbia mountain ranges north east of Kamloops.

When the Johnsons set out from home that warm summer day, food, clothes and sleeping bags packed the trunk of their cream-colored, 1979 Plymouth Caravelle; fishing tackle, lawn chairs, and camping equipment packed its roof-carrier.

* * *

During the summer of 1982, George and Edith Bentley were luxuriating in the freedom of retirement. Although both were in their sixties, age hadn't dampened their enjoyment of camping. The previous year, they had indulged themselves in a new, red and silver Ford camper truck and a ten foot Vanguard camper. In the spring of 1982, they slapped a ten and a half foot aluminum boat onto the roof of the camper and set off on a continent wide tour.

After a four month absence, George and Edith returned to British Columbia, arriving at Wells Gray Park on August 3, and eagerly looking forward to seeing their daughter, son-in-law, and granddaughters again.

On August 6, the same day the Johnsons said goodbye to their Alberta friends, Edith called her youngest daughter, Sharon Sarchet, from Clearwater, a small community thirty-two kilometres south of Wells Gray Park. Edith told Sharon that she and George were having a wonderful time and that they were going to meet the Johnsons the following day.

No one heard from Edith or George or the Johnsons again.

* * *

Experience had taught told Kurt Krack and Albert Aechler where to find the best mushrooms and berries. On August 22, the two friends set out for Wells Gray Park on a mushroom and berry picking expedition. Rather than continuing up Wells Gray Road towards the park's headquarters, they detoured off to the right, heading north east on Battle Creek Trail. Eighteen hundred metres up the trail, they left the main road and trekked deeper into the bushes.

Kurt and Albert had travelled less than thirty metres when they spotted what appeared to be the rusting remains of an abandoned car almost entirely obscured by the dense foliage and underbrush. Annoyed that someone would desecrate the park that way, they voiced their complaints to a couple out riding horses. The riders spent a few minutes commiserating with Kurt and Albert, but never actually saw the vehicle.

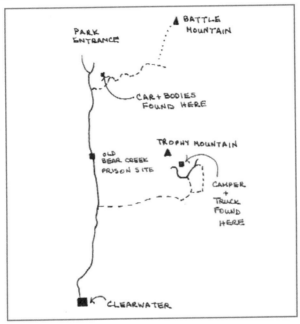

The following day, Al Bonar of Gorman Brothers called the Kelowna RCMP to say he was worried about one of his employees. In his twenty plus years with the company, his sawyer, Robert Johnson, had missed a grand total of three days. Expected back from his holidays on August 16, Robert was now a full week late returning from his family camping trip.

Kelowna RCMP relayed the message to Sergeant Frank Baruta of the Clearwater detachment who followed through on the report by making general inquiries. His inquiries produced nothing, and the Johnson and Bentley families were officially listed as missing.

While Sergeant Baruta continued to hunt for the missing families, their relatives, circulated posters hoping someone would recall seeing the missing families. Someone did. An Avola Petro Canada service station attendant remembered talking to George and Jackie and the two girls. She had told them there was good berry picking in the Blue River area.

Based on that tip, Robert's parents, his sister Elaine, his brother Art, and Jackie's brother and sister, Brian and Sharon, assisted by more than four hundred RCMP officers, parks personnel, volunteers, and friends of the Johnsons and Bentleys, walked, rode horses, piloted helicopters, small aircraft, and boats, and drove motorcycles, jeeps, and other all-terrain vehicles, in an exhaustive search of the area. But despite their best efforts, the search party came away empty-handed. It was as though the Johnsons and Bentleys and their vehicles had vaporized.

The growing publicity concerning the search for the missing families nevertheless stirred the memories of the horseback riders who recalled the conversation they had had with the mushroom and berry pickers back on August 22. They contacted authorities and provided them what little information they had. On the basis of that information, Clearwater RCMP once again conducted a search for the missing families, and, once again, found nothing.

Then, on September 2, Kurt Krack, who had been following the search for the Johnsons and Bentleys as avidly as other area residents, called the Abbotsford RCMP and gave them the exact location of the car he and Albert had seen two weeks earlier. On September 13, thirty-eight days after the Bentleys and Johnsons had last been heard from, Sergeant Baruta, accompanied by Constable Mike Glas, undertook a search of the Battle Creek Trail area. Armed with precise directions, this time the officers spotted a set of tire tracks veering off into the bush, 1800 metres up the trail. Following the tracks for forty-five metres down a slight incline, Sergeant Baruta and Constable Glas located what remained of the Johnson's cream-colored Caravelle.

Fueled by an unknown accelerant, the entire vehicle had been incinerated. Heat from the blaze had evaporated the tires and windows; door handles, headlights, and taillights were gone. A set of scorched and rusty car keys dangled from the lock on the trunk. Flames had eaten the car's rooftop carrier, leaving nothing but the charred remains of tin cans, melted beer bottles, and a handful of blackened potatoes. Whatever had caused it, the blaze had also gutted the dashboard and seats and fused the steering wheel into a misshapen mass of melted metal and plastic.

As devastating as the damage to the vehicle was, what Sergeant Baruta and Constable Glas saw as they peered through the gaping holes where the windows should have been was infinitely worse. In what was left of the back seat, they found human remains.

Sergeant Baruta and Constable Glas immediately sent for the pathologist, the coroner, and Kamloops detectives. When the detectives arrived, they pried open the trunk of the car and discovered more human remains. All the remains had been so completely consumed by fire it was not until after the coroner determined there were six skulls amongst the carnage that police were able to confirm the number of bodies.

Even without positive identification, everyone knew that the "bones, bits of hair, and lumps of charred flesh" found in the makeshift crematorium were the remains of Robert, Jackie, Janet, and Karen Johnson, and George and Edith Bentley. Though the discovery finally resolved the mystery of the families' disappearances, it opened a second pandora's box of endless questions. When had the families been killed? Had they been killed where they were found? Had they been burned alive or had they been killed prior to being placed in the car? Who could have done such a thing and, most importantly, why?

Had the Bentleys and Johnsons been the victims of some kind of road rage that had escalated to murder? Had they been killed in an automobile accident and the driver of the other vehicle had tried to destroy evidence of the fatality? Had they inadvertently stumbled upon a marijuana growing operation and been killed for their troubles?

As unlikely as the scenarios were, police knew from experience that stranger things had happened. Without entirely discounting the other possibilities, because the camping equipment was missing, and because the Bentley's boat, camper, and truck were gone, police believed a more reasonable explanation was that the Johnsons and Bentleys had been killed during a robbery.

But, reasoned police, if that were the case, it was unlikely the robbery had taken place six hundred metres up Battle Creek Trail. Fortunately, they were luckier locating the scene of the crime than they had been in locating the missing families. During the course of their investigations, police received reports of two sightings of the Bentley's truck and camper at the old prison site. The officers in charge of what was now a homicide investigation drove to the site and found seating for six circling the fire pit. In the fire pit's ashes they found three Extra Old Stock bottle caps, Robert Johnson's favorite beer. Further afield they found blocks used for levelling a camper, and a spot where a tent may have been pitched.

The discovery of six spent cartridges from a .22 offered further proof that the Bear Creek prison site had been the scene of the crime, and confirmed police suspicions that the victims had been shot. Because the bodies had been reduced to little more than a pile of charred bones, at the time of their discovery, police had been unable to give an absolute cause of death, even though a hole found over the left eye of one of the children's skulls and an x-ray showing a bullet, probably from a .22, lodged in the skull of another of the other victims had certainly pointed to shooting.

Satisfied they now had answers to where and how and perhaps why the families had been killed, police next grappled with the question of when. They knew that Edith had spoken to Sharon Sarchet on the sixth of August; they knew that Edith and George had met up with the Johnsons the following day. The discovery of a scorched watch, its hands frozen at 10:00, gave them an approximate time of the fire, but could not confirm the time or day of death, or tell them whether the hands were frozen at 10:00 in the morning or 10:00 in the evening.

The nearest police could come to pinpointing a time of death was sometime between August 7, the day the Bentleys and Johnsons were scheduled to meet, and August 16, when Robert was due back at work. However, the discovery of only three beer bottle caps in the fire pit, suggested the families had died sooner than later.

What police now faced was answering the question of who.

Though there were any number of possibilities – an ex-con familiar with the area, a hitchhiker gone sour, a crazed mountain man rumored to exist – the one thing most people, including police, agreed on was that there had been at least two individuals involved. "Lifting Robert Johnson and George Bentley into the back seat of the Caravelle," said retired RCMP officer Norman Lee, "could not have been accomplished by one individual acting alone."

It was Lee's opinion that the crimes had been committed by two "local kids," probably teenagers, from the Clearwater area. Police may have initially thought the same thing, but on August 24, they received a tip from a Vancouver Island man saying he had recently seen the Bentley's truck and camper being driven by two French-speaking males in North Battleford, Saskatchewan.

While police welcomed the tip as a promising lead, others were less convinced. Many people, including Detective Lee, doubted the truck and camper would be used as the getaway vehicle for the simple reason that whoever was driving it "would automatically be linked to the murders." It was Lee's opinion that "the vehicle was hid almost immediately."

The idea that the truck and camper were being driven by the two French Canadians nevertheless gained weight when police received further reports stating that Frenchmen had been seen driving the truck and camper in the Clearwater area at the same time the families disappeared.

Appalled by the thought that the murders could have been committed by anyone who lived in the area, given a choice between two "local boys" or two "frenchmen," Clearwater residents much preferred the latter. Members of the community heaved a universal sigh of relief when lead investigator, Sergeant Michael Eastham announced that, "our theory is that everything points to the truck and camper heading east being driven by two French-Canadians," and police released descriptions and a composite drawing of the two men thought to be driving the truck and camper:

> One man is described as five feet nine inches and 150 pounds with blond, shoulder length hair, with a shaggy moustache and a bump on his nose. He was last seen wearing a tan jacket and blue jeans. The second man is about six feet, 220 pounds, with black shaggy hair and a black beard and moustache. He was last seen wearing jeans and a jean jacket. The men speak little English.

Following the release and distribution of the composite drawing, tips began to pour in. Thirteen hundred witnesses reported seeing the "two scruffy males" driving Edith and George's truck and camper in Clearwater, British Columbia, North Battleford, Saskatchewan, Sherbrooke, Quebec, Windsor, Ontario, and dozens of other towns and cities. Spurred on by the numerous sightings, for the next twelve months, police pursued the elusive "foreigners" across Canada, certain that when they found the vehicle, they would find their murderers.

Then, on October 18, 1983, thirteen months after the Johnson's burned-out Caravelle was found off of Battle Creek Trail, Peter Miller and Doug Kehler, two Clearwater forestry workers, spotted Edith and George's burned-out truck and camper 1400 metres up Trophy Mountain, twenty-four kilometres north of Clearwater, three kilometres north of the prison site campsite, and thirty-two kilometres south of where the Caravelle and its gruesome cargo were found.

To the anger, dismay, and frustration of police, all the time and money spent on their cross-country pursuit, and all the manpower hours logged in following up the thirteen thousand tips had been for naught. For all those months, the Bentley's truck and camper had been resting undisturbed three kilometres from the scene of the murder.

As dispiriting as the news was to police, it was no less so to area residents. "It just drags it all back to our back doorsteps again," said Wells Gray Hotel bartender, Bruce Hystad. The burning question became "which one of their neighbors could have done such a thing?"

In what must have seemed to police a bitter twist of irony, once their investigation focused on "one of the neighbors," the answer came quickly.

Shortly after the discovery of the burned out truck and camper, police received a tip about a a local resident named David Shearing. The informant suggested that police look into David's connection to an unsolved hit and run fatality that had occurred back in 1980.

Later that same day, David's name came up for the second time when one of the investigators was handed a piece of paper with David Shearing's name on it.

Then, while conducting a house to house search of Clearwater, the name David William Shearing came to the attention of the police for the third time. One woman they questioned during their canvass had turned to her husband and said: "aren't you going to tell them about what David Shearing said about re-registering that truck with the bullet hole?"

If three times wasn't enough to raise suspicions, David's name came up for the fourth time during a conversation Sergeant Michael Eastham had with Sergeant Ron Graham of Tumbler Ridge. After learning that David was working in Tumbler Ridge, Sergeant Eastham had called Sergeant Graham to inquire into David's movements. Before Sergeant Eastham had a chance to ask any questions, Sergeant Graham jumped in. "Look. I've got a bit of a weird duck up here. He said he used to live in Clearwater, and I figured I could ask him some questions if you wanted me to. His name's David William Shearing."

It was simply too much of a coincidence for David Shearing's name to come up four times during the course of the investigation and Sergeant Eastham dug deeper. He soon learned that David had a criminal record for possession of marijuana, assaults, drinking and driving, and was presently facing charges of possession of stolen merchandise. Though he now lived in Tumbler Ridge, 965 kilometres north of Kamloops, at the time of the murders, David had been living close to the old prison site, and his job had required him to pass by the Bear Creek Prison site twice each day. Most disturbing though was uncovering the fact that Shearing was partial to young girls.

Using as pretense the 1980 hit and run fatality, on November 19, Sergeant Eastham and his partner, Constable Ken Leibel, brought David in for questioning. Slowly and deliberately, Sergeant Eastham and Constable Leibel worked a confession out of David, first for the hit and run, and then for the Johnson-Bentley murders. It was a bitter sweet victory. After fifteen months of sixteen hour days, once David Shearing was brought in for questioning, it took Sergeant Eastham and Constable Leibel less than six hours to close the case.

* * *

David Shearing had first spotted the Bentleys and Johnsons one evening as he was driving home from work. The families had parked their camper and pitched their tent on the old Bear Creek Prison site, just north of Fage Creek, three kilometres from his home on his family's one hundred and sixty acre ranch near the outskirts of Clearwater. That same evening, he had parked his truck at home before doubling back on foot to a small knoll, which afforded him an unobstructed view of the Johnson-Bentley campsite. Though the early evening darkness shadowed their faces, the flickering light from their campfire was enough for him to distinguish the figures of four adults, two men and two women, and two young girls.

While David sat savoring the cool fragrant air and listening to the light babble of Fage Creek, he made up his mind, he later confessed to Sergeant Eastham, that he wanted the girls and, "he was going to have to kill those other four to get to the girls."

The following night he returned to his spot on the knoll, taking his pump action .22 Remington rifle with him. For forty-five minutes he watched the Johnson and Bentley families laughing and talking and enjoying their time spent together. He waited until Janet and Karen were safely tucked into their sleeping bags inside the tent before putting his plan into action. Circling back to Fage Creek, he turned up Wells Gray Road and approached the campsite from the rear. Veiled by the wall of pine trees surrounding the clearing, he crept up between the tent and the camper.

Jackie noticed him first. Alarmed by his unexpected appearance, she attempted to rise, but David stepped into the clearing and raised his gun, shouting, "don't move!"

Acting on impulse, Robert jumped to his feet. Suddenly there was a thunderous roar. A bullet ripped into Robert's throat, pitching him to the ground. Inside the tent, Karen and Janet screamed and Jackie instinctively ran towards them. George made a dash for his truck, but David gunned him down. Shifting his attention to Jackie, he silenced her screams. Edith made a frantic, and futile, scramble for the camper. Spinning around, David raised his gun to her head and fired.

In less than sixty seconds, David had accomplished what he had set out to do.

With Herculean strength, David then gathered the bodies of "those other four" strewn about the campsite and piled them into the back seat of the Johnson's Plymouth Caravelle. Keeping those things he wanted – a camera, a compass, a tool box – he tossed the remainder of the Johnson and Bentley's gear into the camper. After obliterating all signs of his massacre, David crawled into the tent with Karen and Janet.

It isn't clear how many days David held the girls captive. But whether it was one, two, or ten, the results were the same. After sexually molesting them, he shot them both in the head and dumped their bodies into the trunk of the Plymouth.

David then drove the car, and its grisly cargo, 1800 metres up Battle Creek Trail. He bulldozed the car into an area of dense brush another forty-five metres down a small incline, doused it with twenty litres of gasoline, and set it ablaze. Leaving the fire to burn itself out, he returned to the prison site clearing. Next, he transported George and Edith's boat to a spot close to his house, and, together with the boat's gas tank and life jackets, hid it under some bushes. Finally, he drove the truck and camper one and a half kilometres up Trophy Mountain and set it ablaze.

Through it all, luck had favored David. No one had heard his shots. No one had seen his fires. No one had seen him him driving either of the vehicles or hiding the boat. And, for the next two weeks, no one had known the Johnsons and Bentleys were missing.

* * *

On November 21, 1983 David was charged with the murders of Robert, Jackie, Janet, and Karen Johnson, and George and Edith Bentley. Because the evidence weighed heavily against him – his confession, his possession of the Bentley's motor, boat, and tools, his possession of the murder weapon – the Crown chose to proceed to trial via direct indictment. But there would be no trial. Rather than face a judge and jury on six first-degree murder charges, David chose to plead guilty to six second-degree charges. On April 16, 1984, six days after his twenty-fifth birthday, David stood next to his defense lawyer, Fred Kaatz, and faced the clerk of the court to hear the charges against him.

"David William Shearing stands charged count number one, that he, the said David William Shearing, between the sixth day of August A. D. 1982, and the thirteenth day of August, A. D., 1982, inconclusive, at or near Clearwater, in the Province of British Columbia, did commit second degree murder on the person of Edith Bentley, contrary to section 212 of the Criminal Code of Canada. David Shearing, having heard count one read, how do you plead? Guilty or not guilty?"

"Guilty."

David's first guilty plea was followed by another five, after which there was nothing left to be done but have the judge accept the pleas, listen to sentencing arguments presented by both the defense and the Crown, and announce his sentencing.

For his part, David's lawyer, produced testimonial after testimonial attesting to David's good character. The strongest came from David's brother, Greg, who wrote, "I was completely shocked and unbelieving that he, who was a kind, considerate brother, could even contemplate thinking of such a thing. Both myself and the whole family were completely taken aback and still find it hard to believe. . . . What happened to this young man of good character? He was kind, sympathetic, and a sensitive person. I know him to be a hard-working, compassionate, sensitive man, with above average intelligence. Since his arrest, I have visited David regularly in prison. . . . He shows extreme remorse as to what he has done. He is in pain with himself . . for the terrible deed he has committed." As compelling as the defense argument was, the Crown's was better.

"There is never an excuse for murder, My Lord," said Chief Prosecutor Robert Hunter, "but there is usually a reason. Here the Crown submits that there was not even that. There was no alcohol or drugs involved. There is not the slightest suggestion that these six people annoyed the accused or even insulted him. There is nothing. It was the senseless killing of six innocent and defenseless strangers."

The following day, Tuesday, April 17, 1984, David stood before Justice Harry McKay, the same judge who had heard Clifford Olson's case only two years before, to receive his sentencing:

"I must emphasize," began Justice McKay, "that there are degrees of second-degree murders, just as there are differences between murders. It was for those reasons that parliament gave to sentencing judges a discretion ranging from a minimum of ten years of ineligibility to a maximum of twenty-five years. At the lower end of the range of culpability is the second degree murder with which we are too familiar involving one or more such things as lack of actual intent to kill, a family dispute, real or imagined grievances, sudden anger, provocation falling short of the provocation which justifies reduction of murder to manslaughter, defense of the person falling short of justifiable killing in self-defense, diminished capacity by reason of alcohol, drugs or mental impairment and so on. That is not the case before me . . . What we have, put very simply, is a cold-blooded and execution of six defenseless and innocent victims for no apparent reason other than he possibly coveted some of their possessions. . . . The enormity of the crimes demands the maximum sentence."

In an unprecedented decision, Judge Mckay then sentenced David "to concurrent terms of imprisonment for life without eligibility for parole until you have served twenty-five years of your sentence."

Of the many mysteries that surrounded the Johnson-Bentley murder case, perhaps the most perplexing was finding an answer to why David Shearing could commit the crimes he did. Friends, family, employers, coworkers, and even the police who interviewed him, thought him to be a good guy.

"Where," asks Sergeant Michael Eastham, "did the train switch directions?"

At this writing, David William Shearing is serving his time at a penitentiary in British Columbia. He will be eligible for parole in 2008. If granted, he will be fifty-one when he is released.

Eight
Paul Kenneth Bernardo and Karla Leanne Homolka

I'm the solo creep, I make the girls weep
Committing my crimes while the others sleep

Paul Bernardo

With you in my life I feel complete. I feel whole.

With you by my side, I know nothing can go wrong.

You have done so much for me Paul—

You have taught me what love really is.

You have opened my eyes to a new way of thinking and being.

I will love you forever, no matter what.

I love you. Karla XOXOX.

Karla Homolka

The rapist struck first on May 4, 1987. He may have spotted his victim, a petite, twenty-one year old woman with long dark hair, when she stood up in the brightly lit bus after ringing the bell. Then again, he may not have spotted her until she got off the bus near the intersection of Centennial Road and Lawrence Avenue in Guildwood Village, one of Toronto's affluent bedroom communities in Scarborough. Either way, after she descended into the cool spring air at 1:00 in the morning, he followed.

She made it as far as her own front yard before he seized her from behind and dragged her into the darkness between her house and her neighbor's. Then, while her parents slept peacefully less than six metres away, he held her at knife point and vaginally and anally raped her. Throughout her ordeal, he verbally assaulted her – she was a bitch, a slut, a whore – and demanded she stroke his ego by telling him he was the best.

Ten days later, the scenario replayed itself with horrifying precision. At 2:00 in the morning of May 14, a nineteen year old woman, also petite, also with long dark hair, got off a bus at the same intersection and began walking home. Cautiously hugging the west side of the road where the lighting was better, she reached the driveway to her own house before a man leapt from the shadows and slammed her onto the ground. Even if she had had time to react, her tiny size was no match for that of her six foot, 180 pound assailant.

Immobilized by fear, the young woman could not even manage a scream as her attacker hauled her between two nearby houses and threw her onto her stomach. Using his knees to pin her down, he clenched his fists and pounded her repeatedly. Helpless from fear, she closed her eyes and prayed as he wound a length of electrical cable around her neck, tightened the cord, and for the next twenty minutes anally raped her.

Given the similarity of the attacks, police believed it was the same offender.

Seven months passed before there was another attack. Then, on a cold and blustery winter night, the rapist struck again. At 9:30 in the evening on December 16, shortly after alighting from a bus near Guildwood Parkway and Livingston Road, a five-feet-four-inch, fifteen year old girl, weighing little more than one hundred pounds, became the rapist's third victim.

Wielding his knife, he grabbed the girl by her throat and long dark hair and pulled her into the shadows between two houses. After assuring her he wouldn't hurt her, he asked her name. Terrified, she told him a lie. It was a costly misjudgment. While rummaging through her purse, he found her identification and discovered the truth. In that instant, had she been able to peer into her assailant's cold eyes, the young girl may have caught a glimpse of the loathing he bore all women. As retribution for her deceit, this cunt, slut, whore, bitch of a female would feel his wrath. He slammed her head into the ground and for more than sixty minutes anally and vaginally raped her.

And then he was gone.

So she thought.

Before she had a chance to catch her breath, the assailant was back, binding her wrists, lashing her neck to a fence, thrusting his penis into her mouth, demanding fellatio. When he was finally finished, he forced her to tell him how much she loved him, what a fine lover he was, and how much better he was than her boyfriend – a detail she had no way of knowing.

In addition to her multiple cuts and abrasions, the young girl's medical examination revealed that her anus was torn and her hymen was ruptured. But her most painful injuries were those no one could see. During his marathon of terror, the assailant had shattered the teenager's physical, emotional, and psychological innocence, leaving her with invisible scars that would never heal.

It was clear that a vicious assailant, whom the media now captioned the Scarborough Rapist, was holding Toronto's eastern suburb under siege.

A mere seven days later there was a fourth attack. Just before 1:00 a.m. on December 23, having spent the previous evening shopping and visiting friends, a seventeen year old girl stepped off a bus near the intersection of Lawrence Avenue and Bathgate Drive. Proceeding north on Bathgate, eerily deserted at that time of the morning, the teenager unexpectedly heard the crunch of a footstep on the powdery snow behind her. In the next instant, a gloved hand was covering her mouth and a muscular white male in his early twenties was holding a knife to her throat. In a repetition of his previous attacks, he forced her into the backyard of the nearest house and tied her to a fence using her belt. Other than the fact that this time the victim was tall and blonde and weighed 150 pounds, there was nothing to differentiate this assault from the others. For over an hour the young woman's assailant threatened her life, verbally degraded her, and assaulted her so violently he lacerated her uterus.

This latest attack gave rise to the formation of the Scarborough Rapist Task Force. Set up in March 1988, it was created in time to investigate the April 18 attack on the rapist's fifth victim.

It was an unseasonably cold Monday night when the nineteen year old student, returning home from her part-time restaurant job, exited a bus at the corner of Markham Road and Brimorton Drive. Hastening down Brimorton, she failed to see the figure crouched in the bushes until he was on her. She screamed and struggled and paid for her resistance with a fractured collarbone, a broken left humerus, a bleeding hymen, and a crippling blow to the head. After sexually assaulting her for more than thirty minutes, her attacker poured dirt over her hair and body and ground it in. As Gregg McCrary, distinguished profiler with the FBI's Behavioral Sciences Unit in Quantico, Virginia said, "Could there be any clearer message about his attitude towards women?"

Based on victims' reports taken during the previous year, the Task Force had been able to gather bits and pieces of information about the assailant. In each of his assaults, he adopted the same MO. He likely stalked his victims prior to attacking them. He blitzed from behind under the cover of darkness and the seclusion of tree-lined side streets. He terrorized with a knife and prevented his victims from seeing his face by forcing their heads to the ground, or ordering them, under threats of death, to shut their eyes. He was a trophy collector, taking from the scene of his rapes some kind of memento, more often than not pieces of identification belonging to his victims. For the perpetrator, the souvenirs helped him relive his assaults; for the victims, the knowledge that their attacker knew where they lived held them in a state of perpetual fear.

He also displayed a unique "signature," the term coined by the criminal profiler John Douglas to describe a criminal's personal compulsions – not what they need to do to commit the crime, but what they need to do to achieve satisfaction. He compensated for his own sexual inadequacies by verbally degrading his victims while simultaneously exacting from them remarks on his sexual prowess. As a means of intensifying their pain and his own perverse pleasure, he anally raped them.

Further, anal and vaginal swabs identified him as a non-secretor. In approximately eighty percent of the population, antigens found in a person's blood will also show up in their body fluids, i.e. their saliva, sweat and, in men, spermatozoa. A man with type-O blood, for example, will have the O-antigen in his secretions. A non-secretor is therefore a medical term used to describe a man whose saliva, sweat and spermatozoa fail to indicate a blood type.

The Task Force was also aware of one particularly disquieting reality, the viciousness of the attacks was rising. "His controls are shot," said Judith Hoilett, coordinator of the Whitby Hospital Sexual Assault Care Centre. "He has become more violent and will be more violent still."

Because he had been attacking in twos – two in May, two in December – after the April attack, Hoilett warned he "probably will strike again soon."

He probably did. On May 29, four days after police on a stakeout gave chase to a man believed to be the Scarborough Rapist, an eighteen year old woman was attacked as she walked down Lakeshore Boulevard in Mississauga at 1:30 in the morning. Police were uncertain whether to attribute the attack to the Scarborough Rapist. As with four of the previous five victims, the woman was small and had long dark hair. But unlike the other assaults, on this occasion the attacker had spoken to the woman before committing his assault. Still, the attack itself bore all the characteristic trademarks Scarborough Rapist. After asking the woman for directions, the man had dropped back and seized her from behind. He had then dragged her into a nearby wooded area and forced her to the ground. He had bound her wrists, and verbally and physically abused her, including inserting twigs into her anus.

Police wondered if the Scarborough Rapist was attempting to throw them off his scent by shifting his area of attack. After coming so close to being captured four days earlier, his guard would be up and he may have sought safer hunting grounds. He may have also guessed that police were staking out bus stops and employing undercover policewomen as decoys on city transit buses. There was no denying that the woman's description of her assailant closely matched those of the other victims – a clean-shaven male in his early twenties, roughly six feet tall, fair hair, fine features, and blue eyes, the latter a characteristic previously unknown. Still, the forty-eight kilometres from Scarborough to Mississauga was a significant distance. Despite their uncertainties, based on the victim's description Mississauga police produced a composite sketch and released it locally.

Following this, possibly the sixth Scarborough Rapist attack, FBI profilers Gregg McCrary and John Douglas flew to Toronto to prepare a psychological profile of the assailant. After interviewing those officers involved with the case, reading their reports, and visiting the sites of the assaults and the bus stops from which the victims had been followed, McCrary and Douglas concluded that the Scarborough Rapist was an anger-retaliatory rapist, impulsive and explosive. Even a momentary delay of obedience enraged him and he applied far more force than was necessary to subdue his victims. Both profilers also believed the rapist was a psychopath who lived in the area of the attacks, most probably with his parents. He was single, nocturnal, and thrived on taking risks. Most frightening though was their belief that "the violence had become eroticized, because when that happens, the doors to hell have truly been opened."

Dr. John Bradford, one of Canada's leading authorities on serial rapists, agreed. Just as McCrary and Douglas had done, he predicted that the escalating violence of the assaults could very well catapult the attacker from serial rapist into serial killer.

Meanwhile, spring turned to summer and summer to fall before the man police "knew" to be the Scarborough Rapist reappeared and carried out his next assault. On November 16, he seized an eighteen year old woman near the corner of Sheppard Avenue and Birchmont Road. After dragging her into a secluded spot close to her home, he slashed her leg seriously enough to require sutures and sexually assaulted her.

On December 27, a little over a month later, at 9:00 in the evening, a man followed a twenty-three year old woman home from her bus stop. When she turned into her driveway, he jumped out and attacked her. Screaming and scratching, she managed to fight him off.

Midway through 1989, after a six month hiatus, the attacker gave notice he had no intention of halting his siege. On June 20, he made an unsuccessful attempt to assault a nineteen year old woman as she was walking home from a friend's at 3:00 in the morning. During her struggle, the woman struck and scratched her assailant so forcefully police suspected he may have sustained serious cuts to his face and asked citizens to be on the lookout for an individual bearing such injuries. The woman's valiant fight, combined with her loud screams, brought neighbors running and frightened her attacker away.

As with the Mississauga attack, police were unsure whether to attribute this attempt to the Scarborough Rapist. The would-be assailant had not produced a knife, nor had the woman been accosted after getting off a bus. Nonetheless, the attack *had* occurred in the community of Guildwood, the site of the first two attacks and, other than the man's height, the woman's description of her assailant matched those provided by the other victims – a five foot eight white male in his early twenties with light brown hair.

If police harbored lingering doubts about the identity of the assailant in June's aborted attack, they had none about the man responsible for the assault that came two months later. On the evening of August 14, the Scarborough Rapist followed a twenty-two year old woman home from her bus stop and watched as she got ready for bed. Noting the time she got off the bus, the route she took to get home, and the fact she lived alone, he waited until the following evening before he attacked her. Having learned from his two previous and unsuccessful experiences to silence his victims, he pulled off her vest and shoved it down her throat to keep her from screaming. He then forced her into some bushes at the rear of a house on Packard Boulevard near Ellesmere and McCowan Roads where he bound her wrists and legs and pummelled her body and face. Almost as though he were punishing her for his preceding two failures, he then viciously assaulted her for two hours.

The rapist quickly followed up this assault with the rape of a North York teenager. In a carbon copy of his other rapes, on November 21 at 1:00 in the morning, he forced the fifteen year old girl to a nearby building and assaulted her.

It was close to 3:00 in the morning, during a record-breaking cold spell, when he struck again. On December 22, a nineteen year old girl drove into the underground garage on Sandhurst Circle near Finch Avenue and MacCowan Road. As she approached the elevator, a man holding a knife grabbed her in a half nelson and forced her into the stairwell. Shoving her up against the wall, he raped her. The bright lighting in the stairwell afforded the woman a good look at her attacker – a clean-shaven white male about five feet nine inches tall and about eighteen-years-old with sandy-blond hair and a thin nose.

Two days later, in the early hours of Christmas Eve, the same man came very near to claiming yet another victim. After she got off a bus, a young man approached a woman. Suspicious of his attentions, she fled.

By the end of 1989, the list of possible Scarborough Rapist victims, including the three failed attempts, had grown to at least thirteen. A $50 000 reward for information leading to his arrest jumped to $150 000, the third largest in Toronto history, and the team of detectives working the case expanded to twenty. But try as they would – stakeouts, female decoys, rewards, hundreds of man hours – the police seemed no closer to catching their man. "Sometimes," said Justice Archie Campbell in his 1996 review of the investigation, "motivation, investigative skill, and dedication are not enough."

It would be another five months before police finally got their break. Sadly, it came at the cost of another young victim. At 1:45 on the morning of May 26, 1990, a nineteen year old woman got off a bus at the intersection of Midland and Sheppard Avenues. Walking north on Midland, she heard someone fall into step behind her. Spinning around, she sighed with relief. There was no way the nice looking young man could be a serial rapist. He was too sweet looking. Too clean cut. Too much the well-groomed, college-boy type.

"You scared me," she said with a nervous laugh.

As they headed towards Agincourt Collegiate, they shared a few social niceties – "Nice night. Yes, it is, isn't it?" Then, just as they neared a secluded area north of the schoolyard, the sweet-looking man dropped back and hit the girl from behind. Drawing a knife, he forced her deeper into the shadows, bound her with twine, and assaulted her for an hour. Twice he pretended to leave, only to return and resume his attack. During her ordeal, the woman suffered numerous bruises and lacerations, including a bite mark to her breast.

As grim as it was, the rape provided police their first glimmer of hope. In this, his most recent wake of terror, the assailant left behind one vital clue – a more detailed description.

Three years after the initial attack, Toronto Metropolitan Police finally had sufficient information to produce a composite drawing and release it to the public.

> Male, white, eighteen to twenty-two years old, light colored eyes – possibly blue, medium to heavy build – muscular, blonde hair – parted and feathered back to the sides, hair to the ears and to collar at back, clean shaven, smooth tanned complexion, no accent, wearing baby blue coloured top and tan knee length shorts, running shoes.

On May 29, the face of the Scarborough Rapist stared up at the readers of the *Toronto Star*, *The Globe and Mail*, and the *Toronto Sun*. The caption accompanying the picture in *The Globe and Mail* and the *Toronto Star* asked, "Is This 'Boy-Next-Door' the Scarborough

Rapist?" The caption in the *Toronto Sun* read, "Have You Seen This Man?" Several people thought they had. The face bore a remarkable resemblance to Paul Bernardo.

On November 20, after an employee at the Royal Bank where Paul did his banking, and Paul's childhood friend Alex Smirnis and Alex's wife Tina pointed out the similarities to authorities, police brought Paul in for questioning. Asked where he was on May 26, he said he could not sure, but thought he was probably with his girl-friend. Asked for a blood sample, Paul willingly complied. His alibi for May 26 was never confirmed and it would be another two years before his blood DNA was finally tested. Nonetheless, following Paul's visit to the police, the Scarborough rapes ended abruptly.

Then, on April 6, 1991, almost a year after the Scarborough Rapist seemed to have gone underground, a fourteen year old girl was raped in St. Catharines. The girl had been grabbed from behind while out walking on Henley Island at 5:30 in the morning. The circum-stances surrounding the assault were all too familiar. The girl had been dragged into a secluded area where her assailant bound her hands and verbally and sexually assaulted her. Police would later learn that the reason the Henley Island attack was so similar to the Scarborough attacks was because the Henley Island Rapist and the Scarborough Rapist were one and the same person.

* * *

Leslie Erin Mahaffy was two years into what for her were turn-ing out to be her troublesome teens. She had taken up smoking, had been caught shoplifting, and her grades reflected the fact she had been skipping school. The older kids she began socializing with had introduced her to beer, sex, and marijuana, and, early in 1991, she began challenging what she perceived as an unreasonable curfew imposed by her parents, Dan and Debbie. She was almost fifteen. All her friends got to stay out later than she did. What harm could there be?

On Friday, June 14, at 7:00 p.m., Leslie left her Burlington, Ontario home to attend a memorial service for Chris Evans, an acquaintance from school who had been killed in a car crash that had claimed another three lives. She promised her parents she would be home by 11:00 that evening. Her intentions were good, but time slipped away.

When Leslie's curfew came and went, Debbie Mahaffy, angry that her daughter had defied her again, locked the doors and went to bed.

It was already 12:30 when Leslie's friend, Martin McSweeney began walking her home. The young couple were in no rush; Leslie could not get into any more trouble than she was already in. They dawdled along, stopping to smoke a couple of cigarettes and share memories of Chris, and did not reach the Mahaffy residence until 2:00 in the morning.

Trying the side door, Leslie discovered it locked. She and Martin then circled to the front of the house where Leslie, fearing an embarrassing scene with her parents, assured Martin the door would be open. The teenagers made their goodbyes, including promises to see each other at Chris's funeral in another few hours, and Martin disappeared into the night.

After his departure, Leslie tried the front door only to discover it locked too. Likely more upset by the locked doors than by being out alone in the middle of the night, she headed for a pay phone in a nearby strip mall where she called her friend Amanda Carpino. When Amanda picked up the phone, Leslie asked if she could spend the night. Amanda was unsure. A month earlier, there had been friction between Mrs. Carpino and Mrs. Mahaffy over a similar situation and Amanda was reluctant to give cause for a repeat performance. The girls nevertheless talked until 2:30 when Leslie announced she would return home, ring the doorbell, and face the consequences of breaking curfew.

The doorbell never rang.

At 4:30 p.m., after Dan and Debbie learned that Leslie had failed to show up for Chris's funeral and all attempts to locate her had failed, they reported her missing. A police officer came and dutifully took her description: five feet five, 110 pounds, blue eyes, blonde hair, pierced ears, and braces on both her upper and lower teeth. Born on July 1, 1976, she was just two weeks shy of her fifteenth birthday.

The officer departed, confident that Leslie would soon show up, penitent but unharmed. He had good reason to be optimistic. After all, only two months earlier Leslie had run away twice, once for as long as two weeks and on both occasions had returned safely.

* * *

Early in the evening of June 29, two canoeists and two fishermen discovered five concrete blocks buried in the mud near the shore of Lake Gibson, a small Rorschach, ink-blotch shaped recreational lake that separates St. Catharines, Ontario from the city of Thorold. Encased in one were a human thigh, a lower leg, and a foot. Officers from the Niagara Regional Police, together with forensic investigator, Terry Smith, rushed to the scene. Their expanded search produced another two blocks.

The following morning, two men and a woman, fishing from a bridge upstream from where the concrete blocks had been found, were horrified to spot a female torso floating in the lake. The gruesome discoveries were hoisted up and transferred to the forensic pathology unit of the Hamilton General Hospital. The next day, after Smith carefully measured and weighed each of the blocks, he and pathologist David King began the grisly process of excavating the dismembered parts.

What emerged was the body of a female, five feet five, 110 pounds, aged somewhere between her mid-teens and mid-twenties. Whoever she was, she had brown eyes, blonde hair, pierced ears, and wore braces on both her upper and lower teeth. A distraught Debbie Mahaffy believed it was Leslie. Based on the body's eye color, police assured her it was not.

On July 2, police discovered the torso's tomb, a ponderous 150 pound concrete block. The significance of the find was disturbing. Whoever had tipped the block into the lake was either extraordinarily strong or worked with an accomplice. What was equally disturbing was learning that lime in concrete colors the eyes' irises a murky brown.

One week later, dental records positively identified the body as Leslie Erin Mahaffy, thereby sentencing Debbie Mahaffy, Martin McSweeney and Amanda Carpino to tortuous life terms of endlessly repeating, "if I had only not locked the doors; if I had only stayed long enough to make sure Leslie got safely into her house; if I had only agreed to let her come and stay the night."

* * *

From all accounts, Kristen Dawn French was a remarkable young lady. Oozing with self-confidence, she was blessed with intelligence, athleticism, winning looks, and an engaging smile. It was also her good fortune to enjoy an infectious spirit and genuinely warm personality which had been carefully nurtured and safeguarded by a close and loving family and a doting boyfriend. Donna and Doug French beamed on their daughter with justifiable pride.

At 2:45 p.m. on Thursday, April 16, 1992, the start of the Easter long weekend, Kristen left Holy Cross, her St. Catharines's High School and headed for home, a kilometre away. Between then and 3:00, five people saw her. Friends Andy Morin and Mark Lobsinger spotted her slogging along Linwell Road in the drizzling rain; an unidentified woman saw her speaking to the light-brown haired, twenty-two to thirty year old driver of a yellowish-green, Camaro style car; Barbara Joan Packham saw her being shoved into the back seat of a plain looking, light colored sports model car, with a sloped front like a Camaro, but wrote the struggle off as teenage shenanigans, and one of two drivers who almost collided with what looked like a cream-colored Camaro as it tore out of the Grace Lutheran Church parking lot and sped east on Linwell Road thought he had seen the front seat passenger pushing down arms that were flailing up from the back seat.

At 5:45, when the invariably punctual Kristen still was not home from school, her mother called the police.

The morning after Kristen's disappearance, Horst Keuhn and his wife Heidi arrived at Grace Lutheran Church for early morning service. Sighting a lone shoe lying in the parking lot, Horst picked it up and dangled it over a sign at the parking lot entrance. A short while later, Michelle Tousignant, a friend of Kristen's, out with her parents searching for the missing girl, noticed the shoe. Because of its distinctive arch support and oxblood coloring, she immediately recognized it as Kristen's. The police arrived, taped off the parking lot, and began the painstaking hunt for evidence. Although the rain guaranteed there would be no tire tracks, the search did produce a tiny lock of Kristen's hair and a portion of a map. Common sense said that Kristen had been abducted by someone asking for directions.

While police conducted a door-to-door canvass of the area surrounding the church, twenty-five hundred volunteers, including Holy Cross students wearing green ribbons as a symbol of hope, scoured St. Catharines for any sign of the missing girl.Despite their untiring efforts, there were no leads.

With Kristen's disappearance, talk of a serial killer became more voluble. On April 16, 1990, two years to the day before Kristen's kidnapping, twenty-one year old Lynda Shaw had been abducted after stopping at a Burger King on Highway 401. Lynda's car was found two days later, her body four days after that. She had been sexually assaulted and her body had been mutilated and burned. At the time of Kristen's disappearance, Lynda's murder remained unsolved. On August 12, 2005, without revealing his name, police said they knew the identity of the man who had killed her. He had been out on parole after serving twelve years for another murder when he killed Lynda. They also said that the man had died in 1994. On August 18, three days after Leslie Mahaffy's funeral, police found the body of eighteen year old Nina de Villiers who had disappeared while out jogging in the pre-dawn morning of August 10. Nina's assailant, Jonathan Yeo shot himself a few days later. He was out on bail for a sexual assault at the time. That same year, on November 30, Terri Anderson, who resided in a townhouse very close to Holy Cross High School, vanished after attending a party with friends. Terri's body was later found in Lake Ontario and her death ruled accidental. Though many members of the public and the media believed the murder of Leslie Mahaffy and the abduction of Kristen French were linked to these crimes, at the time, police had no way of knowing if any, all, or none of them were.

* * *

On April 30, while scavenging for scrap metal along the back-roads north of Burlington, Roger Boyer stopped his truck to check out an illegal garbage site just south of Sideroad One. Parking his truck on the side of the road, he tramped through the brush and stubbly grass to take a closer look. He poked about through the discarded odds and ends at the dump site – treadless old tires, musty old car seats, rusty old washing machines, corroding pieces of metal – and found the body of a girl.

Exactly two weeks after she had disappeared, and ten days before her sixteenth birthday, Boyer stumbled upon the body Kristen French.

Initially, the lack of decomposition on Kristen's body led police to believe she may have been kept prisoner for up to two weeks, detonating an explosion of rumors about the unthinkable horrors she may have endured during her confinement. Thankfully, the autopsy, which revealed she had been sexually assaulted and asphyxiated, also revealed she had been murdered within twelve to twenty-four hours of her abduction.

Nagged by unsettling thoughts, the day after police recovered Kristen's body, Van Smirnis, brother to Alex and best man at Paul Bernardo and Karla Homolka's wedding, spoke to Ontario Provincial Police Constable Rob Haney about Paul's possible connection to Kristen's murder. Haney in turn spoke to officers assigned to what police were calling the Green Ribbon Task Force, named in honor of the campaign of hope initiated by Kristen's school friends. Van Smirnis and Rob Haney were not the only people bothered by Paul's possible complicity. According to the Campbell Report, police also received tips from the Royal Bank, Sergeant Kevin McNiff, someone named Madden, and one other individual simply identified by the initials I.L.

On July 21, CHCH television in Hamilton, in conjunction with the Green Ribbon Task Force, aired *The Abduction of Kristen French*. The telecast shocked its one million plus viewers when police announced that based on eyewitness accounts, they were convinced that Kristen had not been abducted by one man, but two. FBI agent Gregg McCrary, who had been peripherally involved in the case, came on via satellite halfway through the program to offer his expertise regarding the type of individuals who would commit such a crime.

According to McCrary, one was the dominant perpetrator of the crime, "a true predator and a psychopath." He was "a manipulator, a cold-blooded killer, with no sense of guilt or remorse. He clearly hated women, and the primary woman in his life would suffer for it. He'd have a history of criminal sexual offenses like flashing, exhibitionism, obscene telephone calls, or rape." The accomplice was a follower who may not have become a sex killer if it weren't for his association with the dominant partner.

McCrary's comments drew out the psychics, the crazies, the confessors, and the more than 20 000 calls. They would ultimately prove horrifyingly accurate.

* * *

Paul Kenneth Bernardo is the youngest of Ken and Marilyn Bernardo's three children. His brother David was born in 1962, his sister Debbie in 1963, and Paul on August 27, 1964.

Everyone agrees he was an adorable child: curly blonde hair, beautiful blue eyes, and a disarming smile, all traits he carried into manhood.

Paul's family life was decidedly less attractive. His brother David was considered taciturn, reclusive, and "odd"; his mother Marilyn, while considered bright and pleasant "enough," was seen as flabby, overweight, slovenly and uncouth. His father Ken was seen as distant and cold and rumored to be a sexual pervert. Not only did gossip speculate Ken was a peeping Tom, it also hinted he sexually abused his daughter. In 1993, at the same time Paul was arrested for the Scarborough rapes and the Mahaffy-French murders, Ken's conviction on sexual assault charges confirmed the earlier rumors.

However convenient it would be to attribute Paul's aberrant sexual behavior to Ken, it would be wrong. In 1981, when Paul was sixteen, Marilyn informed him he was illegitimate. In addition to branding him a bastard, the news killed what little respect Paul had for his mother. Recast as an object of his hatred and scorn, he reduced her status to that of a filthy, fat tramp and made no attempts to conceal his contempt.

In spite of his dysfunctional family, or perhaps because of it, Paul determined to one day make it big. After graduating from the business and commerce program at the University of Toronto, he articled with the accounting firm of Price Waterhouse and, in 1989, leased a new, champagne-gold, two-door Nissan 240SX sports car.

Convinced that image and looks paved the road to success, he became obsessed with his appearance. A self-described "pretty-boy," he began to bleach his hair and press weights. He shed his casual clothes in favor of the haute couture of a man of fashion and tallied a growing list of past and present relationships ranging anywhere from one night flings to long-term, but not, on his part, exclusionary affairs.

To all outward appearances the young man with the Hollywood good looks seemed well on his way to realizing his dreams. He wore the right clothes, drove the right car, dated an endless stream of attractive young women, and assumed the appearance of the successful young professional poised for success.

But lurking beneath the façade were signs that something wasn't quite right.

Like other young men, Paul fantasized about women and sex. But his fantasies always carried a hard, cruel, unpleasant edge. Reminiscent of the chilling wishes of Leonard Lake, partnered in crime with Charles Ng, Paul often spoke of "how satisfying it would be to have a stable of girls – a virgin farm – stocked with beautiful virgins with only one purpose in life: to do your exclusive bidding."

A need to dominate and control factored into his relationships, and he punished those of his female partners who questioned his authority by assailing them with a storm of vulgar epithets. In 1986, Paul offered a glimpse into his dark nature when an anonymous caller made a number of obscene telephone calls to one of Van Smirnis's ex-girlfriends. The ex-girlfriend, suspecting it was Paul, called the police. The police traced the calls back to Paul and confirmed her suspicions.

Nothing had changed by the time Paul met Karla Homolka, an attractive seventeen year old high school student from St. Catharines. Their inauspicious beginning took place on October 17, 1987, in the Atrium Restaurant of Scarborough's Howard Johnson hotel. Paul was there with his best friend Van Smirnis, trying to shake his despondency over problems with two of his girlfriends. Karla was there with coworker Debbie Purdie, attending a pet convention and staying in the hotel.

Within an hour of saying hello, Karla and Paul were up in the girls' hotel room, two metres from Debbie and Van, engaged in their now infamous sexual orgy that went on for the next three to four hours. While their behavior raised eyebrows, the two participants thought it "fantastic."

Though Paul lived in Scarborough and Karla in St. Catharines, they managed to keep their budding long-distance romance alive. Over the next few months, Paul commuted back and forth to wine and dine his new romantic interest and sweep her off her feet. On December 24, 1989, two days after the rape of his nineteen year old victim in the underground parking lot at Sandhurst Circle, Paul presented Karla with a $4500 engagement ring.

In February 1991, two months after the tragic, accidental death of Karla's younger sister, Tammy Lyn, and two months before the Henley Island rape, Paul and Karla moved into a quaint salmon-colored Cape Cod style rental home in Port Dalhousie, a picturesque community adjacent to St. Catharines. Though by then Paul no longer worked for Price Waterhouse, his new occupation as a cross-border cigarette smuggler was lucrative enough to provide him ample income to pay the $1150 monthly rent.

Despite Paul's continuous and frequent liaisons with other women, the couple wed on June 29, 1991, the same day police began removing Leslie Mahaffy's remains from Lake Gibson. The newlyweds honeymooned in Hawaii where, as an unexpected wedding gift, Paul beat up his beautiful new bride and informed her that he was the Scarborough Rapist.

* * *

On January 5, 1993, one and a half years after her wedding, Karla Homolka-Bernardo was taken to St. Catharines General Hospital with what one emergency room doctor called "the worst case of wife assault that he had seen." Her walking was labored; her face was swollen; her head was spongy and covered in lumps. Chunks of her hair had been pulled out by the roots and her left eye was puffy and bloodshot from hemorrhaging. Ugly blue, black, and yellowing bruises discolored 75% of her body and her legs were swollen to the touch.

The hospital reported the beating to police who in turn charged Paul with assault. He made his court appearance and was released on bail.

Karla spent three days in the hospital before being secreted away to an aunt and uncle's. Safely out of Paul's reach, she began to unburden herself, describing the litany of depraved sexual, physical, emotional, and psychological abuses she'd suffered at the hands of her estranged husband.

As Karla was wrestling with her past and present demons and taking the first tentative steps toward recovery, police were zeroing in on the Scarborough Rapist and Mahaffy-French murderer. By the time Karla was hospitalized, they had scaled their list of rape suspects to six, their list of murder suspects to seven. Paul's name figured prominently on both.

A month after she left the hospital, members of the sexual assault squad visited Karla's temporary asylum to interview her about their ongoing investigation into a number of their unsolved cases. Karla said little until after they left. Then she began to talk. Really talk. She admitted to her aunt that Paul was the Scarborough Rapist and that both she and Paul were culpable in the Mahaffy-French murders. In light of her confessions, the next day Karla's aunt and uncle arranged for her to meet with a lawyer.

On February 1, six days before Karla's disclosures, and twenty-six months after he had submitted his DNA sample to police, forensic evidence positively tied Paul to three of the Scarborough rapes. In an attempt to gather more evidence, police promptly placed him under surveillance, trailing him as he cruised about town, surveying the stores and shopping malls for attractive young women. At 3:30 p.m. on February 17, following a particularly nerve-racking night during which he entertained a young woman at his home, they took him into custody. Two days later he was formally charged with the Scarborough rapes, informally the murders of Leslie and Kristen. (He would not be officially charged with their murders until May 18.)

Interestingly, Paul's closest friends expressed no surprised at his arrest. What perplexed them was wondering who could be the accomplice described during *The Abduction of Kristen French* telecast. Not for a moment did they consider Karla.

After his apprehension, police secured a search warrant for Paul and Karla's Port Dalhousie home. Forensic experts descended and began scouring the house for evidence. Their search yielded significant, albeit circumstantial evidence: a hunting knife, a test tube containing the sleeping medication Halcion, a stun gun, dozens of books of prurient content, a one minute and fifty-eight second sex tape involving an Atlantic City prostitute and an under-age friend of Karla's (who would come to be identified only as Jane Doe), handcuffs, boxes similar to those used to encase the concrete that held Leslie Mahaffy's body, a variety of workshop tools, and a rip in the front seat of Paul's Nissan, where something heavy, like a block of concrete, had sliced through the fabric.

There were only two items that held any real forensic promise: a quilt with a reddish-brown smear and a stained piece of carpet.

Two and half months later, on May 6, after concluding their exhaustive search, police gave Ken Murray, Paul's defense lawyer, permission to enter the house and retrieve some of his client's personal belongings. Amongst other things, Murray took from the house a package of video tapes police had been told existed but had been unable to find.

Several months after that, DNA testing confirmed that the reddish-brown smear found on the quilt was Leslie Mahaffy's blood; the stain on the carpet was Kristen French's vomit mixed with Paul's sperm. Although the evidence linked Paul to the crimes, and the vomit inexorably proved a sexual encounter with Kristen, neither was strong enough to charge him with anything other than second degree murder.

Their backs to the wall, Crown attorneys negotiated a plea bargain with Karla's lawyer, George Walker. In exchange for his client's testimony against Paul, they would reduce her sentence and provide her "blanket immunity against prosecution for any offense alleged to have been committed by me, or any offenses that I am alleged to be a party to." Rather than be tried for murder, Karla would plead guilty to two counts of manslaughter and serve two concurrent ten year sentences.

In mid-April, before the deal was officially ratified, there was a startling turn of events. Karla confessed that the accidental death of her youngest sister two and a half years earlier had been no accident. Tammy Lyn Homolka had been her and Paul's first victim.

The particulars of Karla's confession were nothing short of reprehensible.

As a means of helping Paul live out his fantasy of having sex with Tammy, the quintessential young, virgin schoolgirl he so often dreamed about, two days before Christmas 1990, Karla helped Paul drug Tammy using drinks laced with Halcion sleeping pills. Paul then raped the unconscious fourteen year old while Karla held a cloth soaked with Halothane, a liquid anesthetic, over Tammy's mouth. When finished, Paul demanded that Karla rape her as well.

Within moments of her sister's assault, Tammy vomited and quit breathing. Paul attempted mouth-to-mouth resuscitation. Karla dialed 911. An ambulance rushed Tammy to the hospital, but it was too late. She was officially pronounced dead Christmas Eve morning.

Although there were puzzling features about Tammy's death, particularly the unexplained bright red burn marks across her mouth and nose, Doctor Rosloski, the coroner ruled her death accidental; Tammy had died of asthma and coronary arrest after asphyxiating on her own vomit.

As appalled as Crown prosecutors were by Karla's confession, it did not alter their primary objective – to get Paul, the "true predator." But in order to achieve that goal, they felt they still needed Karla's testimony. They affixed another two years to the original ten year sentence and put the proposal on the table. Karla accepted the offer, making what Ken Murray labelled the Crown's "sweetheart deal with the devil." Once the documents were signed, Karla was transported to the Kingston Prison for Women to wait until called to testify at her husband's trial.

The following year there was a second, even more startling, turn of events. In August, 1994, Murray withdrew as Paul's attorney, citing an overwhelming workload. The next month the video tapes he had smuggled out of the Bernardo-Homolka residence found their way into the hands of the police and the prosecuting team.

The tapes, which have since been destroyed, categorically proved what a sick and sadistic psychopath Paul really is. The fact they even existed attest to his depraved and twisted mind. In graphic detail, their images recorded the rape of Tammy Lyn Homolka and the sexual torture of Kristen French and Leslie Mahaffy.

They also bore unassailable testimony to Karla's active participation in the crimes.

When word of the tapes leaked out, recrimination upon recrimination followed. Why had police not found the tapes during their search? When he learned what was on them, was Murray not legally, ethically, morally required to divulge their existence?

Furthermore, the footage was more than enough evidence to damn Paul without Karla's testimony, and the Crown's "sweetheart deal with the devil" came under heavy attack. Two concurrent twelve year sentences hardly seemed adequate punishment for Karla's role in the atrocities.

The victims' families attempted to have the tapes banned from court, but media lawyers argued that to do so would violate two chartered rights, freedom of the press and the right to an open court. Judge LeSage, who would hear Paul's case, compromised. The tapes would be shown to jurors, lawyers, and the defendant. All other trial spectators would only hear the audio portions.

Jurors were presented the case on May 18, 1995.

"Let us look upon the accused and harken to his charge," the court registrar began. "Two counts of first-degree murder, two counts of aggravated sexual assault, two counts of forcible confinement, two counts of kidnapping, and one count of performing an indignity on a human body. And harken to the evidence."

With those words, Paul Bernardo's trial was underway.

While the French and Mahaffy families sat fifteen metres from the man who had brutalized and murdered their daughters and sisters, dozens of witnesses paraded back and forth. The video tapes were played and replayed. Then the Crown's star witness took the stand. For nine days between June 19 and July 14, Karla Homolka recounted what the tapes had already shown; she and Paul were guilty of some of the most heinous offenses in the annals of Canadian crime.

On Friday, September 1, 1995, Paul Bernardo was found guilty on all counts and sentenced to a minimum of twenty-five years with no chance of parole. The Crown immediately launched a dangerous offender application. During those proceedings, Bernardo admitted to thirteen sexual assaults, eleven of which were full-blown rapes. In his review of the case, Justice Campbell wrote that Bernardo was guilty of at least 18 assaults; Karla believed there were even more. On November 3, 1995, Judge LeSage deemed Paul Bernardo a "dangerous offender" and sentenced him to be "detained in a penitentiary for an indefinite period of time." In February 2006, the public learned that, in November 2005, Paul Bernardo admitted assaulting an additional ten women.

* * *

Paul Bernardo and Karla Homolka's crimes outraged the world. No one failed to raise a glass when the court handed Paul the punishment he deserved. Many people, probably most, felt he deserved more. Yet for all its disgust and abhorrence, the public seemed to resign itself to his behavior, accepting his acts as those of a depraved and cold hearted sexual predator.

What people cannot come to grips with is Karla. Perhaps Doctor Stephen Hucker, the Crown's lead forensic prosecutor during Paul's trial, has best expressed it. "She has disturbed the Canadian psyche so deeply," said Hucker, "that she'll become an icon of the diabolical woman remembered long after her partner in crime, Paul Bernardo, has vanished from memory."

Canadians can not understand how a bright and seemingly normal young woman, from a seemingly normal middle-class home, could participate in the atrocious sexual torture and murder of two young schoolgirls, and the rape and death of her own sister. Nor can they comprehend why she remained with a man who heaped upon her blow after blow, degradation after degradation.

Friends harkened back to the early days of Karla's relationship with Paul. As smitten as Karla had been by her new boyfriend, some of them had been less impressed. Why, they had wondered, would a twenty-three year old professional be interested in a seventeen year old high school girl? Why would they find handcuffs and a dog collar in Karla's bedroom? And why would they uncover Karla's 'Self-Improvement List':

> Never let anyone know our relationship is anything but perfect;
> Don't talk back to Paul;
> Always smile when you're with Paul;
> Be a perfect girlfriend for Paul;
> If Paul asks for a drink, bring him one quickly and happily;
> Remember you're stupid;
> Remember you're ugly;
> Remember you're fat.

Karla's degree of complicity in the crimes remains debated. Her sympathizers believe that by the time of the Mahaffy-French murders, Karla was so physically, emotionally, and mentally broken, she was no longer capable of rational thought. They believe that over the years, Paul had so successfully ground her down, she was reduced to little more than a personal servant and "play toy," who was unable to resist her husband's demands, regardless of how sordid.

Without question, Paul began manipulating Karla immediately after they began dating. The manipulation was both subtle and effective. He told her how much nicer she looked in one dress than another. How much he preferred her hair long, straight and blonde, to short, curly, and colored. Anxious to please her sophisticated new boyfriend, Karla adapted her hair and clothes to win his approval.

Having successfully altered her physical appearance, Paul then began working on her mind and self esteem. He convinced her that unlike women, it was only natural for men to have more than one sexual partner. He told her that there was little point in her further-ing her education because after their marriage she would only be at home taking care of their babies anyway. He also began to belittle her privately at first, then publicly.

Next he introduced his sexually inexperienced, seventeen year old girlfriend to a new repertoire of sexual activities designed to sat-isfy his, but not her, sexual wishes and fantasies. If she really loved him and wanted to sexually excite him she should talk dirty, role play, and demean herself during sex. She would engaged in fellatio, anal sex, anilingus. She would insert foreign objects into her vagina, participate in sexual bondage, and create pornographic movies starring Paul and herself.

According to Karla, Paul first struck her – a slap across the face – the summer after they met. As with all abusive men, he apologized profusely, shed a few tears, and vowed it would never happen again. The next time he hit her, he did so more violently. Infuriated because she had dropped his camera, he kicked and punched her. The third time he hit her, she hit him back. Feigning contrition, he seduced her into his car, drove to a deserted parking lot, and beat her unmerciful-ly until she apologized.

After they moved into their home in Port Dalhousie, the physical and psychological abuses accelerated. The beatings became more regular and vicious. Paul made her sleep on the floor beside his bed, upon occasion, in the root cellar in the basement. He made her urinate and defecate in front of him, he made her eat feces. He told her she was ugly and stupid. That she was nothing without him.

Karla and her sympathizers believe that Tammy's death was the pivotal moment in her relationship with Paul. Using the tragedy as a bargaining chip, Paul extorted increasingly degenerate behavior from Karla. And the more she cooperated, the deeper the hole she dug for herself and the more impossible it became for her to climb out. By the time of the Mahaffy-French murders, she was programmed to unques-tioningly comply with his bidding, regardless of how depraved or repugnant.

Karla's detractors counter by saying that she knew of Paul's propensity for evil long before things deteriorated; that she is a liar who colluded, rather than complied, with Paul's increasingly twisted demands; that she is so morally vacuous a $4500 diamond engagement ring, a handsome husband, and a pretty pink house in trendy Port Dalhousie were of greater value to her than the lives of three innocent children. At any time she could have said no. "No, you can not beat me. No, I will not help you drug and rape my sister. No, I will not invite young girls home so you can sexually molest them. No, I will not help you kidnap and murder innocent young women."

Karla's detractors insist that she is as narcissistic and devoid of feeling as her ex-husband. In *Invisible Darkness*, Stephen Williams quotes from a letter Karla wrote to a friend shortly after she had been incarcerated. In it she writes:

> enough has been said about Kristen and Leslie. Anyway, if *I* ever decide to tell *my* story it will definitely be done in a book written by *me*. . . . And it will be only a story about the abuse *I* endured.

Karla's detractors also argue that she recreated herself as a battered wife and victim only because her doctors, family, psychologists, and psychiatrists told her she was.

People throughout the world continue to debate whether Karla Homolka is as "morally insane" as Paul Bernardo or if she is merely another victim of the man FBI criminal profiler Roy Hazelwood calls "a textbook sexual sadist." Time may soon tell. Amidst a maelstrom of anger and fear, on July 4, 2005, three days after Leslie Mahaffy should have turned thirty, two months after Kristen French should have turned twenty-nine, and five months after Tammy Homolka should have turned thirty, Karla was released from Saint Anne's des Plaines Prison.

Nine
Vancouver's Missing Eastside Women

"There were times I wish she'd hurry up and overdose many times before she went missing. I loved her so much, but the pain was unbearable. I'd secretly pray, 'Just give yourself enough to finish it,' not only for herself but for us too. It was just too painful to see this beautiful young lady turned into a drug-ridden form of a human being."

Geri Stewart
Catherine Knight's sister

It has often been said that it is not unusual for women who sell sex in the street and are addicted to drugs to disappear. They check in for rehab. They leave the streets. They move to another city. They overdose. They commit suicide. They are committed to hospitals.

But beginning in 1997, an alarming number of prostitutes, "victims of opportunity," began disappearing from Vancouver's Downtown Eastside, a ten block area radiating out from the corner of Main and Hastings, better known in Eastside vernacular as Pain and Wastings.

Eastside's statistics are as staggering as those of a third world nation. According to a Prostitution Alternatives Counselling and Education (PACE) report issued in 2001, Eastside claims the highest infection rate of HIV and hepatitis C in the western world. It is the only place in the developed world where the percent of HIV infected women is greater than that of HIV infected men. And an estimated 80% of those women are engaged in the sex trade, trapped in what PACE's Char Lafontaine calls "survival sex," further exacerbating Eastside's almost unfathomable infection rate.

Notorious as Canada's "poorest postal code," discarded needles and condoms litter the urine stenched streets and alleys that bypass

Eastside's multitude of crack houses, pawn shops, and drug markets. Squalid flop houses and hotels lodge the chronically ill, the indigent, the alcoholics, the drug addicts, and the women who support their drug habit through prostitution.

Eastside records Canada's highest rates of mental health problems, drug addiction, and deaths from drug overdoses. In 1997, after a lethal batch of heroin took three hundred lives, the local health authority declared the community a public health emergency. If these figures are not disturbing enough, Eastside also lays claim to Canada's highest rates of homelessness and crime.

And now, to add to its already grim statistics, if alleged murderer Robert Pickton is found guilty of the twenty-six first-degree murder charges he has been indicted for, he will surpass Albert Guay's record of twenty-three which has stood since1949 (Guay and his accomplices blew up a Douglas DC-3 airplane in a successful bid to rid Guay of his wife), and Eastside will register Canada's highest number of serial killer victims.

It is, as Christine Cellier, a friend of one of Eastside's missing women says, "an evil, evil place."

* * *

Life has not been kind to the Henry family. In 1961, Patrick Henry, an Alert Bay fisherman and father of ten was swept overboard and drowned. After her husband's death, Mrs. Henry found herself unable to cope with her large family and the family began to disintegrate. Some of the children were sent to foster homes, others were sent to Canada's infamous industrial schools.

From there the tragedies multiplied. In 1962, sixteen year old Sandra was raped. In 1967, sixteen year old Lavina was raped and murdered in Nanaimo. No longer able to live with the memories of the abuse she suffered while under foster care, in 1981, twenty-one year old Debbie committed suicide. In 1990, while walking home in the rain, thirty-four year old Stan Henry, Sandra's twin brother, was accidentally struck and killed by a police car. And in 1997, Janet, the baby of the family, vanished into thin air while living in downtown Eastside.

Janet Henry had married Art Chartier in 1982; their daughter Debra arrived two years after that. Another two years into the marriage, Janet began doing drugs and drinking heavily. Her addictions did nothing to help the marriage and in 1988 the couple divorced. Art retained custody of their then four year old daughter.

After the dissolution of her marriage, Janet hooked up with another addict and slipped further into a life of alcohol and drugs. As with all of the missing Eastside women, she then began prostituting to support her and her partner's habits. When Janet's partner died of an overdose, she packed up her things and moved to Eastside. She had been living there for about six years when she was viciously beaten and raped. If she hadn't already, after the rape Janet simply gave up.

The last time Sandra Gagnon (nee Henry) spoke to her sister Janet was on June 25, 1997. That day the women made plans for Janet to travel to Sandra's Maple Ridge home for a brief weekend visit. They arranged to meet for Chinese at King's Kitchen, but Janet never appeared. Puzzled by Janet's no-show, Sandra returned home to wait for her sister to call. But Janet failed to call that day, or the next day, or the next day after that. Because the two sisters spoke on the phone almost daily, Sandra became increasingly worried. She contacted authorities to see if Janet had been in some kind of accident, if she had taken ill, if she had died of an overdose, but none of the logical explanations accounted for Janet's continued absence.

Vancouver police examined Janet's room at the Holborn Hotel in Eastside and found "a suitcase packed, as if she was going somewhere, and a little brown bag with toothpaste, toothbrush and two cassettes." Other than Janet, nothing was missing.

Sandra instinctively knew something was wrong. Janet may have been a drug addict and prostitute, but she also had a family with whom she maintained regular contact. She would never go away without telling someone. What's more, if Janet *had* planned to leave, why were none of her things missing? Why had she already paid her next month's rent? And why had she left $115 in her bank account?

Determined to find answers, Sandra contacted Lindsay Kines at the *Vancouver Sun*, hoping the media attention would shed some light on the mystery surrounding Janet's disappearance. Lindsay responded by publishing, "Taken From her Family – Janet Henry – Missing Since June 28," in the July 24, 1997 edition of the paper, but other than a fleeting moment of interest, the article failed to generate any new information. Unwilling to let the matter die there, Sandra distributed her sister's picture at truck stops, bus stations, and ferry docks, all the time wondering if Janet was cold or hungry or sick. Sandra also combed Eastside, questioning people who lived or worked in the community. Though no one she spoke to had seen Janet since the day after Sandra and Janet's telephone conversation, one woman told her she had heard that Janet had been going to "Uncle Willy's to party." Another told her that the word on the street was that "there were some women who hadn't been heard from in a while."

The word on the street was right. Between January 1 and June 28, the day Sandra reported Janet missing, seven other women had also disappeared from downtown Eastside: Maria Laliberte,

Stephanie Lane, Cara Ellis, Sharon Ward, Andrea Borhaven, Sherry Irving, and "Kellie" Richard Little.

Maria Laliberte, a beautiful, forty-eight year old Native with rich, closely cropped dark hair and big brown eyes had disappeared from Eastside on January 1, 1997.

Ten days later, in the early morning hours of January 11, following her release from hospital after experiencing a drug psychosis, twenty year old Stephanie Lane disappeared from the front of the Patricia Hotel on Hastings.

Before being introduced to heroin, cocaine, and the hooker stroll, Stephanie had been a "pretty and very popular" straight-A student, indulged, perhaps over-indulged, by her doting parents, Michele Pineault and George Lane. Stephanie began her plunge into the Eastside abyss while working at a club called Number 5 Orange.

As far as anyone has been able to determine, twenty-five year old Cara Ellis – all four-feet-eleven, 106 pounds of her – also went missing that January. Although the precise date of her disappearance is uncertain, that summer, Cara's husband's sister, Lori-Ann Ellis, travelled from Calgary to Vancouver in an unsuccessful attempt to find her missing sister-in-law.

Prior to migrating to Vancouver in the mid 1990s, Cara had worked the streets of Calgary. By the time she drifted to Eastside, she was a twelve year veteran of what John Turvey of the Downtown Eastside Youth Activities Society (DEYAS) calls "The Game." In his 2001 book, *Bad Date: The Lost Girls of Vancouver's Low Track*, Trevor Green writes that Turvey's game is a simple one: "find a reason, an excuse, any excuse to take drugs. My mother is sick, so I can take drugs; my mother is well so I can take drugs. I've got a job; I've lost a job. That's the game." Cara had been playing some version of it since she was thirteen.

On February 14, 1997, while lovers showered one another with flowers and chocolates, and children giggled over Valentine's cards sent by anonymous admirers, twenty-nine year old Sharon Ward vanished. A pretty little thing with feathered brown hair and sparkling brown eyes, because she was reported missing in New Westminster, Sharon's name wasn't added to the Vancouver Police Department's (VPD) Missing Eastside Women list until 2005.

Guesswork places the disappearance of twenty-five year old Andrea Borhaven sometime in March, the same month Stephanie Lane and Sharon Ward were reported missing. "Establishing a more accurate date is impossible," says Eastside's much-trusted and much-loved Constable Dave Dickson, because Andrea, a pretty young woman with lovely hazel eyes and a dainty, heart-shaped face, "was all over the place." She just "bounced off the walls," pinballing between Eastside, Vernon, Vancouver Island, and the communities staggered throughout British Columbia's Lower Mainland. Because she was reported missing in Vernon, Andrea's name didn't get added to the Missing Eastside Women list until the spring of 1999.

Both twenty-four year old Sherry Irving and twenty-eight year old "Kellie" Richard Little evaporated into thin air in April. Sherry, a "fun, outgoing, beautiful girl with a smile that would melt many," whose father remembers her as "generous, warm, and good at just about everything, school and sports," especially track and field, was reported missing to the Stl' Atl'lmx tribal police who passed her name on to the VPD in 1999.

Unlike Sherry, Kellie Little was anything but fun, outgoing, or beautiful. She was a five foot three, 120 pound, twenty-eight year old transsexual, with a cleft palate, a disposition for fighting, and, (not without good reason) according to Victoria's police corporal John Ayres, "serious issues."

It was two months after Sherry and Kellie's disappearances that Janet Henry vanished, and one month after Janet vanished, that twenty-two year old Olivia Williams, who had not been seen since December 1996, was reported missing. As disturbing as the situation already was, between the time Olivia officially became a missing person and the end of 1997, another five women vanished. Almost as though they were making up for the voids in May and July, three of those women – Jacqueline Murdock, Helen Hallmark, Marnie Frey – disappeared in August,

Unlike twenty-six year old Jacqueline Murdock, the mother of two small children who disappeared from the corner of Main and Hastings on August 14, all that can be said with certainty regarding the disappearance of thirty-three year old Helen Hallmark is that she was last seen in the Mount Pleasant area sometime in August.

Of the dozens of missing Eastside women pictures, Helen's is one of the most disheartening. Before drugs, prostitution, and Eastside transformed her into a distorted version of her previous self, Helen had been a beautiful young woman with strawberry-blonde hair, a captivating smile, and sparkling hazel eyes. Looking haggard and wan in her missing persons picture, Helen's eyes, her sister Shelly wrote in a poem, "showed the sadness . . . of many years of pain."

Like Helen Hallmark, it is impossible to reconcile pictures of a younger Marnie Frey with pictures of the twenty-four year old Marnie peering out from her missing persons picture.

Before she "got hooked on drugs through a gang in Campbell River," Marnie had been a "cheerful, happy-go-lucky child" with soft, reddish-blonde hair haloing a smiling face. Somewhere along the way Marnie lost touch with that happy-go-lucky child and, at seventeen, began running away. Abandoning her love of animals, poetry, drawing, and sports for drugs and prostitution, Marnie arrived in Eastside in the spring of 1997. Sometime in August, only half a year later, she went missing.

By the time thirty-two year old Cindy Beck vanished on September 30, her five-feet-eight-inch frame weighed a mere 110 pounds. Coarsened by drugs and her life on the streets, Cindy's missing persons picture is a mere caricature of the pretty young woman who had drifted to Vancouver from Ontario.

Cindy Beck's disappearance was followed two months later by the disappearance of a second Cindy – Cindy Feliks. Barely recognizable in her missing persons picture as the once beautiful mother of Theresa, Cindy went missing on November 26, two weeks before her forty-fourth birthday. Cindy's step-mother, Marilyn Kraft, remembers her daughter as "a fighter" – self-confident, stubborn, and at times even defiant. Because Cindy was a woman who "never let anyone get the best of her," it is tragic that she allowed her addiction to drugs to.

A total of thirteen women disappeared from Eastside in 1997, but Vancouver police knew only of four. Because their absences had either not been reported (in many cases this was not for a lack of trying), or were reported missing elsewhere, at the end of the year, the VPD was unaware that Marie Laliberte, Sharon Ward, Cara Ellis, Sherry Irving, Helen Hallmark, Marnie Frey, Jacqueline Murdock, Cindy Beck, Cindy Feliks, and Andrea Borhaven were missing. And even though three missing women were three more than Vancouver police would have liked, the number was hardly alarming enough to hoist a red flag.

* * *

"You would have liked my sister," Val Hughes boasts proudly of her sister, Kerry Koski. "Kerry could dance and she had a smile that could light up a room." Unlike so many of Eastside's missing women, until 1996, Kerry Koski had been a hard-working, middle-class mother of three beautiful daughters aged, twelve, fourteen, and sixteen. Overcome by despair when her partner committed suicide in 1996, Kerry attempted to deaden her own pain with liquor and drugs. In the fall of 1997, she drifted to Eastside. Three months later, she went missing.

Five-foot-four and a meager ninety pounds, sick and undernourished, Kerry spent Christmas 1997 with Val and Val's husband, Terry. During that holiday visit, Val assured Kerry that, "her family would do anything to help Kerry deal with her addiction and get her life back on track." In a positive move, the sisters made tentative plans to spend a day in the near future touring Vancouver's one thousand acre Stanley Park. Unable to confirm their arrangements by phone, Val went to Kerry's Hastings Street hotel only to learn that Kerry hadn't been seen since January 7, 1998.

Just as family members of so many of the other missing women had done, Val checked all the likely places Kerry could possibly be. She called hospitals to see if Kerry was injured or ill. She contacted police to see if Kerry had been arrested. But Kerry had simply, and inexplicably, vanished.

Though the precise date of twenty-nine year old Tania Peterson's disappearance is unknown, police believe it was sometime in February, the same month that Inga Hall disappeared. Blonde, blue-eyed and pretty, Tania looked completely unlike forty-six year old Inga whose world-weary, cheerless green eyes spoke volumes about her wretched existence.

Then, in the cool early morning hours of April 14, 1998, twenty-eight year old Sarah deVries and her friend, Sylvia Skakum, went to work on the corner of Princess and Hastings. Sarah, whose dazzling white smile camouflaged her years of inner anguish and a soul, self-described as "burning with hatred," took up her customary post on the northwest corner, Sylvia the southeast. A few minutes later, a car pulled up to Sylvia's corner. While Sylvia and the driver circled the block, haggling over terms, Sarah disappeared.

Accustomed to hearing from her every two or three days, when Sarah failed to get in touch with her friend Wayne Leng for almost a week, Wayne became worried. He went to the house where Sarah had been living and discovered that no one there had seen her for almost a week either. Fearing something had happened, Wayne went to fill out a missing persons report, only to be told that because he wasn't family, he couldn't. Wayne promptly contacted Sarah's sister, Maggie deVries.

Knowing that Sarah, a resident of Eastside for over a decade, "wouldn't go away of her own volition and not contact anyone," Maggie immediately filed the missing persons report. She and Wayne then began a desperate hunt for answers. They papered Eastside with posters. They circulated through Eastside asking area residents, shop owners, and other women working the streets if anyone had any information regarding Sarah's whereabouts, but no one could recall seeing her since April 14. They visited hospitals and jails, and attempted to get the media involved, but "no one it seemed was interested in covering a story on a missing Eastside hooker."

As pleased as Maggie and Wayne were when, on May 24, Frank Luba at *The Province* finally ran a piece on Sarah's disappearance – "Mother Fears Addicted Daughter Already Dead" – the article didn't bring them any closer to finding Sarah.

Operating against a backdrop of disinterest, Maggie and Wayne posted a reward and set up a 1-800 number and continued to probe for answers. Eventually their search for Sarah collided with searches being conducted by families of other missing women. Struck by the similarities of the disappearances, and united in their common grief and sense of helplessness, several of them formed an allegiance and began compiling a list of Eastside missing women.

Maintaining that list would prove no easy task. On April 30, nine days after Maggie filled out Sarah's missing persons report, thirty-two year old Cindy Beck, officially became a missing person.

In *Missing Sarah: A Vancouver Woman Remembers her Vanished Sister*, Maggie deVries writes that it was shortly after Cindy was reported missing that the VPD told the *Vancouver Sun* it was concerned by the growing number of missing Eastside Women. Because he was already familiar with the disappearance of Janet Henry and had recently been contacted by Wayne and Maggie, on July 3, Lindsay Kines wrote a *Sun* feature captioned "Police Target Big Increase in Missing Women Cases." Frank Luba followed suit by writing a second piece about the disappearances for the July 29 edition of the *Province* – "Messages on pager say prostitute dead" –, so titled because an anonymous caller to Maggie and Wayne's 1-800 number told them Sarah was dead.

It had taken weeks, in some cases months, of dogged perseverance, but finally the press was beginning to show an interest in the growing number of missing Eastside women. While the women's friends and families welcomed the attention, the publicity did nothing to prevent more women from going missing.

Between the time the *Sun* and *Province* ran their articles and early autumn, when the VPD began a serious examination of the situation, nineteen year old Sheila Egan disappeared.

Before she went missing, photographer Lincoln Clarke managed to capture Sheila's ethereal beauty – her long blonde hair, soft blue eyes, and delicate, almost angelic face – in his "Heroines" series, a "photographic documentary of the marginalized women of Vancouver's Downtown Eastside."

The story of Sheila's slide into drug addiction and prostitution mirrors the stories of so many of the other missing women. In her mid-teens Sheila became involved with the wrong crowd and began experimenting with drugs and defiance. She began running away to downtown Vancouver's Granville and Robson Streets where the street kids hung out. Because Granville intersects with Hastings just before the waterfront, Sheila's trip from Granville to Hastings was but a short five minute walk. Sheila disappeared from Hastings on July 14, two weeks before her twentieth birthday.

Responding to mounting pressure from within and without the department, in September 1998, the same month Marnie Frey and Helen Hallmark were reported missing, the VPD began an official search for Eastside's missing women. They assembled the Missing Women's Review Team, a "working group" of investigators from the missing persons, sexual offense, and homicide units, to look into a list of forty missing women dating back to 1971 and prepare what they termed a "real list."

Noting what geographic profiler Kim Rossmo called "an unusual concentration of women missing from Eastside," the Review Team compiled an initial list of sixteen name, seven from 1998, five from 1997, one from 1996, and three from 1995, that met their profile criteria.

The Review Team's list was not destined to remain static for long. In October, the same month they added Jacqueline Murdock's name, Julie Young went missing.

As he had done with Sheila Egan, before she disappeared, Lincoln Clarke managed to capture thirty-one year old Julie on film. Posed symbolically beneath a store window advertising ham, roast beef, pepperoni, turkey, and meat loaf, Julie is dressed more like she's on her way to a Hawaiian luau than waiting to sell some John a blow-job. At five feet four inches and a mere one hundred pounds, her face is gaunt, her cheeks hollow, and her striking blue eyes tired and haunted.

The month after Julie disappeared, Deborah and Ivan Jardine's worst nightmare came true. On November 20, their twenty-seven year old daughter, Angela, vanished. Ostracized her entire life because of her boisterous, aggressive, and erratic behavior – a consequence of her mental faculty of a ten year old– Angela had found a modicum of acceptance in Eastside she had been unable to find elsewhere. Unfortunately it was also there that the overly-trusting young woman found people only too eager to introduce her to drugs and prostitution. Described by her mother as "a young child in a woman's body," Angela was last been seen at "Out of Harm's Way," a day long symposium on drugs and street violence, wearing a bright pink party dress that was as loud and vibrant as she was.

Twenty-nine year old Michelle Gurney had lived in Eastside since she was seventeen. Though her missing persons picture shows a woman hardened by a dozen years on the streets, according to a friend who lived at the Portland Hotel on Hastings Street at the same Michelle lived there, Michelle's tough exterior "hid a strong and loyal friend." It also hid her risk and vulnerability. Michelle disappeared on December 11, five days after Angela Jardine was reported missing.

Like Andrea Borhaven, Cara Ellis, and far too many others, nobody can say for certain when thirty-three year old Ruby Hardy disappeared. Between 1993 and 1998, she regularly called her mother, Violet, and her step-father, Jack Garreau. Then, in 1998, the calls abruptly stopped.

"I do hope she's still alive," Jack said in 2005 interview, "but I have my doubts." Violet clings to hope tighter. "There's no evidence she's one of the people [who were killed]."

Nineteen ninety-eight ended exactly as it had started. On December 27, at 1:00 in the morning, while her mother and her boyfriend waited at her mother's apartment to present her with Christmas gifts and a belated Christmas dinner, Marcella Creison disappeared from the front of the Drake Hotel.

Marcella was sixteen when she moved to British Columbia in 1994. In time, both she and her sister Melanie ended up on Eastside's seedy streets. Though Melanie managed to straighten her life out, Marcella was less lucky. Dark haired and pretty, and, according to a friend, "not very wise street-wise," Marcella was only twenty when she disappeared.

With Marcella's disappearance, the number of women who vanished from Eastside during 1998 rose to ten. Though police were only aware of the disappearances of four of those women – Tania Peterson, Julie Young, Ruby Hardy, and Marcella Creison – by the end of the year, they had learned of the disappearances of Helen Hallmark, Marnie Frey, Jacqueline Murdock, and Cindy Beck, bumping the number of women who had gone missing in 1997 to seven. Unless one was completely obtuse, it was obvious that Eastside had a serious problem.

* * *

As 1998 gave way to 1999, the Review Team held its breath and waited for its list of missing Eastside women to grow. It didn't hold its breath for long. Marcella Creison was reported missing on January 11, and, on February 22, a little more than a month after she disappeared, twenty-three year old Jacquilene McDonell, was reported missing as well.

According to Elaine Allen, executive director of the Women's Information Safe House (WISH), Jacquilene seemed "so out of place on the street. Articulate, fresh and bright," she was "well-read and adventurous," and "fabulous." Still, for all of her many fine qualities, Jacquilene's drug addiction cost her custody of her four year old daughter and hastened her downward spiral. Jacquilene went missing on January 16, a mere three months after she moved into Eastside.

Jacquilene's disappearance came two weeks before Brenda Wolfe vanished on February 1 and a month and a half before Georgina Papin.

Georgina was one of the dozens of Eastside women who never stood a chance. Her father, George, was an alcoholic, her mother, Alice, a drug addict. From the time they were little, Georgina and her eight siblings were parceled out so many times, by the time she was eighteen, Georgina had lived in thirty-two different foster homes and institutions.

Georgina began experimenting with drugs and prostitution as early as the age of eleven and by the time she was thirty, she had four children: Kristine, born in 1984, Stuart born in 1987, Leslie, born in 1988, and Dillon Sky Rain, born in 1993. After the birth of Dillon Sky Rain, Georgina made a valiant effort to get her life back on track. In 1997, she was off drugs, had a new daughter, Autumn Wind, and was living with her boyfriend D'arcy Pelletier. The reprieve was short lived. Following the 1998 birth of her twins, Winter Star and Little Storm, Georgina and D'arcy's relationship began to deteriorate. When their fighting became incessant, D'arcy left.

On April 30, 1999, after celebrating her sister Bonnie's birthday, Georgina announced she was going to Vancouver for a few days and never came back. Georgina was last seen on March 2, a little more than a week before her thirty-fifth birthday.

It was about the time of Georgina's disappearance that the investigation into the missing women took a promising turn. Lindsay Kines's March 3 *Sun* article titled "Missing on the Mean Streets," renewed interest in the case, and friends and families of the missing women, frustrated by what they perceived as a lack of genuine concern on the part of the authorities, became more proactive. Michele Pineault started a petition while other concerned individuals wrote letters to government officials. Encouraged by Detective Constable Lori Shenher of the VPD's Missing Persons section, Maggie deVries lobbied the police and the government to: 1) publicly acknowledge that the dis-appearances of the missing women may be related and may involve abduction and murder; 2) offer a reward that matches the other two rewards currently before the public (the rewards involved one for information leading to the arrest of the persons responsible for a series of Lower Mainland home invasions, and the persons responsible for a rash of armed robberies in West Vancouver garages); 3) set up a task force to deal with whatever information comes in and to bring more points of view to the cases; 4) offer police protection to anyone who may be afraid to come forward with information.

At the beginning of April, Vancouver Mayor, Philip Owen, who also served as chairman of the police board and had approved the two $100 000 rewards mentioned in Maggie's letter, further antagonized the Missing Women lobbyists by turning down their request for a reward and by announcing he was unprepared to finance a "location service for hookers."

Owen's message was as clear as it was cruel and impolitic. Armed robberies and home invasions were of greater concern to the city's senior political and law enforcement official than the mysterious disappearance and probable deaths of what had now grown to twenty Eastside women.

Urged by Vancouver East MP Libby Davis to rethink his position because "continued inaction on the part of the police makes it appear as though there is a lack of care and attention by those in authority about the importance of women's lives in downtown Eastside," less than two weeks later, in a bid for re-election, Owen began backpedaling clumsily. Not, apparently, because of any personal conviction, but rather because "the press are wanting that reward and the public are wanting it and certainly the families are wanting a little more attention and a little more seriousness," Owen announced that it "was worth having a very close look at it." Before another two weeks had passed, he had done a complete about face and was arguing that $100 000 was not reward enough, that the figure should be raised to two million dollars, $100 000 for each of the missing women.

Though Vancouver police seemed as taken aback by Owen's grandstanding as the discerning public, the force's response to the lobbyists' demands did little to ameliorate the mounting animosity between the VPD and friends and families of the missing women. Reluctant to acknowledge that any crimes had been committed, let alone admit that the disappearances were in anyway related, Review Team investigator Sergeant Geramy Field, announced they had, "found nothing that links the women except they were involved in drugs or the sex trade and frequented Eastside." And though her "gut feeling [was] that some of the women have met with foul play," Detective Constable Shenher said the VPD's official position was that "it was strange."

Though willing to concede that Vancouver, flanked as it is "by the sea and mountains was ideal for hiding bodies," the VPD insisted that "until a body is found, the disappearances had to be treated as missing persons cases."

The VPD's persistent "no evidence of a crime" position infuriated those closest to the missing women. "For the police to say no crime has been committed is ludicrous," said Maggie deVries. Deb Mearns, a safety program coordinator for prostitutes, was as equally disdainful. "You're talking about women on welfare who didn't pick up their last welfare cheque, who left their belongings in a dingy hotel room. It's not as though they could just jump on a plane and fly to Toronto."

Despite strong, albeit circumstantial, evidence to the contrary, police maintained that just because the women were missing was not sufficient reason to assume they had been murdered. "There is no evidence," insisted the VPD's media liaison, Constable Anne Drennan, "that the women were killed."

Outspoken community activists Jamie Lee Hamilton and Joanna Russell manager of a drop-in centre for prostitutes, scoffed at such comments. "All of these missing women have been murdered," said Jamie Lee. "They are dead," said Joanne. "Somebody has murdered them. I have no doubt." Stephanie Lane's mother Michele Pineault, concurred. "Twenty women can't just disappear off the face of the earth."

But it was Barb Daniel, a director of Grandma's House – a safe house for prostitutes – and Wayne Leng who asked the two, million dollar questions. "These women have completely disappeared from the face of the earth. If they haven't been murdered, where are they?" asked Barb, and Wayne, perhaps with an eerie prescience, wondered whether the murderer was, "someone who has property here to dispose of them?"

For Jamie Lee, Joanne, Barb, Michele, and Wayne, as well as other advocates of the missing women, the problem was not whether or not the women had been murdered, the problem was where and by whom?

A large and vocal contingent believed the answer to that lay at the feet of a serial killer. Though "there was no conclusive evidence suggesting that one single predator was targeting the women," said Kim Rossmo, "police have to consider that as a definite possibility. Similarities in victimology and the short time period and the specific neighborhood involved – all suggest the single serial murderer hypothesis is the most likely explanation for the majority of these disappearances."

Doctor Deborah Laufersweller-Dwyer, a one-time police officer teaching a course on serial criminals at the University of Arkansas, was less circumspect. "If I had twenty-one prostitutes missing, I would definitely say it was a serial killer. The police either have blinders on or they don't want to alarm the citizens."

Even Elliott Leyton, renown author of *Hunting Humans: The Rise of the Modern Multiple Murderer*, who has expressed sympathy for the inherent difficulties faced by police in tracking serial killers, seemed as equally bewildered by the VPD's no-serial killer position. "When someone is picking up women from such a relatively confined area, from such a small social niche – street women – I mean, God in heaven, by serial killer investigation standards it's relatively easy."

Apparently it wasn't so easy for everyone. "We keep reviewing this because we hear the concern from the community," said Chief Constable Bruce Chambers, "but we've found nothing that would indicate there's a serial killer involved with these people." "To me," said professor Steve Hart of Simon Fraser University, "having one serial killer would be too easy, because it means you could blame one person for all the bad stuff, and that's unlikely." And, WISH's Elaine Allen said, "There's so many women missing, it's almost ridiculous to think it's one person doing it."

While many members of the press anchored themselves to the serial killer theory, it wasn't a universal attachment. On April 14, Allen Garr of the *Vancouver Courier* vigorously opposed what he called the "noisy demand" for reward money because, the reward "will simply play into the so-far-unproved notion that there is one lunatic on a killing spree. Where," demanded Garr, "is the proof? There's no evidence that a crime has been committed."

Doctor Laufersweller-Dwyer criticized that rationale as earnestly as she criticized the notion that the women of Eastside were *not* being preyed upon by a serial killer. "In many, many instances," Doctor Laufersweller-Dwyer pointed out, "serial killers aren't discovered until someone finds a cache of bodies."

On a more philosophical note, Reverend Ruth Wright of the First United Church in Eastside, the church that houses WISH, told reporters, "I really hope it is a serial killer because the alternative would mean there are thirty-one separate killers out there and that much evil would be too much."

A second explanation for the women's disappearances was the possibility that more than one serial killer was stalking Eastside. Proponents of this theory believed that at least some of the disappearances could be attributed to the Green River Killer (Gary Leon Ridgway), the Spokane Serial Killer (Robert Yates), and the string of unsolved prostitute homicides that had been plaguing Edmonton since the late 1980s.

Closely tied to the multiple serial killers hypothesis was the multiple murderers theory. "I don't buy into the single killer theory," said John Turvey. "I just think that a lot of men that have that propensity to be predators have just figured out that these women are ideal victims with very little ramifications if they go missing."

Turvey had grounds, albeit shaky, to hold that view. In his March 3, *Vancouver Sun* article, "Twenty Women Missing, Action Demanded," Lindsay Kines wrote that "at least twenty-five different men [had been] charged with killing prostitutes in B.C. over the past seventeen years."

There were, however, two serious flaws with both the multiple serial killers and multiple murderers theories. First, twenty-five men murdering prostitutes over a seventeen year period throughout all of British Columbia was statistically a far cry from what, by mid-1999, had risen to twenty-one missing, and conceivably murdered, women from one small, ten block area, during the relatively brief span of four years. And second, as Kim Rossmo pointed out, "if there were more than one killer, chances are at least one body would have been found, and that wasn't happening here."

Still others had other ideas. There was talk of the women being used in snuff films, that Chinese pimps were secreting them away to the orient, that they were being murdered and hauled away by a long-distance trucker. At least one person believed that, "it's two guys working together, like the Hillside Stranglers," while another individual believed that at least some of the disappearances were the result of cult activity.

Of the many possible scenarios, one of the most widely supported, bolstered in part by reporter Peter Smith's August, 1999 *Calgary Sun* articles, and later by Trevor Greene's 2001 book, *Bad Date: The Lost Girls of Vancouver's Low Track*, was that the disappearances were tied to "a sex-slave slaughter involving the ships in the harbour." This theory held that the women had been enticed on board international freighters with promises of liquor and drugs. Once on board the women were imprisoned, sexually used, and then tossed overboard after the ships were well out into the Pacific. It was a popular theory, partly because it was based on documented cases, partly because most of the drugs coming into Canada enter through Vancouver's docks, and partly because the theory explained went far to the absence of bodies.

Meanwhile, as advocates of the missing women, the public, the media, and the police continued to hotly debate solutions to the women's disappearances, three significant developments were taking place. First, a memorial service held by 350 friends and relatives of the missing women, many of whom were bearing placards reading "Find These Women Now," received significant media attention. Second, with the increased media attention, the public's awareness of the disappearances was growing. Third, the popular television show, *America's Most Wanted*, was becoming involved.

Back in 1997, three months after Janet Henry disappeared, Sandra Gagnon had written to the show's producers, hoping to have Janet's disappearance featured on one of the program's missing persons segments. At the time, the producers wrote back, telling Sandra that because *America's Most Wanted* received so many similar requests, they couldn't help her.

When Wayne Leng learned of Sandra's unsuccessful bid at getting Janet's disappearance international exposure, he wondered if the producers might be more interested if they knew that several other women had also disappeared, and that there was a strong probability that a serial killer was involved. Wayne contacted producer Tom Morris Jr., who told Wayne they could not help him just then, but to keep him abreast of developments in Eastside. Over the next four months, Wayne did precisely that. Eventually his persistence paid off. *America's Most Wanted* agreed to feature 'The Case of the Missing Eastside Women' on an upcoming telecast. The program would air July 31.

In the meantime, Wayne was interviewed by Peter Warren of CKNW radio for his program, "Where have all these women gone?" During the show, Wayne publicly announced that *America's Most Wanted* was coming to Vancouver.

With suspicious alacrity, the VPD and British Columbia's government erupted into a frenzy of activity. Police added two homicide detectives to the missing persons department and, though still denying the possibility of a serial killer stalking Eastside, contacted authorities investigating serial murders in Washington and New York, seeking information on how they were handling their serial killer cases.

The VPD and the Attorney General's office approved a $100 000 reward and unveiled a corresponding reward poster displaying the faces of an unbelievable thirty-one missing women. In the following list (as well as all subsequent lists), Robert Pickton has been charged with murdering those women whose names appear in bold print. Those marked with an asterisk (*) either do not fit the profile or have been accounted for. In sequence, the information includes the woman's name, her birthdate, the date she was last seen, and the date she was reported missing. Some dates are approximations.

1. Elaine Allenbach (Lisa Morrison, Nancy Boyd), 26 April 1965, 15 March 1986, 11 April 1986
2. Cindy Louise Beck, 17 April 1965, 30 September 1997, 30 April 1998
3. **Andrea Fay Borhaven, 10 January 1972, March 1997, 18 May 1999**
4. *Linda Jean Coombes, 1959, November 1993, 4 April 1999
5. Marcella Helen Francis Creison, 2 June 1978, 27 December 1998, 11 January 1999
6. **Sarah Jean deVries, 12 May 1969, 14 April 1998, 21 April 1998**
7. Sheila Catherine Egan, 4 August 1978, 14 July 1998, 5 August 1998

8. **Marnie Lee Frey, 30 August 1973, August 1997, 4 September 1998**
9. Catherine Gonzalez, 27 September 1968, March 1995, 7 February 1996
10. Michelle Gurney, 11 February 1969, 11 December 1998, 22 December 1998
11. **Inga Monique Hall, 25 January 1952, 26 February 1998, 3 March 1998**
12. **Helen Mae Hallmark (Brea), 24 June 1966, August 1997, 23 September 1998**
13. Janet Gail Henry, 10 April 1961, 26 June 1997, 28 June 1997
14. **Tanya Marlo Holyk, 8 December 1975, 29 October 1996, 3 November 1997**
15. *Rose Anne Jansen, 1948, 23 October 1991, 24 October 1991
16. **Angela Rebecca Jardine, 23 June 1971, 20 November 1998, 6 December 1998**
17. Catherine Maureen Knight, 5 May 1969, April 1995, 11 November 1995
18. **Kerry Lynn Koski, 14 August 1959, 7 January 1998, 29 January 1998**
19. Stephanie Marie Lane, 28 March 1976, 11 January 1997, 11 March 1997
20. **Jacquilene Michele McDonell, 6 January 1976, 16 January 1999, 22 February 1999**
21. **Diane Melnick, 26 August 1975, 27 December 1995, 29 December 1995**
22. Jacqueline Maria Murdock, 28 January 1971, 14 August 1997, 30 October 1998
23. *Patricia Gay Perkins, 1956, 1984, 1996
24. Sherry Lynn Rail, 8 September 1956, 30 January 1984, 3 January 1987
25. *Karen Anne Smith, 1957, June 1992, 27 April 1999
26. *Ingrid Soet, 13 July 1959, 28 August 1989, December 1990
27. Dorothy Anne Spence, 6 August 1962, 30 August 1995, 30 October 1995
28. Kathleen Dale Wattley, 20 October 1959, 6 June 1992, 29 June 1992
29. Olivia Gale Williams, 19 January 1975, 6 December 1996, 4 July 1997
30. *Teressa Anne Williams, 14 February 1973, 1 July 1988, 17 March 1999
31. Julie Louise Young, 17 July 1967, October 1998, 6 July 1999

Though the television show failed to produce any promising leads, it focused the public's attention on events unfolding in Eastside like nothing ever before. Newspapers across Canada picked up the cause. Radio and television talk shows interviewed friends and families of the missing women. *Elm Street Magazine* printed Daniel Wood's "Vancouver's Missing Prostitutes," and *Da Vinci's Inquest*, Canada's popular crime drama, premiered the fall season with a two-part fictionalized version of the case – "A Cinderella Story."

Against the wishes of the VPD, *America's Most Wanted* also threw its weight behind the serial killer theory when host John Walsh proclaimed, "when there are thirty women missing and no bodies have been found and they're all of the same type of background, that always smacks of a serial killer. Anybody can put two and two together."

After two years of downplaying its likelihood, the VPD began to grudgingly allow the possibility of a serial killer. "We're not afraid to acknowledge there could be a serial killer or multiple killers," Constable Anne Drennan confessed in early August.

Despite all the pandemonium, by the end of 1999, following an exhaustive investigation, the Missing Women's Review Team had only managed to eliminate four names from their list. Rose Anne Jansen and Patricia Perkins were discovered alive and well and living elsewhere in Canada. Karen Smith had died of heart failure in an Edmonton hospital on February 13, 1999, and Linda Coombes had died of a heroin overdose on February 15, 1994.

Police also began to wonder if the Eastside nightmare might have ended. Andrea Borhaven and Julie Young had been reported missing in May and July, but they had disappeared in 1997 and 1998, and Georgina Papin and Brenda Wolfe had not been reported missing as yet. As a result, as far as police knew, there had been no new disappearances since Jacquilene McDonell vanished in February. "For a while there," said Sergeant Field, "for the majority of 1999, we felt that we didn't have any more [missing persons] and that either somebody was in custody or the perpetrator had died or moved on, perhaps because of the media pressure."

But whether it had been the result of the publicity or something else entirely, the eight month hiatus in disappearances ended on December 14, 1999 when police learned that Wendy Crawford had gone missing. The forty-four year old mother of two had struggled much of her life with diabetes and Crohn's disease, and though she lived in Chilliwack, was last seen on November 27 near Columbia Street in Eastside.

Wendy's disappearance was followed one month later by the disappearance of twenty-eight year old Jennifer Furminger. "Genteel, feminine, and mellow," Jennifer had been working the streets of Eastside since she arrived there in 1990 at the age of eighteen. Last seen on the cold winter night of December 27 at the corner of Cordova and Jackson Streets, when Jennifer hadn't been seen for awhile, her friend, Noel Paris, thought she may have moved in with a client or gone to Toronto, something she frequently spoke of doing.

Four days after Jennifer disappeared, on an even colder New Year's, and exactly one month before her twenty-fifth birthday, Tiffany Drew disappeared. The tiny, four-foot-eleven, ninety-five pound mother of three, grew up on Vancouver Island, but moved to Vancouver to better to support her heroine addiction. When Tiffaney's sister, Kelly, went to Vancouver to look for her, the once beautiful young woman with the wavy blonde hair and lovely blue eyes had altered so much, Kelly didn't recognize her in her photo ID.

* * *

Not only was little progress made on the case during 2000, there was also another puzzling hiatus. After Jennifer Furminger and Tiffaney Drew went missing in December 1999, there were no disappearances until Dawn Crey vanished on November 1, a full ten months later.

Like so many of the missing women, Dawn Crey got off to a bad start in life. Her father Earnest died of a heart attack while playing with his three year old daughter in the back yard of their home, a trauma Dawn never recovered from. After Earnest's death, Dawn's mother, Minnie, resorted to drinking, and the seven Crey children were parcelled out to foster homes. Abused at the first home she was sent to, at the age of nine Dawn went to live with Jake and Maria Wiebe. Unfortunately, the six unhappy years before she arrived at the Wiebes' had already scarred her emotionally. Then, to add to those emotional scars, Dawn was physically scarred when someone threw acid into her face. After forty years of disappointments and struggles, Dawn went missing.

She, and forty-three year old Deborah Jones, who disappeared four days before Christmas, were both reported missing in December.

* * *

Other than the addition of Dawn Crey and Deborah Jones's names to the missing Eastside women's list, by the beginning of 2001, the investigation into the disappearances had ground to a halt. In the middle of February, the Missing Women's Review Team disbanded and the RCMP Cold Squad took over. In April, a month before the now two year old, $100 000 reward was scheduled to expire, two members of the VPD and two members of the RCMP set up the Joint Missing

Women's Task Force "to review all Vancouver files related to the homicides and disappearances of street trade workers."

The Task Force was just getting underway when a wrongful dismissal suit launched by Kim Rossmo against the VPD and Deputy Chief John Unger came before the courts in June. During the proceedings, Rossmo claimed that as early as 1998 he had advised senior police to issue a press release, warning the public of a possible serial killer and urged them to establish a task force to "investigate whether a serial killer was preying on the women of Downtown Eastside." According to Rossmo, the suggestions were not only met with hostility, but Inspector Fred Biddlecombe, the officer in charge of serious crime at the time, deliberately went out of his way to publicly deny the possible existence of a serial killer.

When Rossmo's allegations became public, a number of families of the missing women were angered and hurt. "I think [warnings of a possible serial killer] might have made a difference," said Deborah Jardine, whose daughter Angela had now been missing for two and a half years. "The women would have taken extra precautions, including my daughter."

But calmer heads prevailed. "If they're heavily addicted and need money," said Eastside's Constable Dave Dickson, "they're probably going to jump in the car with a guy no matter what anyone tells them." Before she disappeared, Mona Wilson told her boyfriend that, "the addiction to the heroin overcomes the fear of being murdered." And Cynthia Feliks's former common-law partner, John Anderson said that, "eventually they will do anything for that bag. I mean anything. Even going to a pig farm and getting murdered and eaten by pigs. If that ain't a tale of a dead end, I don't know what is."

Before the uproar created by the Rossmo civil suit subsided, the disappearances of Cindy Feliks, Georgina Papin, and Elsie Sebastian, missing since 1992, were reported to police and another six women vanished: Patricia Johnson, Yvonne Boen, Heather Bottomley, Heather Chinnock, Angela Joesbury, and Sereena Abotsway.

Patricia Johnson had lived in Eastside for five years before she disappeared on March 3, 2001. The years had taken their toll. Her drawn face and the dark circles around her eyes, made her look forty, not twenty-four. Remembered by her family as a beautiful young woman who could "light up a room by just walking into it," Patricia was reported missing after she failed to pick up her welfare cheque.

Blonde-haired and blue-eyed, strikingly tall and beautiful, thirty-three year old Yvonne Boen disappeared less than two weeks after Patricia. The mother of three boys, Joel, Troy, and Damien, it was Troy who suspected something was wrong when his mother failed to call and confirm a visit she had asked Troy to make to her home in Vancouver. Her family reported her missing five days later.

Twenty-nine year old Heather Bottomley and her "off-the-wall" sense of humor disappeared one month after Yvonne. Unlike the vast majority of the missing women, Heather was raised in a stable, loving home in New Westminster. Freckle-faced and mischievous, as a young girl Heather had loved sports and practical jokes and enjoyed mimicking her favorite Blues Brother, Jim Belushi.

It is uncertain whether thirty year old Heather Chinnock disappeared before or after Heather Bottomley. What is known is that for ten years before she disappeared, the green-eyed, brown-haired, thirty year old mother of one had been a regular visitor to Robert Pickton's farm in Port Coquitlam, enticed there by the booze and drugs that could be had in exchange for sex.

Pretty and blonde, twenty-two year old Angela Joesbury's life spun out of control when she lost custody of her baby girl. She went missing on June 6, 2001 reportedly after going to meet Robert Pickton.

Sereena Abotsway's aunt said that for all of Sereena's short life "she was misplaced." A victim of fetal alcohol syndrome, when she was four the "troubled child" went to live with Anna and Bert Draayers, but was removed from their home at the age of seventeen when she became violent. Placed in a group home with street wise kids, she soon joined their burgeoning ranks. Despite her problems and lifestyle, for the next thirteen years Sereena called Anna and Bert daily. When she failed to make it home for her thirtieth birthday on August 20, Anna and Bert reported her missing.

With six new disappearances in the first eight months of 2001, it was clear that whatever had prompted the ten month suspension of disappearances, had crashed to a convulsive stop.

Then things took a dramatic turn.

To date, no one other than those involved knows precisely what transpired within police circles during the second half of 2001, but whatever it was, it was significant enough to kick the investigation into high gear. Over the course of the previous few months, the number of officers working the Missing Women's case had been whittled from nine to six to four. Then, on September 20, police unexpectedly added six more officers to the Task Force. When asked why, Deputy Chief John Unger would only say that, "without revealing the investigative leads that we have, I can't really go into that. But I can say that we've made significant progress."

Unfortunately, regardless of whatever significant progress Deputy Chief Unger may have been talking about, in October and November two more women disappeared.

Thirty-four year old Diane Marin Rock became pregnant with her first child, Melissa, at age fifteen. At seventeen, Diane got married and had her son Donnie. At eighteen, she had her second daughter, Carole Ann, and got divorced. Finding herself alone with three young children, Diane discovered that stripping paid a whole lot better than working as a nurses aide and that drugs gave her the courage to do the stripping.

In 1992 Diane almost died of an overdose. In an effort to make a fresh start, that same year Diane and her new husband Darren Rock and Diane's three children moved from Ontario to British Columbia where Darren Jr. and Justin Rock were born. For the seven years the Rocks were there, Diane worked in Abbotsford with developmentally handicapped adults and managed to stay straight.

Beginning in 1999, Diane began to slip back into a life governed by drugs which ultimately led to her second divorce. When her addiction began placing her children in jeopardy, her two youngest boys went to live with their father. Diane's father-in-law, Terry Rock, believed it was then "she just gave up." In April, 2001, Diane took a three month leave of absence from work and never went back. A "cute little thing" with pretty blue eyes, and blonde hair, Diane was last seen on October 19, 2001 by the owner of the Marr Hotel, where she was staying.

Steve Rix last saw his girlfriend, Mona Wilson, on November 23, in front of the Astoria Hotel on Hastings. It was the last time anyone saw the twenty-six year old. When she failed to appear at Christmas, a holiday she always spent with her family, Mona's sister Ada, knew something was wrong. A victim of childhood abuse, in the three and a half years Mona worked in Eastside, she had tried several times to kick her habit and get off the streets. Remembered as "a sweetheart" who loved unicorns and pink lipstick, Mona was the last Eastside woman to go missing before things took a dramatic turn.

On December 4, 2001, four days after Mona was reported missing, the Task Force produced a new Missing Women's poster which included an additional eighteen faces, pushing the total to forty-five:

28. **Sereena Abotsway, 20 August 1971, 1 August 2001, 22 August 2001**

29. Angela Arsenault, 20 May 1977, 19 August 1994, 29 August 1994

30. **Heather Chinnock, 10 November 1970, April 2001, 19 June 2001**

31. Nancy Clark (Greek), 29 July 1966, 22 August 1991, 23 August 1991

32. **Wendy Crawford, 21 April 1956, 27 November 1999, 14 December 1999**
33. Dawn Teresa Crey, 26 October 1958, 1 November 2000, 11 December 2000
34. Cindy Feliks, 12 December 1954, 26 November 1997, 8 January 2001
35. **Jennifer Lynn Furminger, 22 October 1971, 27 December 1999, 30 March 2000**
36. **Sherry Irving, 19 March 1973, April 1997, 21 March 1998**
37. Angela (Andrea) Joesbury, 6 November 1978, 6 June 2001, 8 June 2001
38. Patricia Rose Johnson, 2 December 1976, 3 March 2001, 31 May 2001
39. Deborah Lynn Jones, 31 December 1957, 21 December 2000, 25 December 2000
40. Laura Mah, 23 March 1943, 1 August 1985, 3 August 1999
41. Leigh Miner, 24 March 1958, 12 December 1993, 24 February 1994
42. **Georgina Faith Papin, 11 March 1964, 2 March 1999, 14 March 2001**
43. Elsie Sebastian (Jones), 11 January 1952, 16 October 1992, 16 May 2001
44. **Brenda Anne Wolfe, 20 October 1968, 1 February, 1999, 25 April, 2000**
45. *Francis Anne Young, 7 January 1960, 6 April 1996, 9 April 1996

* * *

Two weeks into 2002, the Task Force added yet another five names to its list of missing Eastside women, bringing the total to fifty:

46. Rebecca Louisa Guno, 25 May 1960, 22 June 1983, 25 June 1983
47. **Heather Kathleen Bottomley, 17 August 1976, 17 April 2001, 17 April 2001**
48. **Mona Lee Wilson, 13 January 1975, 23 November 2001, 30 November 2001**
49. **Diane Rosemary Rock, 2 September 1967, 19 October 2001, 13 December 2001**
50. Elaine Phyllis Dumba, 12 March 1955, 1989, 9 April 1998

Then, in a move that speaks volumes, two days after the addition of the five new names, the Missing Women's Task Force expanded to thirty officers. Three weeks later, the Task Force turned the world on its head.

On February 5, police in possession of a fire arms warrant, searched a mixed farm on Dominion Avenue in Port Coquitlam, a municipality of Vancouver on B.C.'s Lower Mainland. The farm, such as it was, was co-owned by Robert, David, and Linda Pickton. As a result of that warrant, police arrested fifty-two year old Robert Pickton, charged him with possession of a loaded, restricted .22 calibre revolver, unsafe storage of a firearm, and possession of a weapon without license or registration, and released him on bail.

Operating within the constraints of the judicial process, police could say nothing about what they found during their search – speculation says an inhaler and identification from the missing women. But whatever it was, it was significant enough for police to secure a second search warrant.

"We are very confident in our reasons for obtaining the search warrant," said Corporal Catherine Galliford, one of two officers assigned to act as official Task Force spokespersons, "and as you know, we need to have some really good information in order for a judge to grant us a search warrant."

Brandishing their second warrant, on February 6, 2002 police again descended upon the Dominion Avenue farm – fourteen acres of boggy land interspersed with abandoned vehicles, including an old bus, a house, fifteen outbuildings including a barn and mobile home – and initiated what would quickly become the most intensive and scientifically complex criminal investigation in Canadian history.

News of the search met mixed reviews. On one hand there was relief in knowing that after a five year investigation, police may have finally caught a break in the Case of the Missing Eastside Women. On the other hand there was outrage.

Joyce Lachance and Lynn Frey, Marnie Frey's aunt and mother, complained that during their search for Marnie, they had reported talk of the Pickton farm to police as early as 1998. According to James Hormoth, the Frey's lawyer, "Lynn kept getting leads that were leading her back to farm and repeatedly turned those leads over to police."

During a Canadian Broadcasting Corporation (CBC) interview, Lynn said that when she spoke to Eastside women after her daughter Marnie's disappearance, several women told her "there's this farm you can go to, and the guy is really dirty, and a lot of the women are going there, and they have a chipper there. I'm not talking no more."

Suzanne Jay, who runs a shelter and Vancouver rape counselling centre, supported Frey's accusations. "We had information about the location of that farm. People called us to say that they had called the police and told them something bad was going on there." Heather Chinnock's boyfriend, Gary Biggs, claimed he reported the farm to police as well, and Trevor Green, author of *Bad Date*, acknowledged that while researching his book he heard women mention "Farmer Willy." But the most damning report focused on a tape recorded message reportedly given to police by Wayne Leng in 1998.

Shortly after Wayne and Maggie deVries had set up their 1-800 number, Bill Hiscox, a former Pickton brother employee, had called the number and repeated information related to him by a woman who was a mutual friend of both him and Robert Pickton. "Billy," she told Hiscox, "you wouldn't believe the IDs and shit out in that trailer. There's women's clothes out there, there's purses. You know, what's that guy doing? It is like really weird."

Unable to fully respond to questions asking why police had not acted upon that information sooner, Detective Scott Dreimel, the other Task Force spokesperson, cautiously danced around them. "Information was received in the past about this case and that information has been acted upon," said Detective Dreimel before suggestively adding that "A police investigation even involves challenging past assumptions." In a particularly unsettling comment, Detective Dreimel also said, "We're not about to go back and defend ourselves for something that happened years ago."

Corporal Galliford's remark that, "over the last few months, this became a property of interest to us . . . as a result of our file reviews," was equally unsettling. Needless to say, the critical question rising from Corporal Galliford's statement was, if the property had been of interest over the last few months, why had women continued to go missing?

On February 16, 2002, amidst the fallout, police, whose first investigative priorities had "included the mobile home and certain outbuildings," expanded their search to the main residence on the Pickton farm. On February 22, Robert Pickton was once again taken into custody, this time charged with the first degree murders of Sereena Abotsway and Mona Wilson.

Several of Robert Pickton's friends and neighbors reacted to the news with disbelief. "He seemed like a totally nice guy," said Chris Diopita. "[The police] are on the totally wrong track," said Rick Contois. "He was always a nice person, generous, and hardworking," said Tom Hyacinthe. "He is a good guy and I like his brother too."

A month later, on March 28, the Joint Missing Women's Task Force added yet another five names to their ever-expanding list:

51. **Tiffaney Louise Drew, 13 January 1975, 31 December 1999, 8 February 2002**
52. Ruby Anne Hardy (Ruby Galloway), 23 March 1965, 1998, 27 March 2002
53. Yvonne Marie Boen (England), 30 November 1967, 16 March 2001, 21 March 2001

54. Maria Laura Laliberte (Kim Keller), 7 November 1949, 1 January 1997, 8 March 2002

55. *Anne Elizabeth Wolsey, 20 December 1972, November 1999, 1 January 1997

Five days after police appended their list, Robert Pickton was charged with the first degree murders of Jacquilene McDonell, Diane Rock, and Heather Bottomley. Exactly one week after that, he was charged with the murder of Angela Joesbury. The one bright spot during the parade of horrors was that Anne Wolsey's father contacted authorities to say that his daughter was alive and well, thereby reducing the Task Force's list of missing women to fifty-four.

On April 17, based on information received from the hundreds of tips that were now pouring in, police executed another search warrant on an eleven acre property the Picktons owned on Burns Road. In 1996, Dave and Robert had incorporated the "Piggy Palace Good Times Society," and converted a barn on the Burns Road property into the Piggy Palace, ostensibly to be used by non-profit organizations, "sports organizations or other worthy groups" for social gatherings, in reality, a place to party. Whether or not the police search of the Burns' Road property had any bearing on the allegation, on May 22, Robert Pickton was charged with the murder of Brenda Wolfe.

Unable to reveal what they found during their searches, or what evidence led to the laying of charges, at the end of May, police announced that the Dominion Avenue site was like the "scene of a massacre," and told the families of the missing women they "shouldn't expect them to find any bodies;" they should only "expect them to find fragments."

On July 26, amidst an already appalling situation, police added another nine names to the missing women list, bringing the total to sixty-three:

55. Yvonne Marlene Abigosis, 23 November 1957, 1 January 1984, 22 May 2002

56. Wendy Louise Allen, 10 December 1945, 30 March 1979, 5 April 2002

57. *Dawn Lynn Cooper (Wood), 4 May 1964, 1996, 26 June 2002

58. Sheryl Donahue, 4 July 1963, 30 May 1985, 31 August 1985

59. *Tanya Colleen Emery, 6 October 1964, 1 December 1998, 13 March 2002

60. *Linda Louise Grant, 18 March 1953, October 1984, 2 February 1996

61. Kellie (Richard) Little, 12 March 1969, 23 April 1997, 30 April 1997

62. Teresa Louise Triff, 17 August 1969, 15 April 1993, 21 March 2002
63. Lillian Jean O'Dare, 8 January 1944, 12 September 1978, 12 September 1978

Police continued their search of both the Burns Road and Dominion Avenue properties, and on September 19, Robert Pickton was charged with the murders of Helen Hallmark, Georgina Papin, Jennifer Furminger, and Patricia Johnson, on October 2, the murders of Tanya Holyk, Sherry Irving, Inga Hall, and Heather Chinnock. On October 25, three weeks after laying their most recent charges, police concluded their search of the Burns Road property.

By the end of the year, police were able to eliminate another two names from their list of missing women. Tanya Emery had been found alive and well and living in central Canada; Dawn Cooper had died of a terminal illness in March 1997. With the removal of Tanya and Dawn's names, at the close of 2002, the Task Force's list of missing women stood at sixty-one, fifteen of whom Robert Pickton had been charged with murdering.

* * *

Robert Pickton's preliminary hearing, held to determine whether there was sufficient evidence to send him to trial, began on January 13, 2003. The previous month, after Robert Pickton's lawyer Peter Ritchie, strenuously argued for severe restrictions on the dissemination of the "explosive nature" of some of the evidence, provincial court Judge David Stone imposed a stringent publication ban prohibiting discussion of "any submissions, representations or rulings respecting evidence or the nature of the evidence taken at the preliminary hearing of Robert William Pickton."

Because of that ban, little is known about the evidence presented during the preliminary hearing. Crown Prosecutor Mike Petrie did confirm that it was "salacious" and "graphic," while Peter Ritchie stated that it was of such a nature that "we don't have to worry in this case about a discharge." Ernie Crey, the brother of Dawn Crey, and one of the voices of articulate calm throughout the entire ordeal, told reporters that what he heard in court "shocked me. It staggered me. It troubled me a good deal."

The hearing lasted a total of sixty days spread across a six month period. On July 20, the day before the hearing was set to conclude, police secured a fourth search warrant and began investigating a site adjacent to the Lougheed Highway in the Mission area. As it had done with the others, the court sealed the search warrant, restraining police from stating why they were investigating the large, building-less site belonging to the first nations Kwantlen band where a human skull had been found eight years earlier.

On July 23, 2003, Judge Stone ruled there was sufficient evidence to commit Robert Pickton to trial. Four days later, the Pickton house was demolished, twelve days after that, police abandoned the Mission site.

In mid-November, after twenty-one months of painstakingly sifting through 290 000 cubic metres of soil, after 103 anthropologists, twenty-six osteologists, and twelve forensic specialists had collected 200 000 DNA samples, and after more than a hundred investigators had amassed 35 000 pages of evidence, police announced they were leaving the Dominion Avenue site and the property would revert to its owners.

* * *

Throughout the lengthy search, gruesome tales of entrails, rendering vats, wood chippers, and frozen body parts had circulated. Then, on March 10, 2004, in response to a news media leak, police issued a disturbing statement that leant credence to some of the rumors. "We do know that conditions at the farm were unsanitary, including areas where animals were slaughtered," said Corporal Galliford. "Because of that, it is possible that some of the meat produced at the farm may have been exposed to disease and other contaminants, as well as to human DNA."

On October 6, 2004, while friends and families of the missing women struggled to come to grips with this latest round of horrors, police released a new poster which included the names of yet another eight missing women, raising the total to a staggering sixty-nine:

62. Sharon Nora Jane Abraham, 15 September 1965, 2000, 2004
63. Sherry Linda Baker, 28 November 1968, 1993, 2004
64. **Cara Louise Ellis (Nikki Trimble), 13 April 1971, 1996, October 2002**
65. *Tammy Heather Fairbairn, 17 June 1971, 1998, December 2004
66. Gloria Christine Fedyshyn, 15 August 1962, January 1990, July 2002
67. Mary Florence Lands, 15 September 1963, 1991, 2004
68. Tania Peterson, 28 December 1969, 1998, 2003
69. Sharon Evelyn Ward, 7 June 1967, 14 February 1997, March 1997

Three weeks later, on October 29, the *Vancouver Sun* reprinted excerpts from a Health Canada study, commissioned by the RCMP to "evaluate potential health risks to the estimated forty persons who may have consumed meat from the Pickton farm." In his summation, Doctor Tony Giulivi is quoted as saying, "It is believed that there is the possibility that human remains were fed to pigs, but the risk of disease to those who may have had contact with the meat was negligible. The psychological effects," said Giulivi, "may be worse than the physical."

* * *

On Wednesday, May 25, 2005, a week before the pre-trial proceedings commenced, Robert Pickton was charged with an additional twelve first degree murders: Andrea Borhaven, Wendy Crawford, Sarah deVries, Tiffany Drew, Cara Ellis, Cindy Feliks, Marnie Frey, Angela Jardine, Debra Jones, Kerry Koski, Diane Melnick, and one Jane Doe. According to police, seven of the new charges stemmed from evidence presented at the preliminary hearing, the remaining five resulted from evidence collected during their searches of the Pickton property. Unlike the fifteen earlier charges, Robert Pickton would stand trial on the twelve new charges through direct or preferred indictment without a preliminary hearing.

The next day police announced they had located Tammy Fairbairn and that as a result of their ongoing DNA testing, had been able to identify remains found in Vancouver in 1988 as those of Teressa Williams.

Two days into the pre-trial proceedings, Justice Geoffrey Barrow, originally scheduled to hear the trial, stood down, claiming scheduling conflicts. On June 1, Justice James Williams took over.

As he had done at the start of the preliminary hearing, Robert Pickton's lawyer, Peter Ritchie requested a sweeping publication ban of testimony presented during the pre-trial hearing. Justice Williams granted Ritchie's request for a publication ban, but would not agree to any extraordinary measures. Still, just as with the preliminary hearing, little is known about what transpired during the pre-trial. One tantalizing detail is that the defense intended to make "allegations that arise from the police investigation concerning potential involvement of others in the murders."

* * *

The voir dire portion of Robert Pickton's trial began on January 30, 2006, four years after his arrest. It began with the defendant formally entering not-guilty pleas to twenty-six of the twenty-seven murder charges. Justice Williams entered a not-guilty plea on Robert Pickton's behalf for Jane Doe murder charge. Not until after the admissibility of evidence presented during the voir dire has been argued and ruled on will jurors be selected and the trial commence in earnest.

At present there are nearly one hundred officers assigned to the Missing Women Task Force. The list of missing women, including those whom Pickton has been charged with murdering, stands at sixty-seven. Although, on March 7, 2006, Justice James Williams threw out the Jane Doe murder charge, saying it did not meet the requirements laid out in the Criminal Code of Canada, the number of first-degree murder charges facing Robert Pickton may increase. At the end of January 2004, police informed the families of Yvonne Boen and Dawn Crey that Yvonne and Dawn's DNA had been found at the Pickton farm, but not of sufficient quantity to charge Robert Pickton with their murders, and late in 2006 police confirmed they had also identified DNA from Nancy Clarke. In August 2006, Justice Williams announced that, initially, Pickton will go to trial on only six counts of murder. The ruling was made because trying Pickton on all counts would "pose an unreasonable burden on a jury."

Clearly, the investigation into Eastside's missing women is far from over. Neither are the criticisms of the VPD's handling of the case.

Author Elliott Leyton once said, "Often the only difference between the serial killer who murders two people and the serial killer who murders twenty people is the quality of the police investigation." From its earliest days, people have charged that the investigation into the missing Eastside women was seriously flawed. There are troubling claims that senior police officials were unwilling to devote sufficient resources to the investigation and that the women's life styles allowed police the "luxury of procrastination."

Police defend themselves by insisting that when the trial is over, when a verdict has been announced and they can talk freely, the public will see that they did a good investigation. "At the end of the day," Vancouver Police Chief Jamie Graham is quoted as saying in November 2002, "I think we'll be able to stand up and be proud of what we did, what the VPD did. I'd love to be able to speak about this case. I'd love to be able to open the books and let you read everything we've done, but I can't, and I won't anyway."

Geramy Field, on the case from the beginning says "We did a pretty good investigation, with what we had." In their September 22, 2001 article, "How the police investigation was flawed," *Vancouver Sun* journalists Lindsay Kines, Kim Bolan, and Lori Culbert listed three primary flaws with the investigation: it was assigned to inexperienced and horrendously overworked officers who lacked sufficient resources to perform their tasks properly; an open distrust and dislike amongst senior officers resulted in counter-productive in-fighting; there were serious problems with data entry.

Kim Rossmo, the one time VPD Detective-Inspector who went on to become one of the world's foremost authorities on geographic profiling after the VPD failed to renew his contract, critically asked, "if we believe, with any degree of probability, that we have a predator responsible for twenty or thirty deaths in a short period of time, do you think our response was adequate?"

As critical as Rossmo and others have been, it is the friends and families of the missing women who are the most outraged. "[Police] refused to put two and two together when all these women started going missing," says Rick Frey. "I'm not letting go until I get accountability and justice," his wife Lynn insists. "If six dogs from the neighborhood had disappeared, there would have been more done" says Kathleen Hallmark-McClelland, Helen Hallmark's mother. "The police were callous, distant, and unprofessional," says Erin McGrath, Leigh Miner's sister, adding that in the eight years after her family reported Leigh's disappearance, police never once called the family.

Since Deborah Jardine filed a neglect of duty allegation in a formal a letter of complaint against the VPD in 1999, three law suits have been filed: the first by Marnie Frey's parents Rick and Lynn, the second by Marcie Creison's father Doug, the third by Angela Joesbury's mother Karin, the latter claiming negligence against the VPD and RCMP that "allowed the killing to continue."

Surrey-Newton MLA Tony Bhullar lodged an official complaint with the Police Complaints Commission over the early investigation into the missing women, seeking a public inquiry into how the case was handled, while Kim Rossmo and retired VPD Inspector Doug McKay-Dunne have called for an investigation as well.

But it isn't just those directly involved with the missing women investigation who have voiced dissatisfaction with the handling of the case. After Robert Pickton was charged with the murder of Sherry Irving, Stewart Phillip, president of the Union of British Columbia Indian Chiefs said that the disproportionate number of aboriginal women among the victims "reflects a dismissive and discriminatory attitude on the part of police agencies who didn't look as hard for these marginalized women as they would have if sixty-three women had disappeared from the British Properties over time." Even Ernie Crey remarked, "I would hope the police would feel regret."

For years, members of British Columbia's police forces have been lobbying for an integrated police unit or a major case management system to deal with serious crime. At present, policing British Columbia's Lower Mainland is undertaken by six different municipal forces – Vancouver, New Westminster, West Vancouver, Delta, Port Moody, Abbotsford – as well as the hundreds of RCMP detachments.

At times this division of labor has hampered sound communication. No where was this problem better exemplified than with Clifford Olson and the Case of the Missing Lower Mainland Children, where poor interdepartmental communication allowed Olson to escape early detection. It is not insignificant that ten months after a Joint Task Force assumed control of the Case of Vancouver's Missing Eastside Women, an arrest was made.

One wonders if Detective Scott Dreimel appreciated the true significance of his words when on February 22, 2002 he told reporters, "This investigation is a very good example of what an integrated approach to solving crime can accomplish."